# THE IMPORTANCE OF NIE

# THE IMPORTANCE OF
# Nietzsche

## TEN ESSAYS

## ERICH HELLER

THE UNIVERSITY OF CHICAGO PRESS
CHICAGO AND LONDON

ERICH HELLER, Avalon Professor of German at
Northwestern University, is the author of many books, including *The Disinherited Mind* and *In the Age of Prose*.

The University of Chicago Press, Chicago 60637
The University of Chicago Press, Ltd., London

© 1988 by The University of Chicago
All rights reserved. Published 1988
Printed in the United States of America

97  96  95  94  93  92  91  90          543

Library of Congress Cataloging-in-Publication Data

Heller, Erich, 1911–
   The importance of Nietzsche : ten essays / Erich
Heller.
      p.    cm.
   Bibliography: p.
   ISBN 0-226-32637-3.   ISBN 0-226-32638-1 (pbk.)
   1. Nietzsche, Friedrich Wilhelm, 1844–1900.   I. Title.
B3317.H43    1988
   193—dc19                          88-18649
                                      CIP

# CONTENTS

Preface     vii

Vocabulary, References, and Acknowledgments     ix

1   The Importance of Nietzsche     1

2   Nietzsche and Goethe     18

3   Burckhardt and Nietzsche     39

4   Nietzsche, the Teacher of "Free Spirits"     55

5   Zarathustra's Three Metamorphoses: Facets of Nietzsche's Intellectual Biography and the Apotheosis of Innocence     70

6   Rilke and Nietzsche with a Discourse on Thought, Belief and Poetry     87

7   Yeats and Nietzsche: Reflections on Aestheticism and a Poet's Marginal Notes     127

8   Wittgenstein and Nietzsche     141

9   Nietzsche's Last Words about Art versus Truth     158

10   Nietzsche's Terrors: Time and the Inarticulate     173

Notes     187

# PREFACE

Friends and readers have encouraged me to assemble in one volume
the following essays, and I have felt on reading them again that it
might be worth the effort. In the winter of the academic year 1986–87
I was asked to interrupt my retirement to lecture on Nietzsche. The
interest my students took in the subject, and their response to it, over-
came what was left of my hesitation.

Revising and sometimes all but rewriting these essays took up more
time and energy than I had anticipated. I hope that the result is a book
on Nietzsche and not simply a collection of separate essays; their inherent unity was made clear to me by the repetition of certain points
and quotations. I have not succeeded in eliminating them completely,
because in some instances they belong—*sit venia verbo*—to the organic
texture of more than one essay, and to remove them altogether would
interfere with the coherence of the argument. They may even serve as
signposts pointing to the meeting place of many perspectives on my
subject.

The first essay provides the title for the book. It may also be regarded as an overture, doing duty as an introduction and briefly stating
the main themes on which the later essays elaborate. And as the titles
of some of these essays suggest, the focus is not always on Nietzsche
alone. In these instances the "and" that joins his name to another
is sometimes meant—for instance, in "Goethe and Nietzsche" or
"Burckhardt and Nietzsche"—to refer to Nietzsche's inescapable ambivalence, to his love for and rebellion against the tradition he inherited. He believed he understood most intimately why in Shakespeare's
drama *Julius Caesar* the real hero is not Caesar but Brutus, his mur-
derer. To win freedom, Brutus killed the man he loved best. What
instantly comes to mind is Nietzsche's relationship to Wagner or even
to Schopenhauer. The other "and"s point to the profound effect
Nietzsche had on the thought and sensibility of men who came after
him. This is true of many, many more than Rilke, Yeats, or Wittgenstein. Nietzsche anticipated much that they, often without knowing it,
had to say.

If I were to mention all those whose friendship, interest, and criticism helped me to write these essays, a long list would have to follow.
Instead, I beg them to be sure of my gratitude. When it came to revis-

ing and collecting what I had written, and to the painstaking task of checking and transcribing reference notes, my student John Standiford was an exemplary assistant, intelligent, reliable, and good-humored. Mrs. Marion Rothey managed once again, most ably, to produce the typescript from my hand-written pages and to decode my system of corrections and additions. My thanks to both of them.

Finally, I wish to account for the absence of biographical acknowledgments. Those who are familiar with the unmanageably voluminous literature on Nietzsche will not need an apology for the omission. I can neither claim ignorance of others' contributions nor, of course, complete knowledge of them. But the impressions that many of them have made on my work are obvious. I am grateful for this, even though other works have not been explicitly discussed.

E.H.

January 1988
Evanston, Illinois

# VOCABULARY, REFERENCES, AND ACKNOWLEDGMENTS

In any presentation or discussion of Nietzsche's thought the term "*Übermensch*" is unavoidable. Together with the equally problem-ridden notion of "Eternal Recurrence" it is at the center of the message delivered by Nietzsche's imaginary prophet Zarathustra. "*Übermensch*" and Eternal Recurrence: I hope to show in some of the following essays that theirs is an incompatible partnership. But as Nietzsche emphatically blessed the union in a ceremony of paradox, it plays a conspicuous part in this book. Whenever the *Übermensch* enters, I call him by his German name. For obvious reasons, the comically popular translation "superman" has become unemployable in serious contexts, and I feel uncomfortable with the coinage "overman" because of its closeness to "overseer," "overlord," "overreacher," "overdone." Even though these verbal associations may seem not quite inappropriate, they bias, I think, an understanding of Nietzsche's meaning.

I have rendered the "*Apollinische*" as "Apollonian" and occasionally, when this seemed best fitted to the rhythm of thought and sentence, as "Apolline."

The late Professor Walter Kaufmann is not only the author of the most successful and best-known book in English on Nietzsche (*Nietzsche: Philosopher, Psychologist, Antichrist* has appeared in many editions, including paperback, since its first publication in 1950 by Princeton University Press) but also the very competent translator of many of Nietzsche's works. He rendered the title of *Die fröhliche Wissenschaft* as *The Gay Science*. Of course, this is sanctioned by Nietzsche himself, who subtitled it "la gaya scienza," using the appellation given to the practice of poetry by Provençal troubadours. Nonetheless, I call it, after Emerson, *The Joyous Science,* and explain my choice in a footnote to the essay "Nietzsche's Terrors."

Apropos footnotes: I have separated these, marked by asterisks, from references marked by numbers. The latter are grouped according to the titles of the individual essays at the end of the book. They contain no comments, and the only information they yield is the source of quotations. The footnote numbers in the text, therefore, need not interrupt the reader unless he wishes to check the context of what is quoted.

Passages from Nietzsche's works are, on the whole, identified twice: first by the particular volume and page of the *Gesammelte Werke, Musarion-Ausgabe* (abbreviated M.A.), 23 vols., Munich, 1922–1929 (for readers of German with access to academic libraries) and then by the English titles of translations. As some of Nietzsche's books have been variously translated, I have generally refrained from citing particular editions, giving instead the numbered section of the work. The problem of how to refer to the voluminous posthumous notes and fragments is insolvable. Only those that constitute *The Will to Power* are fully accessible in English. The two volumes of *Der Wille zur Macht* (Musarion-Ausgabe XVIII and XIX) have been translated by Walter Kaufmann and R. J. Hollingdale as *The Will to Power* (Random House, New York, 1967). The numbering of entries is identical in the German and the English editions. It is impossible to refer to all the other posthumous notes in any other than the makeshift way I have adopted. In these instances, the translations are my own.

With so many editions of Goethe's works extant—especially those of his *Faust*—I have referred to act, chapter, and verse. His scientific writings have been quoted from the *Jubiläums-Ausgabe,* 40 vols., Stuttgart and Berlin, 1902–1912 (abbreviated J.A.). For the sake of the accuracy demanded by the context, I have avoided English verse renderings of, e.g., Goethe's *Faust,* choosing to paraphrase after the German quotations.

All letters are identified according to date and recipient.

These essays, at least in substance and under the same titles, have previously appeared as follows: "The Importance of Nietzsche" and "Wittgenstein and Nietzsche," in *The Artist's Journey and Other Essays,* copyright © 1965 by Erich Heller; reprinted by permission of Harcourt Brace Jovanovich, Inc. "Nietzsche's Last Words about Art versus Truth" is reprinted from *In the Age of Prose,* © Cambridge University Press 1984; and "Nietzsche, the Teacher of 'Free Spirits'" is based on the introduction to Nietzsche's *Human, All Too Human,* © Cambridge University Press 1986, now appearing in greatly revised and enlarged form. Both are reprinted with the permission of Cambridge University Press. "Nietzsche's Terrors: Time and the Inarticulate" appeared in *Salmagundi,* Skidmore College, Saratoga Springs, Fall 1985–Winter 1986, and is also greatly revised and enlarged. "Nietzsche and Goethe," "Burckhardt and Nietzsche," and "Rilke and Nietzsche" are reprinted by permission of The Bodley Head from *The Disinherited Mind*. "Zarathustra's Three Metamorphoses" was the annual *Salmagundi* lecture, delivered at Skidmore College, April 20, 1972, and is reprinted by permission of *Salmagundi*.

"Yeats and Nietzsche" was first published by *Encounter* in December 1969, © 1969 by Encounter, Ltd. Quotes in that essay are reprinted by permission of Macmillan Publishing Co., Inc., from these works in *Collected Poems* by William Butler Yeats: "Meru," © 1934 by Macmillan Publishing Co., Inc., renewed © 1962 by Bertha Georgie Yeats; "Sailing to Byzantium" and "Among School Children," © 1928 by Macmillan Publishing Co., Inc., renewed © 1956 by Georgie Yeats; "The Second Coming" and "Michael Robartes and the Dancer," © 1924 by Macmillan Publishing Co., Inc., renewed © 1952 by Bertha Georgie Yeats; "The Phases of the Moon," © 1919 by Macmillan Publishing Co., Inc., renewed © 1947 by Bertha Georgie Yeats; "The Withering of the Boughs"; and "Under the Moon."

# THE IMPORTANCE OF NIETZSCHE

In 1873, two years after Bismarck's Prussia had defeated France, a young German who happened to live in Switzerland and taught classical philology in the University of Basle wrote a treatise concerned with "the German mind." It was an inspired diatribe against, above all, the German notion of *Kultur* and against the philistine readiness to believe that military victory proved cultural superiority. This was, he said, a disastrous superstition, symptomatic in itself on the absence of any true culture. According to him, the opposite was true: the civilization of the vanquished French was bound more and more to dominate the victorious German people that had wasted its spirit upon the chimera of political power.[1]

This national heretic's name, rather obscure at the time, was Friedrich Nietzsche. What he wrote almost a century ago about the perverse relationship between military success and intellectual dominance proved true: not then, perhaps, but half-a-century later. Defeated in two wars, Germany appeared to have invaded vast territories of the world's mind, with Nietzsche himself as no mean conqueror. For his was the vision of things to come. Among all the thinkers of the nineteenth century he is, with the possible exceptions of Dostoevsky and Kierkegaard, the only one who would not be too amazed by the amazing scene upon which we now move in sad, pathetic, heroic, stoic, or ludicrous bewilderment. Much, too much, would strike him as *déjà vu:* yes, he had foreseen it; and he would understand: for the "Modern Mind" speaks German, not always good German, but fluent German nonetheless. It was, alas, forced to learn the idiom of Karl Marx, and was delighted to be introduced to itself in the language of Sigmund Freud; taught by Ranke and, later, Max Weber, it acquired its historical and sociological self-consciousness, moved out of its tidy Newtonian universe on the instruction of Einstein, and followed a design of Oswald Spengler's in sending, from the depth of its spiritual depression, most ingeniously engineered objects higher than the moon. Whether it discovers, with Heidegger, the true habitation of its *Existenz* on the frontiers of Nothing, or meditates, with Sartre and Camus, *le Néant* or the Absurd; whether—to pass to its less serious moods—it is nihilistically young and profitably angry in London or rebelliously debauched and buddhistic in San Francisco—*man spricht deutsch*. It is all part of a story told by Nietzsche.

As for modern German literature and thought, it is hardly an exaggeration to say that they would not be what they are if Nietzsche had never lived. Name almost any poet, man of letters, philosopher, who wrote in German during the twentieth century and attained to stature and influence—Rilke, George, Kafka, Thomas Mann, Ernst Jünger, Musil, Benn, Heidegger, or Jaspers—and you name at the same time Friedrich Nietzsche. He is to them all—whether or not they know and acknowledge it (and most of them do)—what St. Thomas Aquinas was to Dante: the categorical interpreter of a world which they contemplate poetically or philosophically without ever radically upsetting its Nietzschean structure.

Nietzsche died in 1900, after twelve years of a total eclipse of his intellect, insane—and on the threshold of this century. Thinking and writing to the very edge of insanity, and with some of his last pages even going over it, he read and interpreted the temperatures of his own mind; but by doing so, he has drawn the fever-chart of an epoch. Indeed, much of his work reads like the self-diagnosis of a desperate physician who, suffering the disease on our behalf, comes to prescribe as a cure that we should form a new idea of health and live by it.

He was convinced that it would take at least fifty years before a few men would understand what he had accomplished;[2] and he feared that even then his teaching would be misinterpreted and misapplied. "I am terrified," he wrote, "by the thought of the sort of people who may one day invoke my authority." But is this not, he added, the anguish of every great teacher? He knows that he may prove a disaster as much as a blessing.[3] What he did not add was that on some of the pages of his writings he unmistakably enabled that "sort of people" to quote him verbatim in justifying their abominable designs. Still, the conviction that he was a great teacher never left him after he had passed through that period of sustained inspiration in which he wrote the first part of *Zarathustra*. After this, all his utterances convey the disquieting self-confidence and the terror of a man who has reached the culmination of that paradox which he embodies, a paradox which we shall try to name and which ever since has cast its dangerous spell over some of the finest and some of the coarsest minds.

Are we then, at the remove of two generations, in a better position to probe Nietzsche's mind and to avoid, as he hoped some might, the misunderstanding that he was merely concerned with the religious, philosophical, or political controversies fashionable in his day? And if this be a misinterpretation, can we put anything more valid in its place? What is the knowledge which he claims to have, raising him in his own opinion far above the contemporary level of thought? What the discovery which serves him as a lever to unhinge the whole fabric of traditional values?

It is the knowledge that God is dead.

The death of God he calls the greatest event in modern history and the cause of extreme danger. Note well the paradox contained in these words. He never said that there was no God, but that the Eternal had been vanquished by Time and that the Immortal suffered death at the hands of mortals: God is dead. It is like a cry mingled of despair and triumph, reducing, by comparison, the whole story of atheism and agnosticism before and after him to the level of respectable mediocrity and making it sound like a collection of announcements by bankers who regret they are unable to invest in an unsafe proposition. Nietzsche, for the nineteenth century, brings to its *perverse* conclusion a line of religious thought and experience linked with the names of St. Paul, St. Augustine, Pascal, Kierkegaard, and Dostoevsky, minds for whom God was not simply the creator of an order of nature within which man has his clearly defined place, but to whom He came rather in order to challenge their natural being, making demands which appeared absurd in the light of natural reason. These men are of the family of Jacob: having wrestled with God for His blessing, they ever after limp through life with the framework of Nature incurably out of joint. Nietzsche is just such a wrestler; except that in him the shadow of Jacob merges with the shadow of Prometheus. Like Jacob, Nietzsche too believed that he prevailed against God in that struggle, and won a new name for himself, the name of Zarathustra. But the words *he* spoke on his mountain to the angel of the Lord were: "I will not let thee go, except thou curse me." Or, in words which Nietzsche did in fact speak: "I have on purpose devoted my life to exploring the whole contrast to a truly religious nature. I know the Devil and all his visions of God."[4]

"God is dead"—this is the very core of Nietzsche's spiritual existence, and what follows is despair *and* hope in a new greatness of man, visions of catastrophe *and* glory, the icy brilliance of analytical reason, fathoming with affected irreverence those depths hitherto hidden by awe and fear, and, side-by-side with it, the ecstatic invocations of a ritual healer. Probably inspired by Hölderlin's dramatic poem *Empedocles,* the young Nietzsche, who loved what he knew of Hölderlin's poetry, at the age of twenty planned to write a drama with Empedocles as its hero. His notes show that he saw the Greek philosopher as the tragic personification of his age, as a man in whom the latent conflicts of his epoch attained to consciousness, as one who suffered and died as the victim of an unresolvable tension: born with the soul of a *homo religiosus,* a seer, a prophet, and poet, he yet had the mind of a radical skeptic; and defending his soul against his mind and, in turn, his mind against his soul, he made his soul lose its spontaneity, and finally his mind its rationality. Had Nietzsche ever written the drama *Empedocles,* it might have become, in uncanny anticipation, his *own* tragedy.[5]

It is a passage from Nietzsche's *Gaya Scienza,* his *Joyous Science,* which conveys best the substance and quality of the mind, indeed the whole spiritual situation, from which the pronouncement of the death of God sprang. The passage is prophetically entitled "The Madman" and might have been called "The New Diogenes." Here is a brief extract from it:

> Have you not heard of that madman who, in the broad light of the forenoon, lit a lantern and ran into the market-place, crying incessantly: "I am looking for God!" . . . As it happened, many were standing there who did not believe in God, and so he aroused great laughter . . . The madman leapt right among them . . . "Where is God?" he cried. "Well, I will tell you. *We have murdered him*—you and I . . . But how did we do this deed? . . . Who gave us the sponge with which to wipe out the whole horizon? How did we set about unchaining our earth from her sun? Whither is it moving now? Whither are we moving? . . . Are we not falling incessantly? . . . Is night not approaching, and more and more night? Must we not light lanterns in the forenoon? Behold the noise of the gravediggers, busy to bury God . . . And we have killed him! What possible comfort is there for us? . . . Is not the greatness of this deed too great for us? To appear worthy of it, must not we ourselves become gods?"—At this point the madman fell silent and looked once more at those around him: "Oh," he said, "I am too early. My time has not yet come. The news of this tremendous event is still on its way . . . Lightning and thunder take time, the light of the stars takes time to get to us, deeds take time to be seen and heard . . . and *this* deed is still farther from them than the farthest stars—*and yet it was they themselves who did it!*"[6]

And elsewhere, in a more prosaic mood, Nietzsche says: "People have no notion yet that from now onwards they exist on the mere pittance of inherited and decaying values"[7]—soon to be overtaken by an enormous bankruptcy.

The story of the Madman, written two years before *Zarathustra* and containing *in nuce* the whole message of the *Übermensch,* shows the distance that divides Nietzsche from the conventional attitudes of atheism. He is the madman, breaking with his sinister news into the marketplace complacency of the pharisees of unbelief. They have done away with God, and yet the report of their own deed has not yet reached them. They know not what they have done, but He who could forgive them is no more. Much of Nietzsche's work ever after is the prophecy of their fate: "The story I have to tell is the history of the next two centuries . . . For a long time now our whole civilization has been driving, with a tortured intensity growing from decade to decade, as if towards a catastrophe: restlessly, violently, tempestuously, like a mighty river desiring the end of its journey, without pausing to reflect, indeed fearful of reflection . . . Where we live, soon nobody will be able to exist."[8] For men become enemies, and each his own enemy. From now onward they will *hate,* Nietzsche believes, however many *comforts* they will lavish upon themselves, and hate *themselves* with a new hatred, unconsciously at work in the depths of their souls. True, there will be ever better reformers of society, ever better socialists, and ever better hospitals, and an ever increasing intolerance of pain and poverty and suffering and death, and an ever more fanatical craving for the greatest happiness of the greatest numbers. Yet the deepest impulse informing their striving will not be love and will not be compassion. Its true source will be the panic-struck determination not to have to ask the question "What is the meaning of our lives?"—the question which will remind them of the death of God, the uncomfortable question inscribed on the features of those who are uncomfortable, and asked above all by pain and poverty and suffering and death. Rather than allowing that question to be asked, they will do everything to smooth it away from the face of humanity. For they cannot endure it. And yet they will despise themselves for not enduring it, and for their guilt-ridden inability to answer it; and their self-hatred will betray them behind the back of their apparent charity and humanitarian concern. For *there* they will assiduously construct the tools for the annihilation of human kind. "There will be wars," Nietzsche writes, "such as have never been waged on earth."[9] And he says: "I foresee something terrible, Chaos everywhere. Nothing left which is of any value; nothing which commands: Thou shalt!"[10] This would have been the inspiration of the final work which Nietzsche often said he would write and never wrote: *The Transvaluation of All Values,* as he sometimes wanted to call it, or *The Will to Power,* the title chosen by his editors for their assemblage of a great many notes from his late years. Fragmentary though these are, they yet give a surprisingly full diagnosis of what he termed nihilism, the state of human beings and societies faced with a total eclipse of all values.

It is in defining and examining the (for him *historical*) phenomenon of nihilism that Nietzsche's attack on Christianity sets in, and it has remained the only truly subtle point which, within the whole range of his more and more unrestrained argumentativeness, this Antichrist makes against Christianity. For it is at this point that Nietzsche asks (and asks the same question in countless variations throughout his works): What are the *specific* qualities which the Christian tradition has instilled and cultivated in the minds of men? They are, he thinks, twofold; on the one hand, a more refined sense of truth than any other civilization has known, an almost uncontrollable desire for absolute spiritual and intellectual certainties; and, on the other hand, the ever-present suspicion that life on this earth is not in itself a supreme value, but in need of a higher, a transcendental justification. This, Nietzsche believes, is a destructive, and even self-destructive alliance, which is bound finally to corrode the very Christian beliefs on which it rests. For the mind, exercised and guided in its search for knowledge by the most sophisticated and comprehensive theology the world has ever known—a theology which through St. Thomas Aquinas has assimilated into its grand system the genius of Aristotle—was at the same time fashioned and directed by the indelible Christian distrust of the ways of the world. Thus it had to follow, with the utmost logical precision and determination, a course of systematically "devaluing" the knowably real.

This mind, Nietzsche predicts, will eventually, in a frenzy of intellectual honesty, unmask as humbug what it began by regarding as the finer things in life. The boundless faith in truth, the joint legacy of Christ and Greek, will in the end dislodge every possible belief in the truth of any faith. Souls, long disciplined in a school of unworldliness and humility, will insist upon knowing the worst about themselves, indeed will only be able to grasp what is humiliating. Psychology will denigrate the creations of beauty, laying bare the tangle of unworthy desires of which they are "mere" sublimations. History will undermine the accumulated reputation of the human race by exhuming from beneath the splendid monuments the dead body of the past, revealing everywhere the spuriousness of motives, the human, all too human. And science itself will rejoice in exposing this long-suspected world as a mechanical contraption of calculable pulls and pushes, as a self-sufficient agglomeration of senseless energy, until finally, in a surfeit of knowledge, the scientific mind will perform the somersault of self-annihilation.

"The nihilistic consequences of our natural sciences"—this is one of Nietzsche's fragmentary jottings—"from its pursuits there follows ultimately a self-decomposition, a turning against itself," [11] which—and this is one of his most amazingly precise predictions—would first show itself in the impossibility, within science itself, of comprehending the very object of its inquiry within *one* logically coherent system, [12] and would lead to extreme scientific pessimism, to an inclination to embrace a kind of analytical, abstract mysticism by which man would shift himself and his world to where, Nietzsche thinks, they have been driving "ever since Copernicus: from the center towards an unknown X." [13]

## 2

It is the tremendous paradox of Nietzsche that he himself follows, and indeed consciously wishes to hasten, this course of "devaluation"—particularly as a psychologist: and at the onset of megalomania he called himself the first psychologist in the world—"there was no psychology before me," [14] a self-compliment which Sigmund Freud all but endorsed when incredibly, or at least not quite believably, late in his life, as he claimed, he came to know Nietzsche's writings. He had good reason to be impressed. Consider for instance, the following passage from Nietzsche's *Beyond Good and Evil:*

> The world of historical values is dominated by forgery. These great poets, like Byron, Musset, Poe, Leopardi, Kleist, Gogol (I dare not mention greater names, but I mean them)—all endowed with souls wishing to conceal a break; often avenging themselves with their works upon some inner desecration, often seeking oblivion in their lofty flights from their all-too-faithful memories, often lost in mud and almost in love with it until they become like will-o'-the-wisps of the morasses and simulate the stars . . . oh what a torture are all these great artists and altogether these higher beings, what a torture to him who has guessed their true nature. [15]

This does indeed anticipate many a Freudian speculation on traumata and compensations, on lusts and sublimations, on wounds and bows. Yet the extraordinary Nietzsche—incomprehensible in his contradictions except as the common strategist of two opposing armies who plans for the victory of a mysterious third—a few pages later takes back the guessing, not without insulting himself in the process:

"From which it follows that it is the sign of a finer humanity to respect 'the mask' and not, in the wrong places, indulge in psychology and psychological curiosity."[16] And furthermore: "He who does not *wish* to see what is great in a man, has the sharpest eye for that which is low and superficial in him, and so gives away—himself."[17]

If Nietzsche is not the first psychologist of Europe, he is certainly a great psychologist—and perhaps really the first who comprehended what his more methodical successors, "strictly scientific" in their approach, did not see: *the psychology and the ethics of knowledge itself;* and both the psychology and the ethics of knowledge are of particular relevance when the knowledge in question purports to be knowledge of the human psyche. It was, strangely enough, Nietzsche's amoral metaphysics, his doubtful but immensely fruitful intuition of the Will to Power as being the ultimate reality of the world, that made him into the first *moralist of knowledge* in his century and long after. While all his scientific and scholarly contemporaries throve on the comfortable assumptions that, firstly, there was such a thing as "objective," and therefore morally neutral, scientific knowledge, and that, secondly, everything that *can* be known "objectively" is therefore also *worth knowing,* he realized that knowledge, or at least the mode of knowledge predominant at his time and ours, is the subtlest guise of the Will to Power; and that *as a manifestation of the will it is liable to be judged morally.* For him, there can be no knowledge without a compelling urge to acquire it; and he knew that the knowledge thus acquired invariably reflects the nature of the impulse by which the mind was prompted. It is this impulse which *creatively* partakes in the making of the knowledge, and its share in it is truly immeasurable when the knowledge is about the very source of the impulse: the soul. This is why all interpretations of the soul must to a high degree be self-interpretations: the sick interpret the sick, and the dreamers interpret dreams. Or, as the Viennese satirist Karl Kraus—with that calculated injustice which is the prerogative of satire—once said of a certain psychological theory: "Psychoanalysis is the disease of which it pretends to be the cure."[18]

Psychology is bad psychology if it disregards its own psychology. Nietzsche knew this. He was, as we have seen from his passage about "those great men," a most suspicious psychologist, but he was at the same time suspicious of the suspicion which was the father of his thought. Homer, to be sure, did not "psychologically" suspect his heroes, but Stendhal did. Does this mean that Homer knew less about the heroic than Stendhal? Does it make sense to say that Flaubert's Emma Bovary is the product of an imagination more profoundly initiated into the psychology of women than that which created Dante's Beatrice? Is Benjamin Constant, who created the dubious lover Adolphe, on more intimate terms with the nature of a young man's erotic passion than is Shakespeare, the begetter of Romeo? Certainly, Homer's Achilles and Stendhal's Julien Sorel are different heroes, Dante's Beatrice and Flaubert's Emma Bovary are different women, Shakespeare's Romeo and Constant's Adolphe are different lovers, but it would be naïve to believe that they simply differ "in actual fact." Actual facts hardly exist in either art or psychology: both interpret and both claim universality for the meticulously presented particular. Those creatures made by creative imaginations can indeed not be compared; yet if they differ as, in life, one person differs from another, at the same time, because they have their existence not "in life" but in art, they are incommensurable above all by virtue of their authors' incommensurable *wills* to know the human person, to know the hero, the woman, the lover. It is not better and more knowing minds that have created the suspect hero, the unlovable woman, the disingenuous lover, but minds possessed by different desires for a different knowledge, a knowledge devoid of the wonder and pride that know Achilles, the love that knows Beatrice, the passion and compassion that know Romeo. When Hamlet has come to know the frailty of woman, he knows Ophelia not better than when he was "unknowingly" in love with her; now he knows her differently and he knows her worse.

All *new* knowledge about the soul is knowledge about a *different* soul. For can it ever happen that the freely discovering mind says to the soul: "This is what you are!"? Is it not rather as if the mind said to the soul: "This is how I *wish* you to see yourself! This is the image after which I create you! This is my secret about you: I shock you with it and, shockingly, at once wrest it from you"? And worse: having thus received *and* revealed its secret, the soul is no longer what it was when it lived in secrecy. For there are secrets which are *created* in the process of their revelation. And worse still: having been told its secrets, the soul may cease to be a soul. The step from modern psychology to soullessness is as imperceptible as that from modern physics to the dissolution of the concept "matter."

It is this disturbing state of affairs which made Nietzsche deplore "the torture" of psychologically "guessing the true nature of those higher beings" and, at the same time, recommend "respect for the mask" as a condition of "finer humanity." (A great pity he never wrote what, if we are to trust his notes, he planned to say in the abortive *Will to Power* about the literature of the nineteenth century. For no literary critic of the age has had a more penetrating insight into the "nihilistic" character of that "absolute aestheticism" that, from Baudelaire onward, has been the dominant inspiration of European poetry. Respectfully, and sometimes not so respectfully, Nietzsche recognized that behind the aesthetic "mask" there was a face distorted by the loathing of "reality." And it was the realistic and psychological novel that revealed to him that epoch's utterly pessimistic idea of its world. How intimately he knew those aesthetic Furies, or furious Muses, that haunted the mind of Flaubert, inspiring him to produce an *oeuvre* in which absolute pessimism, radical psychology, and extreme aestheticism are so intriguingly fused.)[19]

For Nietzsche, however, *all* the activities of human consciousness share the predicament of psychology. There can be, for him, no "pure" knowledge, only satisfaction, however sophisticated, of the ever-varying intellectual needs of the *will* to know. He therefore demands that man should accept *moral responsibility* for the kind of questions he asks, and that he should realize what *values* are implied in the answers he seeks—and in this he was more Christian than all our post-Faustian Fausts of truth and scholarship. "The desire for truth," he says, "is itself in need of critique. Let this be the definition of my philosophical task. By way of experiment, I shall question for once the value of truth."[20] And does he not! And he protests that, in an age which is as uncertain of its values as is his and ours, the search for truth will issue in either trivialities or—catastrophe.[21] We may well wonder how he would react to the pious hope of our day that the intelligence and moral conscience of politicians will save the world from the disastrous products of our scientific explorations and engineering skills. It is perhaps not too difficult to guess; for he knew that there was a fatal link between the moral resolution of scientists to follow the scientific search *wherever*, by its own momentum, it will take us, and the moral debility of societies not altogether disinclined to "apply" the results, however catastrophic. Believing that there was a hidden identity between *all* the expressions of the Will to Power, he saw the element of moral nihilism in the ethics of our science: its determination not to let "higher values" interfere with its highest value—Truth (as it conceives it). Thus he said that the goal of knowledge pursued by the natural sciences means perdition.[22]

3

"God is dead"—and man, in his heart of hearts, is incapable of forgiving himself for having done away with Him: he is bent upon punishing himself for this, his "greatest deed." For the time being, however, he will take refuge in many an evasive action. With the instinct of a born hunter, Nietzsche pursues him into all his hiding places, cornering him in each of them. Morality without religion? Indeed not: "All purely moral demands without their religious basis," he says, "must needs end in nihilism."[23] What is left? Intoxication. "Intoxication with music, with cruelty, with hero-worship, or with hatred . . . Some sort of mysticism . . . Art for Art's sake, Truth for Truth's sake, as a narcotic against self-disgust; some kind of routine, *any* silly little fanaticism . . ."[24] But none of these drugs can have any lasting effect. The time, Nietzsche predicts, is fast approaching when secular crusaders, tools of man's collective suicide, will devastate the world with their rival claims to compensate for the lost Kingdom of Heaven by setting up on earth the ideological rules of Love and Justice which, by the very force of the spiritual derangement involved, will lead to the rules of cruelty and slavery; and he prophesies that the war for global domination will be fought on behalf of philosophical doctrines.[25]

In one of his notes written at the time of *Zarathustra* Nietzsche says: "He who no longer finds what is great in God, will find it nowhere. He must either deny or create it."[26] These words take us to the heart of that paradox that enwraps Nietzsche's whole existence. He is, by the very texture of his soul and mind, one of the most radically religious natures that the nineteenth century brought forth, but is endowed with an intellect which guards, with the aggressive jealousy of a watchdog, all the approaches to the temple. For such a man, what, after the *denial* of God, is there left to *create*? Souls, not only strong enough to endure Hell, but to transmute its agonies into superhuman delight—in fact: the *Übermensch*. Nothing short of the transvaluation of all values can save us. Man has to be made immune to the effects of his second Fall and final separation from God: he must learn to see in his second expulsion the promise of a new paradise. For "the Devil may become envious of him who suffers so deeply, and throw him out—into Heaven."[27]

Is there, then, any cure? Yes, says Nietzsche: a new kind of psychic health. And what is Nietzsche's conception of it? How is it to be brought about? By perfect self-knowledge *and* perfect self-transcendence. But to explain this, we should have to adopt an idiom disturbingly compounded of the language of Freudian psychology and tragic heroism. For the self-knowledge which Nietzsche expects all but requires a course in depth analysis; but the self-transcendence he means lies not in the practice of virtue as a sublimation of natural meanness; it can only be found in a kind of unconditional and almost supranatural sublimity. If there were a Christian virtue, be it goodness, innocence, chastity, saintliness, or self-sacrifice, that could not, however much he tried, be interpreted as a compensatory maneuver of the mind to "transvalue" weakness and frustration, Nietzsche might affirm it (as he is constantly tempted to praise Pascal). The trouble is that there cannot be such a virtue. For virtues are reflected upon by minds; and even the purest virtue will be suspect to a mind filled with suspicion. To think thoughts so immaculate that they must command the trust of even the most untrusting imagination, and to act from motives so pure that they are out of reach of even the most cunning psychology, this is the unattainable ideal, it would seem, of this "first psychologist of Europe." "Caesar—with the heart of Christ!"[28] he once exclaimed in the secrecy of his notebook. Was this perhaps a definition of the *Übermensch,* this darling child of his imagination? It may well be; but this lofty idea meant, alas, that he had to think the meanest thought: he saw in the real Christ an illegitimate son of the Will to Power, a frustrated rabbi who set out to save himself and the underdog humanity from the intolerable strain of impotently resenting the Caesars: *not* to be Caesar was now proclaimed a spiritual distinction—a newly invented form of power, the power of the powerless.[29]

Nietzsche had to fail, and fail tragically, in his determination to create a new man from the clay of negation. Almost with the same breath with which he gave the life of his imagination to the *Übermensch,* he blew the flame out again. For Zarathustra who preaches the *Übermensch* also teaches the doctrine of the Eternal Recurrence of All Things; and according to this doctrine nothing can ever come into being that had not existed at some time before—and, Zarathustra says, "never yet has there been an *Übermensch.*"[30] Thus the expectation of this majestic new departure of life, indeed the possibility of any novel development, seems frustrated from the outset, and the world, caught forever in a cycle of gloomily repeated constellations of energy, stands condemned to a most dismal eternity.

Yet the metaphysical nonsense of these contradictory doctrines is not entirely lacking in poetic and didactic method. The Eternal Recurrence of All Things is Nietzsche's mythic formula of a meaningless world, the universe of nihilism, and the *Übermensch* stands for its transcendence, for the miraculous resurrection of meaning from its total negation. All Nietzsche's miracles are paradoxes designed to jerk man out of his false beliefs in time, before they bring about his spiritual destruction in an ecstasy of disillusionment and frustration. The Eternal Recurrence is the high school meant to teach strength through despair. The *Übermencsh* graduates from it *summa cum laude et gloria*. He is the prototype of health, the man who has learned to live without belief and without truth, and, superhumanly delighting in life "as such," actually *wills* the Eternal Recurrence: Live in such a way that you desire nothing more than to live this very same life again and again![31] The *Übermensch* having attained to this manner of existence which is exemplary and alluring into all eternity, despises his former self for craving moral sanctions, for satisfying his will to power in neurotic sublimation, for deceiving himself about the "meaning" of life. What will he be then, this man who at last knows what life *really* is? Recalling Nietzsche's own accounts of all-too-human nature, and his analysis of the threadbare fabric of traditional values and truths, may he not be the very monster of nihilism, a barbarian, not necessarily blond, but perhaps a conqueror of the world, shrieking bad German from under his dark mustache? Yes, Nietzsche feared his approach in history: the vulgar caricature of the *Übermensch*. And because he also feared that the liberally tolerant, skeptically acquiescent and agnostically disbelieving heirs to Christian morality who had enfeebled the idea of civilized existence and rendered powerless the good would be unable to meet the challenges, Nietzsche sent forth from his imagination the *Übermensch* to defeat the defeat of man.

Did Nietzsche himself *believe* in the truth of his doctrines of the *Übermensch* and the Eternal Recurrence? In one of his posthumously published notes he says of the Eternal Recurrence: "We have produced the hardest possible thought—the Eternal Recurrence of All Things— now let us create the creature who will accept it lightheartedly and blissfully!"[32] Clearly, there must have been times when he thought of the Eternal Recurrence not as a "Truth" but as a kind of spiritual Darwinian test to select for survival the spiritually fittest. There is a note of his which suggests precisely this: "I perform the great experiment: Who can bear the idea of the Eternal Recurrence?"[33] This is a measure of Nietzsche's own unhappiness: the nightmare of nightmares was to him the idea that he might have to live his identical life again and again and again; and an ever deeper insight into the anatomy of despair we gain from this note: "Let us consider this idea in its most terrifying form: existence, as it is, without meaning or goal, but inescapably recurrent, without a finale into nothingness. . . . Those who cannot bear the sentence, There is no salvation, *ought* to perish!"[34] Indeed, Nietzsche's *Übermensch* is the creature strong enough to live forever a cursed existence and even to transmute it into the Dionysian rapture of tragic acceptance. Schopenhauer called man the *animal metaphysicum*. It is certainly true of Nietzsche, the renegade *homo religiosus*. Therefore, if God was dead, then for Nietzsche man was an eternally cheated misfit, the diseased animal, as he called him, plagued by a metaphysical hunger which it was now impossible to feed even if all the Heavens were to be ransacked. Such a creature was doomed: he had to die out, giving way to the *Übermensch* who would miraculously feed on barren fields and finally conquer the metaphysical hunger itself without any detriment to the glory of life.

Did Nietzsche himself *believe* in the *Übermensch?* In the manner in which a poet believes in the truth of his creations. Did Nietzsche believe in the truth of poetic creations? Once upon a time when, as a young man, he wrote *The Birth of Tragedy*, Nietzsche did believe in the power of art to transfigure life by creating lasting images of true beauty out of the meaningless chaos. It had seemed credible enough as long as his gaze was enraptured by the distant prospect of classical Greece and the enthusiastic vicinity of Richard Wagner's Tribschen. Soon, however, his deeply Romantic belief in art turned to skepticism and scorn; and his unphilosophical anger was provoked by those "metaphysical counterfeiters," as he called them, who enthroned the trinity of beauty, goodness, and truth. "One should beat them," he said. Poetic beauty *and* truth? No, "we have *Art* in order not to perish of Truth"[35] and, says Zarathustra, "poets lie too much"—and adds dejectedly: "But Zarathustra too is a poet . . . *We* lie too much."[36] And he did: while Zarathustra preached the Eternal Recurrence, his author confided to his diary: "I do not wish to live *again*. How have I borne life? By creating. What has made me endure? The vision of the *Übermensch* who affirms life. I have tried to affirm life *myself*—but ah!"[37] (There is, I believe, only one example of a confessed *happy* nihilist: the German poet Gottfried Benn. "*Nilismus ist ein Glücksgefühl*," he said. He would be the perfect Nietzschean if his great mentor had died after *The Birth of Tragedy* and not essentially modified or even revoked the central thesis of that early book: that art is the only true "metaphysical activity." And Benn did claim that his "transcendent" appetites found satisfaction in the making of aesthetically successful things: poems, for instance. But in 1933, when Hitler came to power, he wrote not so much poetry, as he did, often brilliantly, in later years, but the most abject mumbo jumbo in praise of the crooked cross, symbol of a very different substitute religion.)*

Was he, having lost God, capable of truly believing in *anything?* "He who no longer finds what is great in God will find it nowhere— he must either deny it or create it." Only the "either-or" does not apply. All his life Nietzsche tried to do both. He had the passion for truth and no belief in it. He had the love of life and despaired of it. This is the stuff from which demons are made—perhaps the most powerful secret demon eating the heart out of the modern mind. To have written and enacted the extremest story of this mind is Nietzsche's true claim to greatness. "The Don Juan of the Mind" he once called, in a "fable" he wrote, a figure whose identity is hardly in doubt:

> The Don Juan of the Mind: no philosopher or poet has yet discovered him. What he lacks is the love of the things he knows, what he possesses is *esprit,* the itch and delight in the chase and intrigue of knowledge— knowledge as far and high as the most distant stars. Until in the end there is nothing left for him to chase except the knowledge which hurts most, just as a drunkard in the end drinks absinthe and methylated spirits. And in the very end he craves for Hell—it is the only knowledge which can still seduce him. Perhaps it too will disappoint, as everything that he knows. And if so, he will have to stand transfixed through all eternity, nailed to disillusion, having himself become the Guest of Stone, longing for a last supper of knowledge which he will never receive. For in the whole world of things there is nothing left to feed his hunger.[38]

It is a German Don Juan, this Don Juan of the Mind; and it is amazing that Nietzsche should not have recognized his features: the features of Goethe's Faust at the point at which he has succeeded at last in defeating the plan of salvation.

And yet Nietzsche's work, wrapped in paradox after paradox, taking us to the limits of what is still comprehensible and often beyond, carries elements which issue from a center of sanity. No doubt, this

*I have discussed the "didactically" perverse and "poetically" paradoxical relationship between *Übermensch* and Eternal Recurrence more fully in the essay "Nietzsche's Terrors: Time and the Inarticulate," later in this book. It is probably the book's most conspicuous case of repetitiveness, the more so as I use some of the same quotations in the later essay. But as the discussion of these two ideas has its organic function in either essay and as, to my knowledge, the inner connection of those themes is shown more directly and succinctly than elsewhere in the literature about Nietzsche, I have not deleted anything, hoping that the reiteration enhances clarity and emphasis.

core is in perpetual danger of being crushed, and was in fact destroyed in the end. But it is there, and is made of the stuff of which goodness is made. A few years before he went mad, he wrote: "My life is now comprised in the wish that the truth about all things be different from my way of seeing it: if only someone would convince me of the improbability of my truths!"[39] And he said: "Lonely and deeply suspicious of myself as I was, I took, not without secret spite, sides *against* myself and *for* anything that happened to hurt me and was hard for me."[40] Why? Because he was terrified by the prospect that all the better things in life, all honesty of mind, integrity of character, generosity of heart, fineness of aesthetic perception, would be corrupted and finally cast away by the new barbarians, unless the mildest and gentlest hardened themselves for the war which was about to be waged against them:[41] "Caesar—with the heart of Christ!"

Time and again we come to a point in Nietzsche's writings where the shrill tones of the rebel are hushed by the still voice of the autumn of a world waiting in calm serenity for the storms to break. Then this tormented mind relaxes in what he once called the *Rosengeruch des Unwiederbringlichen*—an untranslatably beautiful lyricism of which the closest equivalent in English is perhaps Yeats's lines:

> Man is in love and loves what vanishes.
> What more is there to say?

In such moments the music of Bach brings tears to his eyes and he brushes aside the noise and turmoil of Wagner; or he his, having deserted Zarathustra's cave in the mountains, enchanted by the gentle grace of a Mediterranean coastline. Rejoicing in the quiet lucidity of Claude Lorrain, or seeking the company of Goethe in conversation with Eckermann, or comforted by the composure of Stifter's *Nachsommer,* a Nietzsche emerges, very different from the one who used to inhabit the fancies of Teutonic schoolboys and, alas, schoolmasters, a Nietzsche who is a traditionalist at heart, a desperate lover who castigates what he loves because he knows it will abandon him and the world. It is the Nietzsche who can with one sentence cross out all the dissonances of his apocalyptic voices: "I once saw a storm raging over the sea, and a clear blue sky above it; it was then that I came to dislike all sunless, cloudy passions which know no light, except the lightning."[42] And this was written by the same man who said that his tool for philosophizing was the hammer,[43] and of himself that he was not human but dynamite.[44]

In these regions of his mind dwells the terror that he may have helped to bring about the very opposite of what he desired. When this terror comes to the fore, he is much afraid of the consequences of his teaching. Perhaps the best will be driven to despair by it, the very worst accept it?[45] And once he put into the mouth of some imaginary titanic genius what is his most terrible prophetic utterance: "Oh grant madness, you heavenly powers! Madness that at last I may believe in myself . . . I am consumed by doubts, for I have killed the Law. . . . If I am not more than the Law, then I am the most abject of all men."[46]

What, then, is the final importance of Nietzsche? For one of his readers it lies in his example which is so strange, profound, confounded, alluring, and forbidding that it can hardly be looked upon as exemplary. But it cannot be ignored either. For it has something to do with living lucidly in the dark age of which he so creatively despaired.

# NIETZSCHE AND GOETHE

In 1817 Goethe published in *Kunst and Altertum* a little essay entitled "Epochs of the Spirit, based on Hermann's newest records."[1] Inspired by the book *De Mythologia Graecorum Antiquissimorum* of the Leipzig scholar Gottfried Hermann, this sketch, anticipating in its modest way the method of Spengler's historical morphology, speaks of four major phases in the history of man. These "four epochs of the human spirit," "profoundly contemplated," as Goethe claims, "and fittingly named," he calls the Ages of Poetry, Theology, Philosophy and Prose. They are preceded, according to his account, by a state which does not even qualify for a name. It is the chaos before the beginning and before the Word—although even then a few favored spirits might rise above the speechless dark, crudely meditating the uncreated universe and uttering raucous sounds to express their confused astonishment. Theirs is an apparently barren state of mind which nevertheless holds the seeds of observation and philosophy, of giving nature names, and thus of poetry. From these inarticulate mutterings emerges the first Age proper, the Age of Poetry, in which man projects his tender familiarity with himself, his desires and fears, satisfactions and discontents, on to the things which surround him. It is a time of popular myth and poetical fancy; the soul overconfidently and lightheartedly frees itself of the cumbersome abstruseness of the primeval stage. The spirits of myth and poetry wield their undivided power over the community which is, as Goethe says, distinguished by a sensuousness at once free, serious, noble and enhanced by the imagination.

Soon, however, man finds himself, perhaps by force of external circumstances, thrown into new perplexities. The world ceases to be his castle in which the mind and the imagination dwell comfortably between walls covered with allegorical tapestries, and appears once more inadequately understood. The poetically comprehending creature is again beset by apprehension, the idyllic order threatened by a multitude of demons demanding to be placated in their wildness, reverenced in their incalculable dominion, and held at bay no longer by pretty fancies but only through a more energetic activity of the spirit. Gone is the graceful intimacy of the Age of Poetry, and Mystery is reinstated. It is to this epoch that ultimately God is revealed, with the fear and terror of the primeval phase purified into love and awe. We may call it, says Goethe, the Age of the Holy, or the Age of Theology, or the Age of Reason in its highest sense.

Again, it cannot last. For Reason will insist on reasoning and ultimately, as a conqueror often does with the object of his conquests, destroy what it is reasoning about, Analyzing what eludes analysis, systematizing what defies the system, it will in the end deceive itself by pretending that the vainly besieged mystery does not exist. At this point the Age of the Holy gives way to the Age of Philosophy, or, to use a more familiar term, to enlightenment and finally rationalism. We cannot, says Goethe, but acknowledge the noble and intelligent endeavor of this epoch; yet while it may suit some talented individuals, it cannot satisfy whole peoples. The Prosaic Age is bound to follow. The all too radical attempt of the Age of Philosophy at a "humanization" and rationalization of the mystery ends in a perverted miracle. The mystery, cheated of its rightful place, goes underground, reverting to its primeval, unholy and barbarous stage. The human spirit, agitated by historical catastrophes, leaps backward over all hurdles which the guidance of reason has erected, clinging here and there to remnants of tradition, scattered residues of many incompatible beliefs, then plunges headlong into pools of insipid mythologies, bringing to the top the muddy poetry of the depths and proclaiming it as the creed of the age.

No longer are there teachers who teach with calm and reason, but merely men sowing grain and weeds in random confusion. No center holds the human world together and men must lose their bearings; for countless individuals step forth as leaders, preaching their perfect foolishness as the acme of wisdom. In such an age every belief turns into blasphemy, and the proclamation of mysteries into sacrilege. Elements, once evolving naturally one from the other, are now interlocked in perpetual strife. It is the return of the tohu-bohu; yet a chaos not fertile as the first, but so deadening that not even God could create from it a world worthy of Himself.

It is surprising that a peaceful Leipzig scholar, whose attitude Nietzsche once described as the typically *sächsisch* combination of humanism and religious rationalism,[2] should have been the begetter of such a rare flight of Goethe's historical imagination. But although the condensed precision of this seemingly casual prophecy is unique in Goethe's writings, shadows of things to come fall on many a page of his mature work. In the guarded and fortified stillness of *Wilhelm Meisters Wanderjahre* (the work that occupied him at the same time) echoes can be discerned of subterranean rumblings, menacing with future eruptions a society whose exposures and dangers are acknowledged by the very didactic passion of this extraordinary work—a work which struck Nietzsche, in one of his more irreverent moods, as a mixture of "the most beautiful things in the world" and "the most ridiculous triflings."[3] Indeed, a certain parallelism is obvious between the three epochs of the spirit and the three stations in Wilhelm Meister's pilgramage which fill the first book of the novel, so that the monastic sphere of St. Joseph the Second is informed with all the ingredients of the Age of the Holy, with elements of the Age of Poetry lingering on, while the estate of Hersilie's uncle clearly represents the Age of Philosophy, with no picture tolerated in the eighteenth-century portrait gallery that "might point even remotely towards religion, tradition, mythology, legend or fable."[4] And there is finally Makarie's ancient castle, looking so fresh and new—"as though builders and masons had only just departed"[5]—where Goethe's, not Newton's, physics are pursued, a science whose calculations reveal, rather than disturb, the harmony between man's intuitive and rational natures, showing him, not as the ruthlessly dominating, but as "the spiritually integrating part"[6] of the universe. This castle of Makarie's stands like a fortress, built in Goethe's imagination, to ward off, as their most positive alternative, the horrors of the Prosaic Age.

Furthermore, in that masterpiece of ambiguity, *Faust,* the clash between the holy simplicity of the Gretchen world and the reason of the philosopher, aided by the prosaic detachment of the Devil, determines not only the tragedy of Part I, but finds expression also in Part II. Indeed, if we sought in Goethe's works for the most poignant poetic dramatization of the defeat of the holy at the hands of prosaic engineering, we should have to call on the faithful old couple in their little house on the hill, sacrificed to Faust's planning of the future bliss of millions:

| | |
|---|---|
| BAUCIS | *Menschenopfer mussten bluten,* |
| | *Nachts erscholl des Jammers Qual;* |
| | *Meerab flossen Feuergluten,* |
| | *Morgens war es ein Kanal.* |
| | *Gottlos ist er, ihn gelüstet* |
| | *Unsre Hütte, unser Hain;* |
| | *Wie er sich als Nachbar brüstet,* |
| | *Soll man untertänig sein.* |
| PHILEMON | *Hat er uns doch angeboten* |
| | *Schönes Gut im neuen Land!* |
| BAUCIS | *Traue nicht dem Wasserboden,* |
| | *Halt auf deiner Höhe stand!* |

PHILEMON  *Lasst uns zur Kapelle treten,*
*Letzten Sonnenblick zu schaun!*
*Lasst uns läuten, knien, beten,*
*Und dem alten Gott vertraun!*[7]

Human sacrifices had to bleed, the night resounded with cries of anguish; floods of fire poured into the sea, in the morning it was a canal. Godless he is, lusting after our cottage, our grove; boastful neighbor that he is, he demands obedience.—Yet he has offered us a pretty estate in the new country!—Do not trust the watery soil, hold out on your height!—Let us go to our chapel, catch the sun's last radiance, ring the bells, and kneel and pray, and put our trust in God.

What, in the Prosaic Age, is to become of poetry itself, its activity and its enjoyment? How will this very poem *Faust* be received? Goethe asks, five days before his death, in his last letter to Wilhelm von Humboldt. "The absurdity and confusion of the day is such," he writes, "as to convince me that the honest and prolonged labor with which I have built this strange edifice will be but ill rewarded; it will be cast up by the sea as fragments of a wreck, and for some time to come will be buried under the barren dunes of the age. Confused gospels, begetting confused deeds, are abroad in the world, and my business is to enhance and purify what is mine and what has remained with me, as you, my worthy friend, also contrive to do up there in your castle."[8]

In other words, the Prosaic Age is upon us, with its disenchantment of myth and poetry, and its "mystification" of reason itself. It will— to use Goethe's words—"drag into the vulgar light of day the ancient heritage of a noble past, and destroy not only the capacity for profound feeling and the beliefs of peoples and priests, but even that belief of reason which divines meaningful coherence behind strangeness and seeming disorder."[9]

It is, then, the destruction, or rather the mutilation and deformation, of something which Goethe, perhaps for want of a better word, calls "belief," which is one of the symptoms, or one of the causes, of the repulsiveness of the Prosaic Age. As soon as the notion of belief enters into our reflections about Goethe, we have to move with the utmost wariness; for Goethe, of course, was no believer in any doctrinal sense. On the other hand, we need not be too prudish and may take courage from the fact that Goethe, at about the same time, uses the word again in a very much more contaminated neighborhood: namely, in connection with the Old Testament. Meditating on the desert adventures of the Israelites, he says, in his "Notes and Discourses concerning the *Westöstlicher Divan*": "The one and only real and profound theme of the world and of human history—a theme to which all others are subordinate—remains the conflict between belief and unbelief. All epochs dominated by belief in whatever shape have a radiance and bliss of their own, and bear fruit for their people as well as for posterity. All epochs over which unbelief in whatever form maintains its miserable victory, even if they boast and shine for a while with false splendor, are ignored by posterity because nobody likes to drudge his life out over sterile things."[10]

Paradoxically enough, what follows leaves no doubt that Goethe, indulging at this point in a rather ruthless sort of Bible criticism, does not mean the belief of the strict believer in the Old Testament. What, then does he mean? For clearly, this belief can be no trifling matter; it makes and unmakes epochs by its very coming and going; it gives the Age of the Holy its holiness and in parting abandons the next to its prosaic fate; and its struggle with unbelief is proclaimed as the only theme of genuine historical relevance.

The question of what he meant by "belief" would have drawn different answers from Goethe at different times, all equally veiled, ironical—and irritated. For the question touches upon a sphere which Goethe held to be reserved for the initiates—"*Sagt es neimand, nur den Weisen, Weil die Menge gleich verhöhnet*"; "Don't tell anyone apart from the sages, for the herd will instantly laugh at you." Thus it is impossible to state his beliefs in any doctrinal manner, particularly if one wishes to avoid a discussion of that sublime menace besetting all studies of Goethe: pantheism. For there is no creed to be elicited from Goethe's writings. Put together systematically as articulate opinions, his convictions would appear very inconsistent and at times self-contradictory. Yet it is neither his opinions nor their inconsistencies that matter in this context. What matters is the level on which his convictions are formed, or the pressure of spiritual energy by which they are sustained; and the quality and direction of his beliefs are most clearly revealed through Goethe's critique of his age. For there is little doubt that the mature Goethe would have put his contemporary world, in spite of occasional outbursts of Panama Canal optimism, into a rather shadowy place on his map of the world's historical epochs, at some removes, in any case, from the Age of Poetry and the Age of the Holy, and considerably nearer those grey stretches where history writes its most atrocious prose passages. And he would certainly not have discovered in it many glimpses of that radiance which emanates from "epochs of belief."

It would be easy enough, of course, to deny the historical accuracy of Goethe's, or Professor Hermann's, scheme of epochs; but perhaps still easier to show that our seemingly most effective refutation would simply be due to our use of a different code of selection and emphasis in ordering the mass of historical raw material. Goethe's—and Nietzsche's—judgments on their contemporary world are undoubtedly what it is the fashion to call "*wild generalizations.*" But then, this is the same vice in which the prophets of the Old Testament indulged. Perhaps the Israel of their time was, in fact, a very much better community than their indignation suggests. But if we reached this conclusion, and even if it were based on the greatest profusion of historical evidence, our findings would ultimately reflect, not a higher degree of "objective knowledge," but our allegiance to values which the prophets would have denounced as false. And as this mental and moral situation is the precise cause of their indignation, it is we who are under judgment—a position which is generally not regarded as favorable to the forming of unbiased views. Also, I think, our case against the justice of the judges must be aggravated by the fact that their prophecy has come true. The Temple was destroyed.

What the mature Goethe means by belief has this in common with the prophets—that for him too it is the active realization of certain *values* in the lives of men. And our question turns on the nature of these values, a question which, as Nietzsche knew, "is more *fundamental* than the question of the certainty [of knowledge]: the latter becomes serious only if the question of values is answered."[11] Goethe would have accepted this, although it stands as a key phrase within a body of thought which at first sight is worlds apart from the world of Goethe. And Goethe actually did accept it, if not in the radical spirit in which Nietzsche proposed it, nor, of course, with the same intensity of desperate doubt about the worth of knowledge. His opposition to Newton, for instance, is ultimately based not on a conviction of his own *scientific* superiority, but on his commitment to values which he believed were threatened by man's adopting an exclusively mathematical-analytical method in his dealings with nature. Goethe does confuse the issue in his scientific writings; but outside the laboratory, as it were, he makes this abundantly clear, as, for instance, in the words which Wilhelm Meister, here simply the expositor of Goethe's own wisdom, addresses to the astronomer: "I can well understand that it must please you, sages of the sky, to bring the immense universe gradually as close to your eyes as I saw that planet just now. But allow me to say . . . that these instruments, with which we aid our senses, have a morally detrimental effect on man. . . . For what he thus perceives with his senses is out of keeping with his inner faculty of discernment;

it would need a culture, as high as only exceptional people can possess, in order to harmonize, to a certain extent, the inner truth with the inappropriate vision from without. . . ."[12]

## 2

There must have been a time when the religious, aesthetic and moral perceptions were at one."[13] This is not, though it could be, a sentence from Goethe's "epochs of the spirit," but, one of Nietzsche's posthumous notes assembled in *The Will to Power,* the fragments of a work in which he intended to "revalue all values." It is so much a Goethean thought that it seems to have been expanded into the following reflection about Goethe in *Götzen-Dämmerung, The Twilight of the Idols,* one of the last works of Nietzsche:

> Goethe—in a grandiose attempt to get beyond the eighteenth century through the naturalness of the Renaissance, a kind of self-conquest on the part of that century—had within himself its strongest instincts: its sentimentality, its nature-idolatry, its anti-historical bias, its idealism, lack of realism, its revolutionary spirit (which is only one form of the lack of realism). He called in the help of history, of natural science, of antiquity, even of Spinoza, and, above all, of practical activity; he surrounded himself with closed horizons; he did not desert life, but placed himself at its center and took as much as possible upon himself, above himself, into himself. What he aimed at was *totality; he fought against the sundering of reason, sensuality, feeling, will . . .;* he disciplined himself into wholeness, he *created* himself . . . Goethe was, in the midst of an unrealistic age, a *convinced realist. . . .* He envisaged man as strong, highly civilized, skilled in all skills of the body, holding himself in check, having respect for himself as a creature who may be allowed to taste the whole width and wealth of naturalness, who is strong enough for this kind of freedom; who is tolerant, not from weakness but from strength, because he knows how to use to his advantage what would destroy an average character. . . .[14]

Although things of this kind have been said so often in later appraisals of Goethe that they have come to smack of the commonplace, in the context of Nietzsche's "revaluing of values" they have a profundity of their own, and receive in the concluding words of this passage, so far withheld, a surprising twist which we shall, a little later, allow to shock us. For the time being we should like to reflect on the identification in this passage of Goethe's realism with his antagonism to the severance of reason, sensuality, feeling and will; or, in Nietzsche's previous formula, on Goethe's roots in an imaginary period in which religious, aesthetic and moral perceptions were at one—a unity so disastrously destroyed in the Prosaic Age.

The term "realism" had a definite meaning, as the opposite to nominalism, at a time when metaphysical disputes enjoyed the advantages of as rigid a discipline as is nowadays accorded to scientific research. But, of course, this was before the word became used as a coin of uncertain value in that nineteenth-century bazaar of ideas where other counters too, such as transcendentalism, idealism, empiricism, materialism, positivism, bought a few frills of the mind. Thus Goethe's "realism," fallen among the philistines, assumed so often the meager meaning of "down to earth," or "practical," or "you will learn, my boy." Or else, as the name of a literary genre, "realism" was to provide a convenient common denominator for all writers who harness the exuberance of their imaginations to the austere task of calling a spade a spade.

Clearly, this is not what Nietzsche means in speaking of the realist Goethe, a realist, moreover, not from "instinct" but through "discipline." What, I think, Nietzsche does mean I should like to illustrate with the help of three Goethe aphorisms which were first printed together in the same number of *Kunst and Altertum* (V,3, of the year 1826). The first reads as follows: "It is now about twenty years since the whole race of Germans began to 'transcend.' Should they ever wake up to this fact, they will look very odd to themselves."[15] The second, famous enough, is: "In a true symbol the particular represents the universal, not as a dream or shadow, but as the living and instantaneous revelation of the unfathomable."[16] The third seems at first rather obscure: "All that is ideal will ultimately, once it is claimed by the real, consume it, and itself. As paper money consumes the silver and itself."[17] There is, not merely by virtue of their sequence in print, an intimate connection between these three aphorisms. The first, of course, ridicules the German *Transzendentalphilosophie* of Goethe's time; the second provides the happiest condensation of Goethe's own idea of the relationship between the transcendent and the immanent, the "ideal" and the "real"; the third is the epigrammatic abbreviation of the prophecy of the Prosaic Age, this time seen as the destructive, nihilistic outcome of the tearing apart of the real and the ideal spheres.

It is a very long story which these three aphorisms succeed in cutting short, and it would be an invidious business indeed to restore it to its original length. But perhaps a few meditations are permissible.

Goethe's hostility towards all forms of transcendental philosophy has certainly no affinities whatever with a philosophical offensive against the transcendent, waged much later under the name of positivism—a campaign with which Nietzsche is often associated. On the contrary, Goethe's ill feelings against the transcendentalists sprang from the same source which sustained his energetic attacks on the kind of positivism he believed to be inherent in Newtonian physics. He regarded both transcendentalists and positivists (of whom he had the idea, if not the name) as the systematizers of a perception of reality which to him appeared absurd, indeed as that very "absurdity and confusion of the day" which he lamented at so late an hour of his life to Wilhelm von Humboldt. What both these tendencies of the mind—superficially so inimical to each other—have in common is a passion for abstraction. And it is in abstraction that Goethe saw the fatal loophole through which reason could escape into an illusory freedom from its duty toward what is of the senses, of feeling, of the will. He dreaded this emancipation of reason, whether exercised in adventures of transcendental speculation, or in the mathematical calculus which creates, despite its apparent empiricism, the phenomena to be fitted into its abstract order.

Either method of emancipating reason from the totality of the human person appeared to Goethe as the denial of his vision of man, the negation of the values he upheld, the heresy *kat'exochen*. He sincerely believed that this way lay catastrophe.

In the pursuit of transcendentalism he discerned the danger that reason, doped with transcendental ambition, would construct a world too big in its anaemic hugeness for man to live and love in, distracting him at every point from—as Wilhelm Meister puts it—"attending with spontaneous care to the duty of the day, examining the purity of your hearts and the stability of your minds. . . . Only then will you find the right attitude towards the sublime; for it is to the sublime that we dedicate ourselves in all manner of activities and in a spirit of awe. . . ."[18] In a spirit of awe; not of that spiritual conceit of which he suspected the architects of the transcendental Towers of Babel to be possessed.

If in transcendentalism human reason was perverted in the direction of the abstruse, in scientific positivism, so it seemed to Goethe, it was led astray in yet another way: in turning the universe into a plaything for mathematics and the willful assertiveness of experimentation, reason once more placed the world out of the reach of true human comprehension. For the truth of human comprehension resides for Goethe in that balanced vision in which the religious, the aesthetic and the moral perceptions are at one. Only through their concord the world stands revealed as the proper home of man, appearing neither too great for his insignificance, nor too small for his greatness; neither too fantastic for his reason, nor too prosaic for his imagination; neither too unwieldy for his will, nor too unlovable for his affection. In a very profound sense of that word, *propriety* is for Goethe the criterion of truth. This is why Nietzsche admired him as the last of the great aristocratic minds of Europe.[19] For there is indeed something plebeian at work in all other standards of truth which have become, articulately or not, the fashion in modern intellectual activities: elements of either self-abasement or rational conceit, of excessive curiosity, of psychological tactlessness, and a sniggering suspicion of the absence of meaning in anything that evades definition or experimental proof, and above all a disregard for those intangible qualities that make the world a noble habitation.

Goethe's scientific labors were directed and sustained by his intuitive certainty that knowledge can only be true as long as it is not in excess of man's feelings. The problem involved is, of course, an old one, at least as old as modern science itself, and was first lived and struggled through by that extraordinary man in whom the mind of a mathematician clashed with the mind of a mystic—Pascal. His endless concern was with reason and that reason of which reason knows nothing: the reason of the heart; with the *esprit de géométrie* and the *esprit de finesse*. Since then the question and conflict, in innumerable variations, have never ceased to vex some of the finest minds of Europe. In Goethe's case, however, it can hardly be called a problem. For he had no serious doubts about the worthlessness of the *esprit de géométrie*. And where its achievements were beyond dispute, beyond even the negative certainty of Goethe, the utmost homage he was prepared to pay to them was the suggestion that a soul rich with intuition could reach at least as far as the newest telescopes. In the peculiar household of Makarie, the astronomer's business is simply to spot the stars which the lady of the house, harboring all the galaxies in her breast, has seen in her dreams; an astronomical job not very much superior to that of the digger who digs for the water that the diviner has divined.

But beyond such indulgence of a wayward sense of humor, Goethe is deeply convinced that man can only do justice to himself and to the world and its maker by creating from within an image of both himself and the world which does not clash with his idea of the deity. And Goethe's idea of the deity was given to him in that "revealed mystery," that "living and instantaneous revelation of the unfathomable," through the symbolic nature of the particular. From this symbolic nature of the particular, to be grasped only in the concerted receptivity of sense, mind, feeling and will, man was increasingly alienated through the excessive rationalism of both his physics and metaphysics.

The Germans were indeed to look odd to themselves once they woke up to their real status after all the transcending had been done: as odd, one might add, as the scientist confronted with the all but demonic unmanageability of the results of his analytical radicalism. For what is lost between the extremes of transcendence and analysis is the Goethean ideal of personality: a state of balance between what man *is* and what he *can do*. "Man ought not to know more of a thing than he can creatively live up to." Goethe might have said this. It was said by Nietzsche, reflecting on the sterility of philological studies (of which he was a professor) and comparing the quality of mind of his most learned colleagues with Goethe's meager philological equipment; yet, he adds, "he knew enough to wrestle fruitfully with antiquity!"[20] And elsewhere: "Goethe's taste and ability ran parallel."[21] This is a posthumous note from the time of the muted dithyrambus *Richard Wagner in Bayreuth*. Even then he knew what was to become violent polemic in later years: that this could not be said of Richard Wagner. And with the words "the presumptuous" the remark on Goethe leads on to an observation about Richard Wagner's histrionic character.

Indeed, Nietzsche knew who Goethe was. There is the instruction of Goethe in his turning away from Wagner, the Goethean knowledge that it is the discrepancy between human substance and human virtuosity, between what a man is and what he can do, which is a dominant feature of the Prosaic Age. The Age of Talent may be an alternative name for it. The symptoms are displayed by art and life alike. Life is frightened out of its highly enlightened wits by the return of ancient nightmares: the tales of the sorcerer's apprentice, of dwarfs with magic powers. The promise of Heaven for the poor in spirit is understood to mean that, on earth at least, they should be educated into clever people able to manipulate and let loose the technical installations of Hell. And in art, there are sounds most skillfully organized, furies expressed in the most virtuoso fashion and proud of signifying nothing. Whole systems of aesthetics are evolved to justify this state of affairs. A world emptied of meaning seeks to escape from the infinite boredom of its meaninglessness by the magic of words without flesh and forms without content. And, indeed, the attempt to distill poetry from the things or ideas that form our "real" world would be in vain. Poetry, we are told, is enchantment, and all things and thoughts have been robbed of their charm in the bright daylight robbery of utility and abstraction. Yet for Goethe things and thoughts shared that luminous concreteness which is the quality of a world with all its dimensions intact. Remember what he called "thinking" in a passage of his *Second Sojourn in Rome,* where he describes his impression of Raphael's *"Transfigura-zione"*: "The kindred spirits among us were confirmed in their convictions," he writes. "Raphael, they said to one another, is distinguished by the rightness of his thinking." And thus he interprets the two levels of being, represented in that painting: "How can one sever what is above from what is below? The two are one; below there is suffering and neediness, and above active mercy, the one reflecting upon the other in mutual interchange. Is it then, to express the meaning of this painting in a different way, at all possible to separate from the real its ideal relevance?" [22]

In the "Buch Hafis" of the *West-östlicher Divan,* one section has this motto:

> *Sei das Wort die Braut genannt,*
> *Bräutigam der Geist;*
> *Diese Hochzeit hat gekannt,*
> *Wer Hafisen preist.* [23]

Let the word be named the bride, and the spirit the bridegroom; he who sings in praise of Hafis has known this wedlock.

In that section the poet, addressing himself to Hafis, proclaims his faith in a world marked with the imprint of the divine features and sings its praise in defiance of all negation, hindrance, robbery, that words and things endure at the hands of the detractors and abstractors:

> *Und so gleich ich dir vollkommen,*
> *Der ich unsrer heil'gen Bücher*
> *Herrlich Bild an mich genommen,*
> *Wie auf jenes Tuch der Tücher*
> *Sich des Herren Bildnis drückte,*
> *Mich in stiller Brust erquickte,*
> *Trotz Verneinung, Hindrung, Raubens,*
> *Mit dem heitern Bild des Glaubens.* [24]

And so I am your perfect likeness, I who have taken on myself the glorious image of our sacred books: as on that cloth of cloths there was imprinted the countenance of the Lord, so, within my quiet heart, was I refreshed, despite negation, hindrance, robbery, by the serene image of faith.

This, then, is Goethe's belief, or his answer to the problem which is "more fundamental than the question of the certainty of knowledge": the problem of values. The answer lies in Goethe's realism as understood by Nietzsche. It is the *realism of the symbol;* not of the obscure symbol thrown up by the collective unconscious of the symbolists, invading the husks of dead memories with dreamt and undreamt-of significances; nor of the symbol which refers to abstractions, in the manner of an allegory: the kind of symbol which the young philologist Nietzsche in a preparatory note for *The Birth of Tragedy* regarded as the sign of a dying art because it introduced, furtively and in flimsy disguise, abstract notions—but the symbol in its original meaning, defined by Nietzsche in the same note, in a strikingly Goethe-like manner, as "the language of the universal." [25] This realism of the symbol is the common property of all great art. It does not strain after an ideal sphere which may redeem the prosaic unworthiness of this world (as Schiller's art does), nor does it seek deliverance from the terror of truth in the healing unreality of the *"schöner Schein"* (as the young Nietzsche believed), nor does it self-consciously call on dreams and nightmares pleasantly or unpleasantly to ruffle the boring smoothness of life's surface. It describes; and in describing it opens our eyes to what really is. And what really is is not a dream or shadow, nor the meaningless agony of the Will, nor the abstractions of Reason, but the living revelation of the unfathomable. Yet why should the unfathomable be beautiful? Because it can only be comprehended by the unfathomable, and the only truly unfathomable faculty of man is love. Thus the realism of the symbol becomes the artistic vindication of the reality of a lovable world. "That something like Spinoza's *amoi dei* could be experienced again!" [26] This is a note which Nietzsche, during his most radical Anti-Christ period, made about Goethe.

3

At this point we had better return to that passage in Nietzsche's *Twilight of the Idols* from which, in quoting it before, we left out the concluding words. After he has called Goethe a "convinced realist in the midst of an unrealistic age," Nietzsche continues: "Such a mind, having attained to real freedom, lives at the very center of all things with a joyful and confident acceptance of fate, lives in the faith that only the particular in its separateness is objectionable, and that in the wholeness of life everything is affirmed in its holiness—*he no longer denies.* . . . There is no higher faith than this: I have baptized it in the name of Dionysus." [27]

This is very beautiful and true, and shocking only because of Dionysus so suddenly entering an apparently Apolline scene. Goethe, no doubt, would have been baffled by the choice of this godfather, and might have asked for some less inebriating deity to be his spiritual support—Apollo, perhaps, or even Eros. Yet it is precisely this invocation of Dionysus, forced upon Nietzsche (and not only upon him) by his determination to accept and affirm life, which is our theme; and we should lose track of it if we allowed ourselves to be persuaded that it was, as it were, Apollo's child's play for Goethe to persevere in affirmation, or simply due to his superbly fortunate temperament and genius. And our theme would equally be abandoned if we succeeded only in showing that the iconoclast Nietzsche surrounded the picture of Goethe with nothing but admiring marginal notes—significant though even this would be. Goethe would not be the author of Faust and Mephistopheles had he not known—and at times with terrible intimacy—the spirit of the denial of life:

> . . . *Was ist daran zu lesen?*
> *Es ist so gut, als wär' es nicht gewesen,*
> *Und treibt sich doch im Kreis, als wenn es wäre.*
> *Ich liebte mir dafür das Ewig-Leere.*[28]

What can one make of it? It is as good as though it had never been. . . . And yet it rushes round in circles, as if it had some real existence. I should prefer instead eternal emptiness.

These are anticipatory echoes of Nietzsche's Eternal Recurrence of a positivistically self-contained world that has no opening into meaning and sense. Indeed, he was only too familiar with the temptation of calling on magical powers to endow a drably disenchanted life with the poignancy of consuming beauty:

> *Und sollt' ich nicht, sehnsüchtigster Gewalt,*
> *In's Leben ziehn die einzigste Gestalt.*[29]

And shall I not, with all the might of my craving, succeed in bringing to life the uniquely beautiful shape?

This desire, even if realized only for that one fatal moment of ultimate satisfaction, is Faust's very challenge to the Devil. But the challenge is withdrawn at the end, and the *very desire for magical transformation identified with the act of blaspheming and cursing life:*

> *Könnt' ich Magie von meinem Pfad entfernen,*
> *Die Zaubersprüche ganz und gar verlernen,*
> *Stünd ich, Natur, vor dir ein Mann allein,*
> *Da wär's der Mühe wert, ein Mensch zu sein.*
> *Das war ich sonst, eh' ich's im Düstern suchte,*
> *Mit Frevelwort mich und die Welt verfluchte.*[30]

Could I forget my sorcery, and ban my magic, stand, stripped of it
utterly face to face with Nature, then it would be worth while to be a
man. I was one once, before I searched in the sinister sphere, thus blasphemously cursing the world and myself.

This rejection of magic is, of course, not merely a poetical and secularized version of the traditional theological disapproval of that activity. Nor has it anything in common with the conventional idea of
piety. It simply reflects Goethe's final acceptance of life as it is—only
that Goethe's vision of what is, affirms the *reality* of much that in the
consciousness of the Prosaic Age is not. Goethe is exemplary in his
courage to trust in the absolute reliability of that experiment which, in
its utter "subjectivity," is not merely one of many possible, but the
experience of life itself. And at least half of his experiment yields results dismissed by the Prosaic Age with frowning vagueness as "emotional" or "mystical":

> Sie haben dich, heiliger Hafis,
> Die mystische Zunge genannt,
> Und haben, die Wortgelehrten,
> Den Wert des Worts nicht erkannt.
>
> Mystisch heissest du ihnen,
> Weil sie Närrisches bei dir denken,
> Und ihren unlautern Wein
> In deinem Namen verschenken.
>
> Du aber bist mystisch rein,
> Weil sie dich nicht verstehn.
> Der du, ohne fromm zu sein, selig bist!
> Das wollen sie dir nicht zugestehn.[31]

They have called you, Saint Hafis, the mystical tongue; but they, the
scribes, have not recognized the meaning of the word. To them you are
mystical because you inspire foolish thoughts in them, and because they
pour out their impure wine in your name. Indeed, you are mystical, but
only because they do not understand you, you who are blessed without
being pious. And this they will not allow you.

This is the poem *"Offenbar Geheimnis"* from the *Westöstlicher Divan*.
Nietzsche could have written it. It is Goethe's most light-hearted assertion of the oneness of the two spheres, of the revelation of the unfathomable in the reality of the symbol, and of the holiness and blessedness
which is the quality of being *really* alive.

The "ideal" aspect of life, abandoned by transcendentalists and positivists alike to some limbo of ideality, was so inescapably real to

Goethe that he was convinced it would one day avenge itself on the age that has banished it from its "reality." This brings us to the last of the three aphorisms from *Maximen und Reflexionen* which we have selected to epitomize stages on the precarious journey of the European mind. It is the aphorism which follows immediately upon the definition of the symbol from which this discussion has so far taken its bearings and which it leaves now with one of the last jottings among the posthumously published notes of Nietzsche: "The interpreters of poets do not understand that the poet has both: the reality and the symbol. Thus he has the first and the second sense of a totality."[32] It is inspired by Goethe; and Goethe's aphorism, the third and last in our sequence of citations, reads, once more: "All that is ideal will ultimately, once it is claimed by the real, consume it, and itself. As paper money consumes the silver and itself." And this is exactly what has happened within the fifty years of the Prosaic Age, between Goethe's death and Nietzsche's *Zarathustra*. Goethe's realism, on its profoundest level, was driven to despair. And Nietzsche, in order to transform this despair into affirmation, had to call in so un-Goethean a spirit as that of Dionysus. The comparison between the god of Goethe's *amor dei* and Nietzsche's love of Dionysus yields the measure by which we can assess the distance the Prosaic Age has travelled from Goethe's time to Nietzsche's, or the depth to which it has sunk. For with all the radical, and indeed obvious, differences between Goethe and Nietzsche—differences of character, genius, temperament, modes of thought and expression—they nevertheless meet in their concern for the proper state of man. Nietzsche is the outraged believer of Goethe's beliefs, the scandalized and scandalizing upholder of Goethe's values, fighting out within his own soul the battle between belief and unbelief, accepting for himself the fates of the tortured martyrs of either side as well as the role of the adjudicator of victories and defeats.

It is not only Nietzsche's consistent admiration that bears witness to his kinship with Goethe. There is no *internal* evidence either to refute the intellectual sincerity of Nietzsche's repeated assertions that there could not be any bypassing of Goethe when it came to tracing his own intellectual ancestry; and although the names he quotes on the occasions of such stock-taking vary, Goethe is invariably included. In the second volume of *Human, All Too Human,* for instance, he is paired with Spinoza (the other pairs are Epicurus and Montaigne, Plato and Rousseau, Pascal and Schopenhauer). It is their approval that he, Nietzsche, seeks, after long stretches of "lonely wandering";[33] and among his many notes from the time of *Zarathustra,* Goethe again appears as one of his spiritual ancestors, this time together with Heraclitus and, once more, Spinoza.[34]

And in one of his own posthumously published critical comments on the writings of his early period, Goethe is thanked for having freed him from the pessimistic tyranny of Schopenhauer and Wagner: "*Now* antiquity dawned upon me, and Goethe's insight into the nature of great art, and *now* I gained that *simplicity* of vision to see what human existence *really* is; I had the antidote to make sure that it did not turn into poisoning pessimism."[35]

In *Human, All Too Human,* in one of the loveliest passages ever written on the *moral* task and function of literature (and, indeed, there is not much loveliness to be found in the repertoire of writers on this austere subject), the imprint of Goethe's genius is recognizable in every phase: "The works of such poets"—poets, that is, whose vision of man is exemplary—"would be distinguished by the fact that they appear immune from the glow and blast of the *passions*. The fatal touch of the wrong note, the pleasure taken in smashing the whole instrument on which the music of humanity has been played, the scornful laughter and the gnashing of teeth, and all that is tragic and comic in the old conventional sense, would be felt in the vicinity of this new art as an awkward archaic crudeness and a distortion of the image of man. Strength, goodness, gentleness, purity, and that innate and spontaneous sense of measure and balance shown in persons and their actions, . . . a clear sky reflected on faces and events, knowledge and art at one; the mind without arrogance and jealousy dwelling together with the soul, drawing from the opposites of life the grace of seriousness, not the impatience of conflict:—all this would make the background of gold against which to set up the real portrait of man, the picture of his increasing nobleness."[36]

This, quite consistently, is written by the same Nietzsche who, in listing the best books in German prose, reserved no place for either the tumultuous Kleist or the coruscating Heine but chose works of wise repose and quiet humor.[37] But is it, one wonders, written by the same Nietzsche who has appealed to what is most immature in the popular imagination of his country, and largely antagonized that of other nations by "philosophizing with a hammer," proclaiming himself dynamite, preaching the advent of the *Übermensch?* How is one to reconcile this explosive mind with that Nietzsche whom we have observed painting, against a background of gold, the Goethean picture of man "immune from the glow and blast of the passions"?

Throughout Nietzsche's life, and not merely from a certain point onward, his acclamations of Goethe, the dominant voice indeed, are yet interspersed with misgivings. These are invariably concerned with the Goethe-Winckelmann idea of Greek antiquity and with Goethe's "purely epic genius," which rendered him incapable of facing tragedy.

As early as 1870, while he was writing his *Birth of Tragedy,* Nietzsche enters in his notebook the following remark: "With Goethe, in accordance with his epic nature, poetry is the remedy, protecting him from full knowledge; with tragic natures art is the remedy, liberating them from knowledge." [38] All that Nietzsche ever said in criticism of Goethe is contained in this observation of the young philologist. Seven to eight years later, at the time of *Human, All Too Human,* it is applied to Goethe's reaction to Kleist: "What Goethe felt at coming into contact with him was his sense of tragedy. Goethe turned his back on it; for tragedy represents the incurable aspect of nature. He himself was conciliatory and curable." [39]

These criticisms, clearly, are not determined by purely aesthetic considerations. Nietzsche was utterly incapable of dividing up his thought into any such neat academical departments. Thus his criticism of Goethe can be seen as part and parcel of his total strategy: the strategy of despair. Towards the end of his conscious life Nietzsche was convinced that the culture of Europe was doomed; that an eclipse of all traditional values was at hand, and that modern European man, this pampered child of the optimistically rational eighteenth century, must needs go astray in a wilderness without path or guidance. He quoted Pascal, who said that without the Christian belief we shall become to ourselves what nature and history will become to us—"un monstre et un chaos." We, Nietzsche adds, have made this prophecy come true. [40] The sections of his *Will to Power* which are concerned with the coming of European nihilism read like a vast elaboration of that dictum of Pascal's as well as of Goethe's prophecy of the Prosaic Age. Nietzsche believed that its approach was *inevitable.* But the paradox, which is the very life of true prophecy, also sustained—until madness possessed him—the prophet Nietzsche; that prophetic paradox within which historical inevitability is defeated through an act of spiritual conquest: "God has decided to destroy the Temple. In the name of God, rescue the Temple from the wrath of God." This is the paradox of every true prophet.

What was inevitable, according to Nietzsche's prophecy, was the coming of nihilism. Its conqueror, more powerful than fate itself, was the Dionysian spirit, the spirit that ruled Greek tragedy. The Dionysus of Greek tragedy transformed the despair at the fate of man into the bliss of ultimate acceptance, thus transcending the very thing it accepted. There is an amazing consistency running right through Nietzsche's contradictions. The young philologist and philosopher had, in the *Birth of Tragedy,* celebrated the god of ecstasy, redeeming the spectacle of man's ultimate failure in the rapturously accepted wholeness of life in which there is nothing but ultimate succeeding. The writer of the *Will to Power,* seventeen years later, demanded from European man that he should perform the very same drama on the stage of the world and, caught in the doom of his historical fate, transcend it through the act of tragic affirmation.

For him who believed he had recognized this, *Faust* could no longer stand as the "tragedy of knowledge," "*die Tragödie der Erkenntnis.*" "Really? I laugh at Faust."[41] Salvation was no longer to be had from the "*Ewig-Weibliche.*" This was still merely comfort, a religious illusion hiding the mercilessness from above against which not man, in his weak and fallen state, will assert himself, but only the creature graced with the grace of Dionysus: the *Übermensch.* As far as man is concerned, no *chorus mysticus* concludes Nietzsche's "tragedy of knowledge," but Mephistopheles:

> *Kein Weg! Ins Unbetretene,*
> *Nicht zu Betretende; ein Weg ans Unerbetene,*
> *Nicht zu Erbittende. Bist du bereit?—*
> *Nicht Schlösser sind, nicht Riegel wegzuschieben,*
> *Von Einsamkeiten wirst unhergetrieben.*
> *Hast du Begriff von Öd' und Einsamkeit?*
>
> *Nichts wirst du sehen in ewig leerer Ferne.*
> *Den Schritt nicht hören, den du tust,*
> *Nichts Festes finden, wo du ruhst.*[42]

No way! Toward untrodden ground, where none may tread; a way toward the unprayed-for, beyond all prayer. Are you prepared? There are no locks, no bolts to thrust aside; you will be driven hither and thither by hosts of loneliness. Do you know what void and loneliness mean? . . . You will see nothing in that expanse of eternal emptiness, you will not hear your own step, you will find nothing solid for you to rest upon.

In those voids, the first sound that will be heard again, indeed be met by the resonance of a transfigured world, will be the voice of the *Übermensch.* He will, Nietzsche dreams, find the firmest of footholds precisely where man loses the ground under his feet.

To insist on the Mephistophelean prospect, and yet not to despair, and yet to glorify, indeed to transfigure existence—this is the goal of Nietzsche's desperate strategy. He was determined to go to the very end of disillusionment, shed skin after skin of comforting beliefs, destroy every fortress manned by protective gods, in fact, to banish the last vestiges of "magic" which still save man from the final exposure to his tragedy—and *then* bring to life once more Goethe's vision of the glorious integrity of all things. Until this was done, even the nearest German approximation to Dionysian acceptance, even Goethe, would fail us. For he had an inclination to play truant when life was teaching its most desperate lessons. At the approach of the terror of ultimate knowledge, Goethe withdrew into the healing darkness of the unconscious, trusting to intuition that it would restore the brightness of day in the created work of art. But Nietzsche dreamt—and dreamt in vain—of an artist of the future who would reach in his art that turning point where the highest degree of consciousness and self-consciousness transforms itself into a new spontaneity, primitivity and innocence—[43] just as he strove to realize the utmost of nihilistic despair to arrive at a new faith, and mobilized all forces of negation to defeat all denial. In one of the last paragraphs of *The Will to Power* he says: "To have paced out the whole circumference of modern consciousness, to have explored every one of its recesses—this is my ambition, my torture, and my bliss. Really to overcome pessimism—; and as a result, *ein Goethischer Blick voll Liebe und gutem Willen.*"[44]

The desperate *experimentum crucis* failed desperately. Nietzsche's tragic failure is spiritual impatience. He was a Faustian, after all, in his deep-rooted belief that in the beginning was the deed as it is in Faust's self-willed translation of St. John. But it is certainly not in the end, and this increases the probability that it was not in the beginning either. He saw the end and took the initiative. He had before him a world without faith or hope or love; and how much he was of the nineteenth century in attempting to create from his own impatience that trinity of spiritual survival which may be "all in the waiting." From the bottom of his wounded heart he believed that

> . . . such is the infection of the time,
> That, for the health and physic of our right,
> We cannot deal but with the very hand
> Of stern injustice and confused wrong.
> (Shakespeare, *King John V, 2*)

But such war-like preparations have a habit of producing the precise state in which the "paper money consumes the silver and itself."

Nietzsche, with an intellectual courage, penetration and impatience which have no equal in the nineteenth century, made himself, with the most splendid invocations, the claimant of the ideal on behalf of the real; but in his time and place, already so hopelessly exposed, he merely succeeded in vindicating Goethe's prophecy that this will be the point at which the severed spheres consume each other.

3

# BURCKHARDT AND NIETZSCHE

When in 1495 Raphael was apprenticed to Pietro Perugino at Perugia, this city was one of the many Renaissance centers of political strife, moral outrage and ruthless violence. Matarazzo, the chronicler of the Perugia of that time, relates the story of the two rival families, the Oddi and the Baglioni, interlocked in a deadly struggle for the possession of the city. The Baglioni had been victorious and remained for some time the overlords of the Republic. The Oddi and their soldiers lived as exiles in the valley between Perugia and Assisi, being attacked by, and counter-attacking, the Baglioni in a perpetual war which devastated the rich Umbrian land, turned the peasants into beggars or robbers, and the vineyards into jungles where wolves fed on the dead of the battles. One day, however, the soldiers of the Oddi succeeded in taking Perugia by storm. Coming up from the valley, they overwhelmed the defenders at the city gates and reached the piazza. But there, in front of the cathedral, they were defeated by Astorre Baglione. The contemporary reporter describes the daring feat of courage and martial skill that Astorre performed; at the last moment and against superior numbers, he threw himself into the battle, sitting upright on his horse, with a falcon on his helmet and with his golden armor glittering in the sun. He looked and acted, Matarazzo says, like the God of War himself.

Jacob Burckhardt, in his *The Civilization of the Renaissance in Italy*, draws freely on such sources, and, in this particular case, reflects whether it is not the hero of this episode whom we can see in Raphael's early paintings of St. George and St. Michael; adding that in the figure of the celestial rider in the Heliodorus fresco Astorre Baglione has found his final glorification.

Again, using Matarazzo as his source, Burckhardt tells the story of Atalanta, the beautiful mother of Grifone Baglione, who was for some time ruling prince of Perugia. He had fought his way to power against rival members of his own family. His mother Atalanta was on the side of his enemies. On her son's victory she cursed him and fled from the city. But Grifone's rule was shortlived. He was soon overpowered by his rivals and mortally wounded. When Atalanta heard he was dying, she returned with her daughter-in-law. At the approach of the two ladies, the tumultuous crowd on the piazza parted, both sides fearing the wrath of the bereaved mother. She, however, went straight to her son, and far from contemplating further violence, implored him to forgive those who had dealt the deadly blow. After he had thus re-nounced the spirit of revenge, he died with the blessings of his mother. Then the two women left the city again, and the crowd, partisans of both camps, knelt down and wept as they crossed the piazza in their bloodstained garments. It was for this Atalanta that Raphael later painted his *Deposizione*. Thus, Burckhardt writes, "her own suffering was laid at the feet of the most sublime and sacred agony of a mother." After all this the cathedral of Perugia, which had stood in the midst of these many scenes of felony and murder, was washed with wine and consecrated anew.[1]

Anecdotes of this kind occur frequently in Jacob Burckhardt's book on the Renaissance, which was first published in Basle in 1860, when its author had reached the age of forty-two. Are they, the historian of today may ask, worthy of a self-respecting scholar? Have they not the romantic flavor of a fanciful dramatization rather than the authentic ring of precise recording? What is the value of a source like Mataraz-zo's chronicles? Was he not a partisan himself, bent upon building up a heroic reputation for the Baglioni, and, at the same time, a storyteller determined to entertain and edify his public rather than to instruct it?

We may, in the context of such queries, note that, when he began his university education in Basle as a student of theology, Jacob Burck-hardt soon developed a very skeptical attitude towards his subject. He was the son of a Protestant minister of the Church, and it was his father's—and originally his own—wish that he should become a cler-gyman himself. Soon, however, he decided to give up theology be-cause the rationalist Bible criticism of his teacher de Wette had under-mined his faith in orthodox beliefs. "De Wette's system," he wrote in a letter to a friend, "grows before my eyes to colossal dimensions; one *must* follow him, nothing else is possible; but, alas, every day there disappears under his hands a fragment of the traditional teaching of the Church. Today I have finally discovered that he regards the birth of Christ as a myth—and I with him. It was with a shudder that I thought of a number of reasons why it all but had to be like this. . . ."[2] Did this critical passion leave him during his subsequent training as a historian? And, after all, this history of the Renaissance was published by a pupil of Ranke's—Ranke whom he always respected, though without much affection, and in whose seminar he had learned how to handle sources and be critical of them. Are we not, therefore, entitled to expect some-thing more sophisticated than heroic tales from this professor of His-tory, holding a chair at the University of Basle?

Before raising such questions we may first ask ourselves: what is the picture produced in our minds by these unverified, and probably unverifiable, anecdotes? It is composed of intense evil and sublime beauty; of hatred and charity; of degradation and purification; of the unscrupulousness that inflicts pain and the reverence felt for suffering; of sin, contrition and atonement. Indeed, the source from which it springs is not chosen for the sake of factual exactitude. Its authority is of a different nature. It has for Burckhardt the authenticity of the mind, imagination and spirit of the Renaissance, and if it yields a negligible *quantity* of reliable facts, it nevertheless reveals something more important to him: the *quality* of the life of the period, or as he would have called it, the *Geist* of the epoch. To reproduce this is the concern of what he calls History of Culture as distinct from Political History. If he is to recapture the quality of life lived by a certain age, the historian must bring to his study not only industry, intelligence and honesty, but also something of the sensibility and intuition of the artist. History of Culture has a critical method of its own, still more difficult to acquire than the ordinary techniques of critical investigation. In fact, it is not a technique at all, but rather creative sympathy. If we do not possess this we are perpetually misled by the egocentricity of our intellectual concepts; for we are prone to overrate the power as well as the range of application of our abstract thinking. Notions, for instance, like "freedom" and "slavery"; "tolerance" and "intolerance"; "tyranny," "aristocracy," "democracy"; "belief" and "superstition," which we assume we are using objectively, applying them to certain observed phenomena, are, in fact, "value judgments" charged with all the sentiments and resentments of our contemporary perception of human affairs. The very sound in our ears of the word "slavery" may render our imagination impotent in its dealings with the particular quality of Greek civilization, and the emotional charge contained in the term "freedom of thought" or, indeed, "objectivity" itself, may practically blot out all our understanding of the quality of the knowledge and wisdom of a medieval sage. Yet there is a possible scale of human achievement on which a wretched feudal drudge may appear to approach the degree marking absolute freedom, and the constitutionally free citizen of a free republic the state of absolute slavery.

To come back to Burckhardt's Renaissance scenes: who can, as long as he remains within his restricted moral senses, assess the spiritual power present in a society and ready to be spent on the transformation of a ruthless prince into the Raphael picture of a warrior of Heaven, and of a cunning and power-seeking woman into a *mater dolorosa*? And when it comes to our contemporary debates, we might become considerably more economical and subtle in drawing historical parallels and comparisons if we were inspired by only one spark of what Burckhardt meant by historical understanding. We might not have to risk in every attempt at, for instance, appreciating the spiritual life and character of the Middle Ages, the release of cataracts of moralizing recriminations about religious wars, crusades, inquisitions and other pestilences.

Indeed, Burckhardt, like his teacher Ranke, is convinced of the fundamental importance of original sources and warns his pupils against textbooks, digests and interpretations, not because he upholds the superstition of perfect objectivity emerging like the vision of a god from the assiduity of the source collector, but because he believes that the activity of the imagination can be stimulated as well as purified by an ever-renewed contact with the documents which reproduce the impact made upon particular minds by an event in human history. Such a mind—and here the method of the historian of a culture differs from that of the political or economic historian—may be a naïve chronicler like Matarazzo or, indeed, an inspired painter like Raphael. Did they report or paint what *really* happened? Of course not, if "real" is to denote the pure abstract of an event, which is, in fact, no event whatsoever. For something that happens becomes an event only when it is mentally and emotionally perceived and registered. Matarazzo, therefore, in all his naïvete, and Raphael, with all the transforming power of his art, are both sources for the historian of a culture, who is, as Burckhardt once put it in his unphilosophical manner, as much concerned with "represented history" as with what "literally happened," forgetting that nothing happens literally—unless we are determined to make our own perception the criterion of the perception of truth itself, and to say that what *really* happens is precisely what we would have noticed had we been on the spot. Thus it is with some justification that Burckhardt maintains, in a neat overstatement, that for the history of culture the facts to be assessed are *identical* with the sources. Claiming for his method *primum gradum certitudinis,*[3] he upholds in defiance of the fact-worshippers that even records of things that have not happened at all may be important by virtue of the typical mode of their inventions, distortions or misinterpretations. Of Aeneas Silvius he says in his *Renaissance:* "One may distrust the testimony of that man completely, and yet one would have to admit that there are not many other men in whose minds the picture of the age and its intellectual culture is reflected with such perception and liveliness."[4]

The idea, however, of arriving at any positive certainty by accumulating more and more sources until that point of completeness is reached at which we may, in Bury's words, "grasp the complete development of humanity," is, of course, dismissed by Burckhardt as a chimaera. The very attempt, he holds, would interfere with any comprehensiveness of vision. Pedantry to him is one of the most cunning enemies of truth, luring the search into the dusty lumber rooms of the past where only mice may hope to find something to eat. Mind and imagination must needs choke in them, and Buckle, for instance, he says, owes his paralysis of the brain to his exclusive obsession with the Scottish sermons of the seventeenth and eighteenth centuries.[5] The very spiritual poverty of what Burckhardt calls his "pretty century" drives many of its academic studies into some narrow recess of the past where the ideal of precision and completeness may hide from the adept the absence of true comprehension. It is in those holes of the mind that the indiscriminate and diffused suspicion is bred which tends to dismiss as vague generalizations *all* historical assessments based on a broader vision. For the modern mind, in some of its most vocal representatives, has yielded to the inferior magic of facts, numbers, statistics, and to that sort of empiricism which, in its passion for concreteness, paradoxically reduces experience to a purely abstract notion of measurable data, having cast aside the "immeasurable wealth" of authentic experiences of the spirit and imagination. The specialization in trifles which results from such abstractions seeks its justification not only in the arithmetical deception that a thousand futilities add up to a large piece of significance, but also in the strange belief that the great issues have all been fully explored and the outstanding sources exhausted. For Burckhardt, however, it merely brings to light that waning sense of significance which he finds and deplores in his age, the crumbling of all central convictions and the spontaneous disinclination of mediocrity to expose itself to the impact of what is great. It may be, he says, "that there is still hidden in Thucydides a fact of capital importance which somebody will note in a hundred years time."[6] For the present, Burckhardt maintains, "a single source, happily chosen, can, as it were, do duty for a whole multitude of possible other sources, since he who is really determined to learn, that is, to become rich in spirit, can, by a simple function of his mind, discern and feel the general in the particular."[7]

This is an echo from Goethe's world. For Goethe knew the difference in quality between a writer who, starting with preconceived ideas, assembles his particulars to fit the needs of his generalities, and a poet who "discerns and feels" the universal in the particular phenom-

enon.[8] Like Stifter, with whom he has so much in common, Burckhardt felt himself to be one of "Goethe's family." As a young man he
hoped he would become a poet—and he actually did publish a number
of poems—and throughout his life history remained for him a poetic
activity. "As a historian," he once wrote, "I am lost where I cannot
begin with *Anschauung*."[9] It is a Goethean word and hardly translat-
able. Its connotations are visual, and it means the mental process by
which we spontaneously grasp, through observation aided by intuition, a thing in its wholeness. Goethe uses it as the opposite of analysis, the mental approach which he feared would establish itself as the
dominant habit of an age fascinated by Newtonian physics, only to
destroy all culture of the intellect. Sometimes Burckhardt even felt it
to be a nuisance that the historian, in presenting his historical narra-
tive, was bound by the chronological order compelling him to tell one
thing after the other, when the true order "could only be represented
as a picture."[10] With such a mind it is not surprising that he agrees with
Aristotle and Schopenhauer in claiming for poetry and art a higher
rank in the hierarchy of understanding and knowledge than history
could ever hold. In those lecture notes which he prepared in the years
1868–71, posthumously published by Jacob Oeri in 1905 under the
title of *Weltgeschichtliche Betrachtungen* (*Reflections on World History*), he
states in a fashion leaving no doubt about the degree of his certainty:
"The rivalry between history and poetry has been finally settled by
Schopenhauer. Poetry achieves more for our knowledge of the truth
about mankind; even Aristotle said: "Poetry is more philosophical and
profound than history," and this is true because the faculty which gives
birth to poetry is intrinsically of a higher order than that of the greatest
historian; further, the end to which it is created is much more sublime
than that of history. . . . Hence history finds in poetry not only one of
its most important, but also one of its purest and finest sources."[11]

Saying this, Burckhardt refers to a number of specified passages
from Schopenhauer's *World as Will and Representation;* they contain almost all that is needed for an understanding of Burckhardt's philosophy. Has he, then, a philosophy? He has no "philosophy of *history*";
indeed, it is repugnant to him if by this forbidding term there is to be
understood what dominated the philosophical and historical scene in
his time: the attempt to transform history into philosophy and, indeed, into theology. In other words, Burckhardt hates the philosophy
of Hegel. This fundamentally irreverent intimacy with Providence,
this "bold and insolent anticipation of a world plan,"[12] as he calls it, is
not for him. All the introductory remarks to his *Reflections on World*

*History* are directed against Hegel. "Our task in this course," he writes, "consists in linking a series of historical observations and findings to an all but arbitrarily chosen line of thought and then again to another one."[13] Further: "Above all, we shall not give any philosophy of history."[14] And a few lines later, so as to leave no doubt as to what has prompted this renunciation of all philosophy of history, the name of Hegel is introduced: "Hegel . . . tells us that the only idea which is 'given' in philosophy is the simple idea of reason, the idea that the world is rationally ordered: hence the history of the world is a rational process, and the conclusion yielded by world history *must* be that it was the rational, inevitable march of the [World Spirit . . .] Hegel speaks also of the 'purpose of eternal wisdom,' and calls his study a theodicy by virtue of its recognition of the positive in which the negative (in popular parlance, evil) vanishes, subjected and overcome. He develops the fundamental idea that history is the record of the process by which mind becomes aware of its own significance; according to him, there is progress towards freedom. In the East only one man was free, in classical antiquity only a few, while modern times have set all men free. Thus we find him putting forward the doctrine of perfectibility, that is, our old familiar friend called progress."[15]

But in spite of his disclaiming it, Burckhardt has, of course, a philosophy; that is, he thinks philosophically about history. He has, however, no system which could be expounded apart from, and beyond, his historical and philosophical thinking. His metaphysical beliefs and fundamental thoughts, therefore, have to be perceived through his reflections about things. Yet there is one philosopher in whom he finds the dispersed elements of his own thought crystallized into a definite system. It is Schopenhauer, whom Burckhardt in conversations with Nietzsche called "our philosopher."[18] The introduction to his *Reflections on World History* is in part a précis of what Schopenhauer has to say about the subject and, above all, about Hegel's hypostasis of history. "The Hegelians," Schopenhauer says, "who regard the philosophy of history as the aim of all philosophy, ought to be taught some Plato, who indefatigably repeats that the object of philosophy lies in the unchangeable and in what lasts, and not in the things which are now like this, and now again like that. All those who postulate such constructions about the world in motion, or, as they call it, history, have not grasped the fundamental truth of philosophy: that, philosophically speaking, what *really* is is the same at all times. . . . The fools, however, believe that it will develop and one day arrive. . . . Thus they regard the whirling world as they perceive it as the ultimate reality, and see its final meaning in a meager bliss on earth which, even if cultivated evermore by man and favored by fate, will remain a hollow, deceptive, fickle and sorry thing of which nothing essentially better can ever come through either constitutions, or legal codes, or steam engines, or telegraphs. Those philosophers and glorifiers of history are therefore realistic simpletons, optimists and eudaemonists, which is to say, mediocre fellows and obstinate philistines and, in addition, bad Christians. . . . A real philosophy of history ought to bear in mind what for ever *is* and never *develops*. It can, indeed, not consist in raising the temporal aims of man to the rank of absolutes, and furthermore, in constructing in an artificial and fanciful manner man's progress; but it ought to be based upon the insight that, in all those endless variations and turmoils, we have before us merely the one creature, *essentially* identical and unchangeable, busying itself with the very same things today, and yesterday, and forever. . . . This identity, preserved through all changes, is founded on the fundamental qualities of human hearts and brains, many bad, few good. . . . For someone bringing philosophical intentions to history, the study of Herodotus is sufficient. There he will find everything that has gone into the making of all subsequent world history: the activities, afflictions and fortunes of the human race. . . ." [17]

Schopenhauer's philosophy pervades the whole work of Jacob Burckhardt, and letter after letter shows how deeply he was in agreement with it. For instance, in the Introduction to his *Reflections* he sys: "Our point of departure is the one and only thing which lasts in history and is its only possible center: man, this suffering, striving and active being, as he is and was and will be for ever. . . . The philosophers of history see the past in opposition and as a preliminary to us as the more developed; *we* shall study what is *recurrent, constant* and typical as echoing in us and to be understood by us." [18]

In this context Burckhardt, as though casually, makes a remark which strikes at the very center of what can, after all, be called his philosophy of history. Man, he had previously asserted, not a Hegelian *Weltgeist,* is the center of history. Is this to be taken as the declaration of a humanistic creed, pure and simple? In a sense, it is—in as far as it draws a definite line between the study of the *historical* aspect of human life and all theology. But while he definitely attacks the Hegelian brand of *secularized* theology, he acknowledges, without accepting it for himself, the particular justification of a genuinely religious interpretation of history, the great model of which he sees in Augustine's *De Civitate Dei.*[19] It is, however, none of his business. He is concerned with man, he says, and not with God. Is he, therefore, simply a humanist? We might be allowed to assume this more lightheartedly were it not for the remark which I have hinted at, and which concludes the paragraph that allots to man the central position in Burckhardt's studies. It says: "Hence our study will, in a sense, be pathological in kind." In other words: the perpetual agent of human affairs is a pathological creature, the Fall the beginning of history, original sin its driving force and redemption its end. Although this may sound very much like a surreptitious opening of the theological floodgates, it is, in fact, implied by Burckhardt when he regards the study of history as an essay in pathology.

He may have lost his faith in Christianity, very much as "our philosopher" Schopenhauer had lost it; he may have abandoned the belief that the offer of redemption reached man in the shape of an historical event and was rejected by a creature bent on the *continuation* of his history. But, again like Schopenhauer, he accepts an *order or things* identical with that accepted by the Christian believer. It is the only order of things in which the religion of Christ can make sense; and if it is the *true* order of things, it is, at the same time, a profoundly *senseless* pattern *without* the religion of Christ. To look upon man, as Schopenhauer and Burckhardt did, as the fallen creature, on sin and evil as constituent and ineradicable factors in human history, on human affairs as pathological, without believing in the reality, existence, possibility and indeed the definite offer of spiritual health, must needs create a profound spiritual predicament. A tougher form of humanism than that of Burckhardt, a humanism coupled with rationalism, knows nothing of such difficulties. But it is astonishing how few people can really and truly attain to such toughness. Those who believe they can do without metaphysics are usually only those who cannot do with metaphysics, indulging instead in sentimentality and other secret betrayals of *ratio,* and in the kind of metaphysics which escapes being diagnosed as such merely by virtue of its diffuseness and conventional respectability; as, for instance, the metaphysics of equating scientific discoveries with the discovery of Truth, or the metaphysics of perfectibility and progress. For the rest the predicament persists; and it did, throughout their lives, persist for men like Schopenhauer and Burckhardt. They bore it nobly, and with a strength of spirit and character which is rare among human beings. They represent the true aristocracy of the nineteenth century. Within the German language writers like Stifter, Grillparzer, Mörike, Gottfried Keller are of their kin. They are few indeed; and to all of them one could, in some measure, apply

Nietzsche's words describing Schopenhauer in the image of Dürer's "Knight with Death and Devil," that man in armor "who bravely travels along his path of horror, unperturbed by his terrible companions, and yet without hope."[20]

Set up against such stoicism, those Germans who, in the nineteenth century, cried out their despair, appear somewhat obtrusive and vulgar. But who is able to judge whether in them—and I am thinking of men like Kleist, Büchner, Nietzsche himself—the sense of spiritual loss had not penetrated deeper? However this may be, it certainly was not met with the same inner resources of natural strength and tradition which saved Schopenhauer and Burckhardt.

2

Nietzsche, who for a short time was Burckhardt's much younger professorial colleague in the University of Basle, once described him in a letter as "that elderly, highly original man, given, not to distorting truth, but to passing it over in silence."[21] He goes on to say that he deeply enjoys listening to Burckhardt's lectures "with their profound thoughts and their strangely abrupt breaks and twists as soon as they touch the danger point." Passing over the truth in silence, sudden twists as soon as the matter approaches a critical point: Nietzsche appears to imply that Burckhardt is in fact more of a rebel than he is inclined to show, and more profoundly desperate about the intellectual and spiritual situation of the age than his professorial equilibrium would betray. Indeed, Nietzsche was convinced to the very end of his conscious life that Burckhardt knew the desperate truth which he believed himself to have discovered and exposed, and that the resigned serenity of Burckhardt's life in Basle was a mask put on for the sake of self-defense. Again and again, from the depths of his loneliness, Nietzsche begged Burckhardt's understanding and sympathy. He was probably mistaken. The core of Burckhardt's being was not affected by his pessimism. There was no need for him to attempt, in the manner of Nietzsche, any metamorphosis of spiritual gloom into Dionysian ecstasy. He knew, as certainly as Nietzsche, that the civilization of Europe which he loved was doomed. To one of his German friends, who placed high hopes in the pre-1848 revolutionary and nationalist movement, he wrote—to quote only one example out of a very great number of similar statements: "None of you has any idea yet what a people is and how easily it deteriorates into a barbarous mob. You do not know yet what a tyrannical rule is to be set up over the spirit. . . .

We may all perish; but I for one shall choose the cause for which I am going to perish: the culture of old Europe." [22]

Burckhardt could not bear with Nietzsche's iconoclastic philosophizing. He had lost his religious faith, but, unlike Nietzsche, the loss was registered by the intelligence alone. The "shudder" with which, as a young student, he discovered that he did not believe in the recorded circumstances of the birth of Christ did not disturb the core of his being. "Religions," he said in his *Reflections on World History*, "are the expression of the eternal and indestructible metaphysical need of human nature." [23] This he accepted as a self-evident and empirical truth—in the same way in which it was accepted by Schopenhauer, who in his *World as Will and Representation* called man the *animal metaphysicum* in a chapter entitled "About the Metaphysical Need of Man." And believing, as he did, in a fundamental correspondence in the world between needs and possibilities of satisfaction, Burckhardt could not share Nietzsche's suspicion that man—the diseased animal, for Nietzsche—was an eternally cheated misfit within a universe catering, on the whole, to the natural needs of its creatures. Should man alone have been cursed with an everlasting appetite, to feed which all the Heavens may be ransacked without result? Nietzsche did believe this; and his *Übermensch* was the child of his fancy, miraculously feeding on barren fields and finally conquering the metaphysical hunger itself. Burckhardt, on the other hand, was of a more robust spiritual nature and more firmly rooted in the Christian tradition of Europe. He continued to eat the bread and drink the wine, and called them by the names of culture and tradition. Religious crisis he regarded as only one more historical variation and change embedded in the spiritual *continuum* without which history would have meant nothing to him. To Burckhardt, therefore, Nietzsche's burdening himself obsessively with the problem of nihilism must have appeared almost offensive, and yet it must have set in motion those elements of despair which were inherent in his own philosophy. The all but inhuman coldness with which he responded—or rather did not respond—to Nietzsche's entreaties for a word of encouragement can hardly be accounted for in any other way. We are reminded of Goethe's forbidding aloofness in his dealings with men of whom he sensed that too close a contact with them might endanger the subtle balance which he had achieved, because they embodied the *alter ego* of his own being, the *ego* of despair.

Nietzsche, however, remained convinced of Burckhardt's "mask." One of his notebook jottings from the years 1875–76 says: "Those who are restrained, like Jacob Burckhardt, out of desperation," [24] and there is little doubt who is in his mind when in *Beyond Good and Evil* he remarks: "There are 'scholarly men' who make use of scholarship because it gives them a classically serene façade, and because scholarship suggests that the man is superficial:—they *wish* that people should arrive at a wrong conclusion about them." In the same context Nietzsche also speaks of "buffoonery" as another possible disguise of "desperate, all too certain knowledge." [25] Clearly, he meant himself, referring to his own display of paradoxical formulations, witty extravagances, provocative exaggerations. The two supposed masks of despair, Burckhardt's scholarship and his own "buffoonery," are mentioned once more: in the last letter Nietzsche wrote to Burckhardt after the catastrophe, foreseen by Burckhardt, had taken place, and clinical insanity had descended upon him. It is one of the most extraordinary and most revealing documents ever composed by a madman, which begins with the words: "Dear Herr Professor, when it comes to it I too would very much prefer a professorial chair in Basle to being God; but I did not dare to go as far in my private egoism as to refrain for its sake from the creation of the world," and in which the writer refers to himself as "being condemned to entertain the next eternity with bad witticisms." [26]

There were two men in Nietzsche's life whom intellectually he had abandoned, but whom he continued to love, respect and admire: Schopenhauer and Burckhardt. With regard to all others—and he was alone at the end—he identified their unwillingness to follow him intellectually with weakness of character, and discarded them. But to Burckhardt, about whose rejection of his own philosophizing he was left in no uncertainty, he submitted, as it were, his resignation in what are the only lucid words in an otherwise deranged note, written two days before the letter just quoted: "Now you are our great—our greatest teacher." [27]

In the case of Burckhardt, Nietzsche's love survived even humiliation. What then did, in so commanding a manner, hold Nietzsche's affection for Schopenhauer and Burckhardt? Undoubtedly what Goethe had praised in Schopenhauer: intellectual honesty. And something else as well: the spiritual vitality which enabled them to live on, and to remain sane, in spite of their profound pessimism. This is precisely the same strength which the young Nietzsche, in his *Birth of Tragedy*, discerned in the Greeks, and which he passionately and lyrically exalted—so passionately and lyrically, indeed, that the work was, of course, rejected by the sound scholars of his day. Despair, reconciled to life through the love of beauty: this is Nietzsche's interpretation of the Greek view of the world. It is identical with the view of Greek antiquity which pervades the pages of Burckhardt's *History of Greek Culture,* another of his lecture courses posthumously published between 1898 and 1902. Obviously, he had read his younger colleague's book on the *Birth of Tragedy.* Burckhardt, too, is attacking the conventional enthusiasts of classicism, who look upon ancient Greece as a prolonged jamboree of suntanned optimists and philosophizing athletes, and he gives to tragic pessimism the central position in the picture he draws of their culture.

It is this tragic pessimism which, at the beginning of their acquaintance, Burckhardt and Nietzsche had in common. But Nietzsche soon went further, and the very way he went reveals—much to Burckhardt's dismay—the precariousness of the position they had held in common. Nietzsche was more deeply wounded by the loss of positive religious convictions than Burckhardt, which is as much as to say that his nature was more in need of an articulate religious faith. The aesthetic comfort offered by the contemplation of the human tragedy proved insufficient to counteract Nietzsche's despair. For Burckhardt history, or rather the history of culture, was the medium of such selfless contemplation. Had his talents allowed him to become an artist, it would have been so much the better for him; as it was, the history of culture had to take the place of poetry. Here at least he could contemplate the *manifestations* of art. For it is the work of art (and with it, to a certain degree, culture itself) through which, according to Schopenhauer, man escapes from the drudgery of the Will and leaves behind the fetters of selfhood. Thus it testifies to man's share in a creative intelligence beyond the purely historical realm, the realm of original sin. Therefore, Burckhardt believes that it is in the sphere of culture that human contemplation can perceive that spiritual *continuum* which gives meaning to all history. For the performance of this task, he maintains, "the human mind is well equipped," for it represents "the power of interpreting all things in an ideal sense. . . . Our spirit must transmute into a possession the remembrance of its passage through the ages of the world. What was once joy and sorrow must now become understanding. . . . Therewith the saying *Historia vitae magistra* assumes a higher yet a humbler meaning. We wish knowledge to make us, not shrewder (for next time) but wiser (for ever)." And finally: "Contemplation, however, is not only the right and the duty of the historian; it is also a supreme need. It is our freedom in the very awareness of universal bondage and in the stream of necessities."[28]

This is the nucleus of Burckhardt's view of history. It is, at the same

time, the application of Schopenhauer's metaphysics to historical studies. Also, it contains Burckhardt's idea of the historian's objectivity,
which for him does not consist in the seemingly simple and practically
impossible device of suspending moral judgment or, indeed, any other
judgment in the face of a phenomenon, merely because it happens to
be historical. The evil which Burckhardt perceives in history—and he
perceives more evil in it than good—he freely calls by its name; as
freely as he calls beauty beautiful and ugliness ugly. "From the fact,
however," he says in *Reflections on World History,* "that good may come
from evil, and from disaster relative happiness, it does not follow that
evil and disaster are not what they are." [29] *Values,* for him, are as real as
facts and happenings. In this he remains with Schopenhauer a Platonic
idealist, despising what he calls "the frivolous pretense of objectivity"
which, instead of achieving what it aims at, merely loses itself in a
welter of relativities. By the objectivity of true contemplation he
means the *conquest of the self-will,* the philosophical activity *kat'· exochen.* Its goal is certainly not the abolition of judgment, be it aesthetic
or moral, but its purification.

There was a time when Nietzsche was prepared to remain at rest
here with Burckhardt. And indeed, we hardly know of any better rest-
ing-place. It is certainly good enough to deserve our most exacting
efforts in defending it against the onrush of those noisily activist forces
which, in the disguise and with the persuasion of social moralism, are
undermining it from all sides. Burckhardt, in letters to his friends,
called all "these great achievements" in politics, industry and social
organization which are demanded from us at the cost of all peace for
contemplation "thoroughly mediocre, and a nuisance because of the
ever-increasing bother of 'earnest work.'" He speaks of the "frightful
spiritual nullity" of "radicalism," [30] of those "odious windbags of progressive optimism," and fears that "the conditions of Europe may
overnight deteriorate into a kind of gangrene with all truly conservative forces suddenly dying away." [31] In his critique of the age Nietzsche,
consistently enough, was with him. At what point, then, did they part
company?

It was, I would suggest, over a religious and moral issue.

The kinship between Schopenhauer's (and therefore Burckhardt's)
philosophy of contemplation and Eastern forms of religion has often
been emphasized. Yet we have, I think, little understanding of the nature of some aspects of Eastern quietism. What we really appreciate of
it we judge by the tradition of European mysticism. The reward of
this kind of mystical contemplation is the contact established with the

divinity or the supreme spirit. Thus it is not practiced for its own sake, but for the sake of this highest reward, which, as the highest reward, stands in no need of further justification. Schopenhauer's idea of contemplation also knows of some reward; but its reward is, or at least appears to be, the purest aesthetic experience. If life on this earth is sin and self-willed deception, if the misery of it by far outweighs the rare moments of happiness, if it is altogether the continuous and futile drudgery of a fallen creature—and this is, I believe, a faithful summing-up of Schopenhauer's and Burckhardt's views—then, surely, the desire to emancipate oneself from it, and seek reward in the sublimity of a self-detached vision, not of God but, for Burckhardt of *history,* must needs provoke dissatisfaction and moral suspicion in a man to whom life on this earth is agony, precisely because he cannot attain to a vision of ultimate Truth.

This is where the roots of Nietzsche's catastrophic plight lie, and the deepest cause of his final breaking-away from his "great educator" Schopenhauer and his "great teacher" Burckhardt. With God "being dead" for him he could find no lasting spiritual satisfaction in the pure contemplation of a creation deserted by its creator. If history, the dwelling-place of sin and evil, had thus lost its meaning, it had to be abolished; if the fallen creature had ceased to be redeemable, good and evil had to be transcended by the *Übermensch;* and the gloom of the Eternal Recurrence of a senseless world in motion (and not Burckhardt's spiritual *continuum*) was for him the only alternative to the Second Coming. Nietzsche, to the very end of insanity, spins out the thread of unbelief. In his very spiritual consistency there dwells the madness of desperation. Yet there was in him a mind nobler than the mind of those who, like Hegel's idealist or Marxian train, chose the other consistent alternative, seeking, and presumably finding, in the *historical* dimension of man's existence the promise of salvation, and in his mundane performances sufficient attraction for the *Weltgeist* to settle down among human beings, bringing with it the bliss of perfect harmony or, at least, a classless society.

Rare, however, are those who, on the highest level of spiritual awareness and in this hour of history, are blessed with the power to maintain the equipoise of suspense. Burckhardt was one of them. "At every moment," he wrote in a letter, "I would be prepared to exchange my life for a never-having-been." [32] He knew "what beggars we mortals are at the gates of happiness," [33] but he was determined to "die at peace with the world." Yet his, on the surface, purely aesthetic faith was not the only source that sustained his soul. There was, though it remained inarticulate, much left in him of a faith which was narrower but precise. In his *Reflections on World History,* contemplating the power and the success of evil (and power he regarded as forever predominantly evil, and Napoleon he called a personified absurdity), he dismisses the comfort which the Hegelian assumption of a historical master-plan for the world may give. "Every successful wickedness," he says, "is, to say the least of it, a scandal," and he adds: "The only lesson to be derived from the successful misdeeds of the strong is to hold life here and now in no higher esteem than it deserves."[34] And once, concluding one of his lectures about Greek art with some reflections on the sadness expressed in the faces of the marble images of Greek gods, he made the Vatican Hermes say: "You are astonished that I am so sad, I, one of the Olympians living in perpetual bliss and immortal joy? Indeed, we possessed everything: glory, heavenly beauty, eternal youth, everlasting pleasure, and yet we were not happy. . . . We lived only for ourselves and inflicted suffering on all others. . . . We were not good, and hence we had to perish."[35] This is not the language of a rhapsodist of beauty. It sounds rather like an echo of the voice of Jacob Burckhardt *senior,* Vicar of the Minster of Basle.

# NIETZSCHE, THE TEACHER OF

# "FREE SPIRITS"

Nietzsche's *Human, All Too Human* was first published in 1878. Its subtitle offered it as "a book for free spirits." Neither its author nor its readers could know that eight years later, in 1886, it would be only volume one of a two-volume work by the same title.*

At the time of the book's greatly enlarged appearance, Nietzsche no longer occupied the Chair of Classical Philology at the University of Basle. He had resigned it in 1879, at age 35 and ostensibly because of deteriorating health, but when the original *Human, All Too Human* appeared in 1878 he was still a professor. The book, though, was certainly not what the academic guild expected of one of its members. Nietzsche's preceding works had not met such expectations either— not even his first book about the origins of Greek drama, *The Birth of Tragedy* (1982). Its style was more hymnic than philological and its ideas more subversive than was compatible with the mores of professional behavior. Nietzsche, later, knew this himself. In 1886, in the Preface to the second edition, he called *The Birth of Tragedy* an "impossible book," written by one who should have said what he had to say as a poet rather than a philologist. Although this did not apply to the four publications that followed, summarily called *Thoughts Out of Season,* nobody would have guessed that their author was a professor of classical philology.

The first (1873) of these *Thoughts Out of Season* was a vehement polemic by the future "Anti-Christ" against David Strauss, whose influential *Life of Jesus*—translated into English by George Eliot—had helped to shake many a reader's Christian faith; but the "demytholo-

---

*Two books of aphorisms that Nietzsche had written and published during the in-between years, *Assorted Opinions and Maxims* (1879) and *The Wanderer and His Shadow* (1880) were now joined to it as volume II of *Human, All Too Human.* The whole work was published in R. J. Hollingdale's new translation by Cambridge University Press, the first complete English edition of the work in its 1886 form after its appearance in the 18-volume edition of *The Complete Works of Friedrich Nietzsche,* edited by Oscar Levy (New York, 1909–1911. In this new translation, the three parts that form Nietzsche's own final edition have retained the original numbering of aphorisms. Thus my references are to I (the original *Human, All Too Human*), to II, 1 (*Assorted Opinions*), and to II, 2 (*The Wanderer*), followed by the number of the particular aphorism.

gizing" theologian's last book, *The Old and the New Faith,* infuriated Nietzsche with its comfortably "rational" Christianity and the philistine style that went with it. *Bildungsphilister*—educated philistine— was the enduring coinage of Nietzsche's attack. The second volume of Nietzsche's "untimely" series (1874) dealt with History, its advantages and disadvantages, or rather with the uses and abuses of its study. Later in the same year followed the third book, the panegyric to Schopenhauer the Educator, *his* educator. The sequence was concluded with the fourth; *Richard Wagner in Bayreuth* (1876), a book that is a boon for those who like to read against the grain and who delight in stylistic ambiguities. The essay foreshadowed the darkening of Nietzsche's love for Wagner, his boundlessly admired older friend from earlier days who for him, according to the last part of *The Birth of Tragedy,* had been the recreator of what Attic tragedy was for the Greeks.

The Wagner of Bayreuth is no longer quite the same as the Wagner whom Nietzsche, then still a student in Leipzig, met for the first time in 1868, or the Wagner who was his host in the Lake Lucerne house at Tribschen where a room was always ready for him. No, the new master of Bayreuth had to be reminded, with innuendo and subtle indirection, of the spiritual promise of his beginning. This expectation seemed now endangered by Wagner's unbridled worldly ambition, his ideology (including an anti-Semitism that became ever more repellent to Nietzsche), dynastic flatteries, and mediocre partisans who were prepared to pay handsomely for being uplifted every season from their pedestrian existences. Did Wagner not know, Nietzsche seemed to ask, that his young friend and admirer would detest the spectacle of a successful Wagner-Wotan, increasingly popular with the poor in spirit? But Wagner heard only what was praise in this essay. He was overjoyed, responding with "Friend! Your book is tremendous! How have you come to know so well my innermost being?" Clearly, the essay left him unprepared for the shock of *Human, All Too Human.*

Nietzsche, in April 1878, sent two copies of the book to him and Cosima—with trepidation. He rehearsed several letters to accompany the hesitant present, so hesitant that he had even toyed with the possibility of publishing it under a pseudonym. He did not mail the letters. According to one of those epistolary sketches, he said the book revealed the "secret" that he now shared with Wagner. The writing of it had comforted him, where all other comforts had failed: "Perhaps I have survived only because I was capable of writing it." For the first time, he said, he had succeeded in bringing to light his deepest perceptions of the human world, in traveling the whole circumference of his thought. Had they received the letter, it would have upset the Wagners even more than the work itself, the more so as Wagner, in January, had innocently sent the libretto of *Parsifal* to his "true and faithful friend," jocularly signing himself "R. W., *Oberkirchenrat*," a title bestowed by the Lutheran Church on its most distinguished clergy. In his extraordinary and often inaccurate autobiography *Ecce Homo* (1888), written shortly before his mental breakdown, Nietzsche dramatized the exchange by ignoring the four months that lay between these two postal events. "Through a miracle of meaning and accident," he wrote, the two works arrived simultaneously at their respective addresses. It was like a "crossing of swords." Obviously, it was high time to break with Wagner, as Nietzsche said in 1888, for "incredible! Wagner had become pious." These marks of surprise are indeed surprising, for had Wagner not been "pious" as far back as his 1861 *Tannhäuser?* Whatever *Human, All Too Human* did to Nietzsche's once so ardent friendship with Wagner, it surely could not advance his reputation as a philologist. Philology had become, in every respect, an "unhealthy" career for him. Small wonder he ended it during the following year, 1879.

Nevertheless, he *was* a scholar of unusual gifts, having proved it during his apprenticeship to his teacher, the influential Friedrich Wilhelm Ritschl in Leipzig. Ritschl was so impressed with the academic thoroughness and originality of his favorite student that he recommended him to the University of Basle, indeed recommended him so enthusiastically and persuasively that the young man of hardly twenty-five *was* appointed Professor without even a doctorate to his name; and he initially proved himself an outstanding scholar and teacher.

The notes for his lectures and seminars could serve as the basis for at least a dozen Ph.D. theses. Jacob Burckhardt, the distinguished historian, Nietzsche's older colleague in Basle, remarked later that the university would never have a more inspiring educator. Yet when at the very beginning of 1872 *The Birth of Tragedy* was published—a book that despite its faults counts now as a momentous work, seminal not only with regard to its subject but, above all, to anthropology and psychology—the academic orthodoxy was much displeased. Even the mild-mannered Ritschl, to Nietzsche's dismay, first said nothing, then uttered only the verbal corollary of a shaking head; and the young scholar Ulrich von Wilamowitz-Moellendorff made his own academic promise even more promising by publishing a devastating review that Thomas Mann one day was to call a scandal of German intellectual history. Yet Wagner in Bayreuth was moved to tears by *The Birth of*

*Tragedy* and promoted Nietzsche to the second place in his life—the first after Cosima. Six years later Nietzsche was to forfeit this position—or resign from it, just as he resigned his professorship.

*Human, All Too Human* may well have been the occasion, but no more than the occasion, of both "emancipations," as Nietzsche liked to interpret these breaks. The book certainly brought about the lasting estrangement from Wagner and thereby, perhaps, the "psychosomatic" worsening of Nietzsche's health. It is one of the paradoxes of Nietzsche's life that he regarded his break with academe, and above all his liberation from the spiritual enthrallment to Wagner, as steps towards attaining *"die grosse Gesundheit,"* superior health, while his letters, from that time onwards, increasingly contain wretched "bulletins" of his medical state. Certainly, this may simply have been due to the progressive course of an undiagnosed and—apparently even by himself—unsuspected fatal illness, most probably syphilis in conjunction with other pathological causes. Yet if so, it might at the same time have been the source of the hectic and profound creativity that he took to be a symptom of clairvoyant sanity to the very time of his terminal collapse in 1889. Thomas Mann has made the most of this in *Doctor Faustus,* the Nietzschean story of a great and sick composer.

In April 1878, *Human, All too Human* was sent out to Nietzsche's friends. On his presentation list, Richard and Cosima Wagner—the very first, of course, to receive *The Birth of Tragedy* and *Richard Wagner in Bayreuth,*—took twenty-first and twenty-second place. The book never reached very far beyond this circle. It was an "abominable failure," wrote Nietzsche, when he was informed that only 120 exemplars, out of a printing of 1,000, had been sold within the first year. Nobody as yet had an inkling that the author would before long be recognized, together with Marx and Freud, as one of the makers of the modern mind. For the time he himself seemed to play into the hands of historians of the intellect who bracketed the author of this "book for free spirits" with Voltaire.

In April 1876, during the incubation period of *Human, All Too Human,* he paid his respects to the French genius of the Enlightenment by making a pilgrimage, while spending a few days in Geneva, to Voltaire's late abode in nearby Fernay. Nietzsche was anxious to have his new work published for the hundredth anniversary of Voltaire's death. In this he succeeded, dedicating the book to the memory of this friend of Frederick the Great, and thus to a friendship that uniquely betokened the alliance between Reason and the Will to Power. In addition, Nietzsche inserted on the reverse of the 1886 title page yet another testimony to his new rationalist zeal. The book, he wrote, "that came into being in Sorrento during the winter of 1876–77 might not have been published just now" if it had not served the purpose of paying homage to "one of the greatest liberators of the human spirit." On the same page he quoted a passage from Descartes's *Meditationes de prima philosophia*. The citation is in praise of that Reason which filled the seventeenth-century philosopher's soul "with such joy that it became invulnerable to all worldly things."

Would this were true of Nietzsche's later life. Also, it is worth remarking that the name of Voltiare makes a rather modest appearance in only five of the 638 numbered aphorisms of *Human, All Too Human, I*: in 26, 221, 240, 438, and 463. Nor is Voltaire mentioned among the intellectual constellations that Nietzsche invokes in section 408 of what has become the first part of the second volume of the work (II, 1): "I too have been in the underworld, like Odysseus." There he compares himself to Odysseus descending to the abode of the shades and offering there his sacrifices, praying, as it were, to "four pairs" with whom, he writes, he must come to terms after each long stretch of solitary journeying, examining their minds and his own to find out whether they prove him right or wrong. These four pairs are Epicurus and Montaigne, Goethe and Spinoza, Plato and Rousseau, Pascal and Schopenhauer. Voltaire is not among them.

How could he? Fernay and Bayreuth? Voltaire and Dionysus? Voltaire's wit and literary elegance could not truly prevail over Nietzsche's spiritual intoxications. Impossible. In comparison with Nietzsche's Dionysus, Voltaire was an encyclopedic faun, a brilliant extravagance of the human spirit, while Nietzsche was cursed and blessed with an assignment close to the spirit's center of gravity (as well as with the gift for excesses of the mind). All of Nietzsche's attempts at "French" levity, at liberated sensuality, at pitting Bizet or Offenbach against the severity of Wagner, all his poems in the manner of Theocritus (or, for that matter, Heine) are pastiche to the point of embarrassment. No, his truth is the deep world of Zarathustra's midnight song, where even joy and delight rise from the depth of tragedy. Voltaire a great tragedian? Only one section of *Human, All Too Human* (I, 221) is truly in praise of Voltaire. It makes him the *very last* of the practitioners of French drama to uphold the principles of form and measure that might have counteracted the German tendency towards the chaos of "original genius," fostered by Lessing's extolling of the "barbarous" greatness of Shakespeare. Yet Nietzsche, the author of *The Birth of Tragedy*, must have suspected that the writing of comedy, a genre Voltaire largely neglected, would have been a more natural employment of the Frenchman's great talents.

Voltaire served Nietzsche merely as the stick with which to chastise Wagner. The composer had only to look at the work's dedication to Voltaire to suspect that it was meant as an insult to him or, if not as an insult, as a defiant declaration of independence. The Jewish psychologist Paul Rée, companion of Nietzsche's winter in Sorrento and supporter of what Nietzsche called his new "Réealism," became the target of Cosima Wagner's hostile response to the work. In a letter to a friend she wrote that she refused to read Nietzsche's new book; a few passages that struck her while turning its pages made her put it aside. It was, she believed, the sad consummation of her friend's intellectual development, against which she had struggled in vain. "In the end, Israel took over in the shape of a Dr. Rée, very slick, very cool, . . . representing the relationship of Judea to Germania. . . . It is the victory of evil over good." Had she, perhaps, chanced upon what Nietzsche's new book says about the Jews (I, 475)? That the Jews have helped to make European history "a continuation of the Greek." And, then, Cosima deplores the effect the book has had on their friends. One, while rejecting its message, "yet finds that it is the most beautiful that Nietzsche ever wrote." And Wagner himself? He read only a few lines and put it down. He did not want it to spoil the pleasure, he said, that Nietzsche's previous works had given him. It seems that only Rée and Jacob Burckhardt were pleased. Rée wrote to his "dearest friend" that he had "pounced upon the book like a hungry beast of prey" and devoured it with delight; and Burckhardt called it the superior book of a superior mind.

The reader of today is hard put to understand the agitation aroused by *Human, All Too Human.* Nietzsche's most intelligent friend among philologists, Erwin Rohde, his only distinguished expert defender in the "scandal" of *The Birth of Tragedy,* used metaphors derived from the Roman baths in describing the book's effect on him. Coming to it from Nietzsche's previous writings was like being chased from the *calidarium,* the steamy waters, immediately into an icy *frigidarium,* "a rather shocking experience"; and a dedicated elderly friend wrote to him that she would never forget the day she had spent reading the new work—a terrifying thunderstorm raged on in the sky as well as in her soul, "But now I feel that something has died within me." And there exist many letters reporting such tempestuous responses. How was this? Much of the book's brilliance is as fresh and invigorating as it was on its first day but its *opinions*—and he who reads it only in order to agree or disagree with them is a poor reader—have largely been deprived of their startling effects. The psychological and anthropological inventions or presumed discoveries of the intervening years have seen to that.

What was it that so deeply shocked the admiring readers of Nietzsche's previous works? Nietzsche himself sometimes believed that a new sensibility had emerged with the publication of *Human, All Too Human*, one radically different from that of the author who wrote *The Birth of Tragedy*, heralding Richard Wagner. A sensibility different from that of the detractor of David Strauss's "enlightened" religiousness, the partial advocate of "monumental"—that is heroic—historiography, the evangelist of Dionysus who had "transvalued" Schopenhauer's metaphysical pessimism. Yet if he reversed Schopenhauer's "nay-saying," he did so without abandoning his educator's metaphysics, keeping it intact, in fact, far beyond the apparent metaphysical skepticism or even positivism of *Human, All Too Human*. Indeed, he proclaimed in the most recklessly metaphysical note of the year 1885, written only five years after the publication of the two-volume edition of *Human, All Too Human*, that *"this world is the will to power—and nothing besides! And you yourselves are also this will to power—and nothing besides!"* an assertion that only adds "power" to Schopenhauer's metaphysics of the Will.[2]

Nietzsche himself found it very difficult to explain why *Human, All Too Human* so upset many of his readers. In 1886 he sketched out one preface after another that was to introduce the new edition of his book—and discarded most of them. In one of these unused 1886 introductions he confessed that, looking at the book, he felt considerable embarrassment and was tempted to ask whether it was really he that had produced it—"Is it me? Is it not me?" Two years later, however, in his self-presentation in *Ecce Homo*, he claimed that *Human, All Too Human* showed his "true self." He had rid himself, in an exercise of rigorous self-discipline, of the "higher swindle" that he had allowed insidiously to seduce him, of all "idealism," "pleasurable sentiment," and "other femininities." Now he was bent on the negation of logic as the condition of truth. Also, he was convinced that he had renounced any metaphysical Absolute. All of these Absolutes were empty. Interesting were only *error* and *illusion*. They alone had a chance to be "profound, miraculous, pregnant with bliss and disaster." "The overcoming of metaphysics" was his aim, and ultimately the act of reversing all traditional valuations that merely burdened and misled the human mind. It was this in *Human, All Too Human* that had caused the great shock. For in denouncing as "swindle" what once had seduced him, he also implied that he had seduced his readers. Yet he could speak in this manner only of the original 1878 edition of the work. The criticism was no longer valid in 1886, when he called *Human, All Too Human* a mere "*Denkmal*," a war memorial to one of the "victories" of his ever-embattled spirit.

True, in a letter from the time of the final *Human, All Too Human* he describes himself quite unambiguously as one who desires nothing more than to lose some soothing belief every day, who seeks and finds his happiness in just this. Yet in one of the discarded and fragmentary introductions he declares it to be the function of the "offending" book to help him "to absorb positivism in its entirety and yet remain an idealist."

One of the introductions Nietzsche wrote in 1886, the year so productive of introductions, is to the new edition of *The Birth of Tragedy*. It may well be the strangest and at the same time the weightiest preface ever written. For it essentially rescinded the book he had published in 1872. A fragment of another introduction he had planned in 1886, probably again for *Human, All Too Human*, might have found its proper place there: "I want to inform the readers of my previous works that I have given up the metaphysical-artistic views that dominate them: they are appealing but untenable. He who permits himself to speak publicly early in life, is usually constrained publicly to contradict himself soon afterwards." Nonetheless, he published *The Birth of Tragedy* again—presumably as another "*Denkmal*," a commemorating monument.

If it is a monument, it is at least as much alive as the statue of the Commendatore at the end of *Don Giovanni;* and although it does not drag its reader-victim into Hell, it at least issues to them anew the old *metaphysical forgeries* of his first book and even sends them to Bayreuth. Obviously it is not easy, intellectually, to live with Nietzsche.

Why the "forgeries"? He himself answers the question, and does so very beautifully in the published 1886 Introduction to *Human, All Too Human*. He *created*, he maintains, spiritual companions for himself in order not to feel so unendurably lonely; and tried to *believe* in them even when he ought to have known better. He tried to believe in companionship with Schopenhauer despite the pessimist's stubborn moralism; and with Wagner, despite the musician's inveterate romanticism. He also "forged" or invented the "free spirits" to whom *Human, All Too Human* was dedicated. If they did not yet exist, he persuaded himself that he saw their approach. But his eyesight was very bad, and this vision was yet another self-deception, one among the other illusions, all of them therapeutic measures against loneliness and isolation: psychological necessities.

Psychology was the weapon—the deadly weapon, as he believed—that Nietzsche wielded in the subsequent war against the companionable forgeries, idealism and metaphysics. His new psychological strategy was based upon the persistent suspicion that all "higher values" are merely satisfactions of psychological needs, dams built against the onrush of emptiness, of the "*nihil,*" the spiritual vacuity created by the "death of God." Nietzsche's is the eye that now sees through everything until all that is left to see through is blank nothingness; and even then this eye would turn around, fairy-tale-like, and see through the seer.

Most of the psychological "unmasking" in Nietzsche's works after *Human, All Too Human* is brilliantly performed with instruments constructed in that book. There occurs, for instance, in *Beyond Good and Evil* (1886) a famous passage (269) in which psychology does indeed do away with the greatness of all great poets, and, at the same time, with all traditionally established values:

> The world of historical values is dominated by forgery. These great poets, like Byron, Musset, Poe, Leopardi, Kleist, Gogol (I dare not mention greater names, but I mean them)—all endowed with souls wishing to conceal a break, often avenging themselves with their works upon some inner desecration, often seeking oblivion in their lofty flights from their all-too-faithful memories, often lost in mud and almost in love with it until they become like will-o'-the-wisps of the morasses and simulate the stars . . . oh what a torture are all these great artists and altogether these higher beings, what a torture to him who has guessed their true nature.[3]

Or "seen through them." Only an artist who is himself one of these poets would write so well. But Nietzsche's thought here eschews the miracle, or at least the alchemy, that would have to be at work even if the doctrine of the base origins of the sublime were correct: the transformation of mud into something precious and beautiful, or the expression of such sobering insights in radiant prose. The aphorisms of *Human, All Too Human,* particularly in the section that deals with the psyche of artists and writers, are prolegomena and often anticipations of this devastating psychoanalytical diagnosis.

What is still absent from the book for free spirits is the aversion of the later Nietzsche to the "nihilistic" psychology. This appears, for instance, in the section of *Beyond Good and Evil* that closely follows upon the seen-through "great poets." There (270) he refers to a different kind of "free and insolent spirit" who, on the contrary, shyly desires to conceal the pains he suffered in arriving at his "unholy and all-too certain knowledge." He realizes that it may be the sign of a finer sensibility "to respect 'the mask' and not, in the wrong places, indulge in psychology and psychological curiosity."[4] And only a little further on (275) we even read what certainly could not have been written in the first infatuation with "scientific" sobriety that pervades *Human, All Too Human:* "He who does not *wish* to see what is great in a man, has the sharpest eye for that which is low and superficial in him, and so gives away—himself."[5] Yet we may well ask *when* exactly it would be wrong to employ psychology? Nonetheless, this is probably the last moment in the history of modern psychological suspiciousness when it still had words luminous with the afterglow of that piety that is named in *Zarathustra* IV: Zarathustra is called there "the most pious of all those who do not believe in God." This piety pervades the concluding sentences of the same section 275 of *Beyond Good and Evil:*

> It is possible that, disguised by the holy fable of Jesus' life, there is hidden one of the most agonizing martyrdoms of *one who knows the nature of love:* the martyrdom of the most innocent and most desirous heart that never had been content with any human love, that *demanded* love, wanted to be loved and nothing else, with mad determination and terrible outbursts against those who withheld love from him; the story of one who was unsated and insatiable in his love so that he *had* to invent Hell where to send those who would not love him—, and who, finally, having come to know everything about human love, had to invent a God who was nothing but love, nothing but the *capacity* for love, one who takes pity on human love because it is so feeble and so unknowing! He who does feel like this . . . *seeks* death.—But why inquire into such painful things? Unless one has to . . .[6]

Before too long such a lover might seek out a psychoanalyst rather than invent hells and divinities, and yet would not come closer to the ranks of Nietzsche's free spirits.

Certainly, Nietzsche did explain why he had to "forge." There is a passage in one of the unpublished 1886 introductions to *Human, All Too Human*[7] that makes one wonder whether Kafka, perhaps, knew and remembered it when he wrote his "Hunger Artist." And it is true to say that in a sense he did know it, although it was not yet published during his time: the *Zeitgeist,* the spirit of the age, did read it to him. Nietzsche writes of one who is in danger of starving because he hardly ever "finds *his* table set, *his* food prepared." He is thrown into an age "whose meals he is forced to decline," and thus he may "perish of hunger and thirst—or of nausea if in the end he takes what the cooks offer." This, Nietzsche continues, was the peril of his early years when his soul was undernourished and full of longing and loneliness; and

> the danger became most threatening when one day I recognized *what* sustenance I chose, seduced by the starvation of my soul. This dawned upon me in the summer of 1876. It was then that, from revulsion, I pushed away all the tables at which I used to sit, and vowed that I would live, like cattle, on grass, or live not at all rather than share my meals with the "gang of actors" or the "higher circus-riders of the spirit"— yes, such harsh words I used at the time; for it seemed to me that I had fallen among gypsies and fiddlers, among Cagliostros and men born to be forgers, and enjoyed their alluring luxuries.[8]

The plural is somewhat misleading, for Nietzsche could not possibly have included Schopenhauer among the Cagliostros. No, he meant only one: Richard Wagner. He saw him for the last time in 1876 in Sorrento. Nietzsche and a group of his friends, Rée among them, moved into the Villa Rubinacci at the end of October and soon began to plan (nothing became of the plan) the founding of a kind of free college for free spirits. The Wagners had been staying in a nearby hotel and went to Rome after two weeks. These two weeks, it seems, sufficed to strengthen Nietzsche's determination to part with the acrobats of "the higher spirit," for Wagner talked of *Parsifal* and the trancelike state that the symbolism of the Last Supper induced in him. Also, it is likely that he warned Nietzsche against his Jewish friend Rée who, in Sorrento, was to finish his own book on *The Origin of Moral Perceptions,* a title that surely suggested to Nietzsche his own *Genealogy of Morals* (1887).

During the autumn, winter, and early spring of 1876–77 the Villa Rubinacci became the actual birthplace of *Human, All Too Human* I. A large number of the aphorisms of which the book is made were written there. The first of them announces Nietzsche's break with his metaphysical-idealist past and, at the same time, describes the sort of "scientism" he now embraced. It is entitled "Chemistry of Concepts and Sensations." Chemistry, of course, does not mean chemistry, nor has "scientism" much to do with "science," as the words are used today. Nonetheless, Nietzsche, here as much as elsewhere in this book, is astonishingly Hegelian in the assumption that the range, potency, and effectiveness of *art* is bound to be lessened by the increasing reliance of the modern age on *rationality*. Although he would, of course, not accept Hegel's metaphysics of History, he yet echoes Hegel's *Aesthetics* by saying, at the end of the aphorism I, 222, that "scientific man is the further evolution of the artistic," that is to say, the successor, appointed by History, to the artist who, in *The Birth of Tragedy* and still in *Thoughts Out of Season,* ruled over the domain of the spirit.

Chemistry, then, means psychological analysis and that extreme historical relativism for which Nietzsche used the term "Perspectivism." This is based upon what may well be looked upon as the indisputable "fact" that the beliefs held about life, gods and beauty as expressed in the stone of the Athenian Acropolis are obviously very different from those that have taken architectural shape, for instance, in the cathedral of San Marco in Venice. Is there *truth* in both of these fundamentally different "beliefs"? Truth, therefore, is merely "truth," a matter of perspective. In the posthumous note 481 of *The Will to Power,* Nietzsche asserts that there "are no facts, only interpretations."[9] As this was certainly not meant for the literal-minded, who habitually cite it in their "deconstructive" campaigns, it is advisable to remind them and ourselves of its context—the context of extreme nihilism. For that note first turns against the positivist illusion that there are *only* facts. By no means, Nietzsche replies—it is exactly facts that do not exist. There are only interpretations. "Subjective" interpretations? he goes on to ask. Surely not, he answers, and resolutely crosses the frontier into nihilism. For the concept "subject" is not a "given"; it is itself an interpretative invention. And then: "In so far as the word 'knowledge' has any meaning, the world is unknowable." One is tempted to add: after the death of God, the only "real" knower.* Yet the unknowable world "is variously *interpretable,* it has no *one* meaning behind it, but countless meanings—this is 'Perspectivism,'" and bangs the door in the face of anyone who claims any sure "knowledge." Does it include, one wonders, the knowledge that there is no knowledge?

What is left is the later Nietzsche's persistent problem, the question of "*Rang*"; for although the multitude of interpretations can no longer be said to differ with regard to "truth," they do differ in "*Rang*." To determine their "*Rang,*" that is, the position of any "truth" in the order and hierarchy of "values," is now Nietzsche's superlative task, a task that does not allow for any philosophical solution. Nietzsche, there-

---

*There is an awkward error in Kaufmann's or the printer's English rendering of the sentence: the "un" in "unknowable" is missing.

fore, had to create the *Übermensch* or at least his prophet Zarathustra to pass judgment on "values." They made the recklessly aristocratic decisions.

With the aphorisms of *Human, All Too Human,* Nietzsche, who had never been a systematic thinker, found the form that best suited his intellectual nature. He was not to abandon it again, not entirely even in *Thus Spoke Zarathustra,* his disquieting, indiscreet, and intermittently radiant book of prophecy. His intention to crown his life as a philosopher with a systematic exposition of *The Will to Power,* or, as he sometimes wanted to call it, *The Transvaluation of All Values,* remained unrealized—rightly and fortunately so. For this frustration led to a very great number of preparatory notes, many of which have the kind of definitiveness that only the brevity of aphorisms can afford. What appears in *Zarathustra* as a different style is merely his—very much *his*—"parody," meant to reverse the message of the Gospels.

Philosophical systems? Even the most impressive of them are uncomfortably seated on a throne of rock bottom "stupidity," that self-inflicted unimaginativeness which enables a mind to believe that it, unquestionably itself *part* of the immense world, could make absolutely coherent sense of it *all.* Nietzsche was too intelligent, too skeptical, and too much of a latecomer to the history of German philosophy, a history both glorious and disastrous, to construct a philosophical system. In its pursuit even so honest a thinker as Schopenhauer would, for the sake of a "fit," become something of a "counterfeiter," as Nietzsche notes as late as 1888.[10] Nietzsche, by his intellectual nature, is the very opposite of a "systematizer." His is the brilliance of sudden illuminations, often the wisdom of deeply pondered paradoxes; and sometimes, of course, the shrill foolishness of the fool. At his best, his aphorisms are as good as those of Blaise Pascal, whose mind Nietzsche profoundly admired (although, he once said, Christianity had done much damage to it), or *mutatis mutandis* of the French *moralistes,* or of Lichtenberg (1742–1799), whom he praised as a master of German prose. He did so very strikingly in aphorism II, 109 of *Human, All Too Human,* where Lichtenberg's *Aphorisms* do come immediately after Goethe's *Conversations with Eckerman* on that very short list of German prose books that will remain worth reading. And in 1885 Nietzsche noted: "The profoundest . . . books will probably always have something of the aphoristic and unexpected character of Pascal's *Pensees*" (*The Will to Power,* section 424).

In a rather innocuous, only posthumously published and not a little ironical preparatory piece for *Human, All Too Human,* Nietzsche com-

mends the aphoristic form as particularly suitable for people who
travel much and frequently must interrupt their reading; and the more
monotonous the modern conditions of work are bound to become,
the more people will want to travel. Hence, "Writers who wish to
affect the general views of the public, will have to address travelers."
But Nietzsche did not think of his readers as merely traveling; he
hoped they would be underway to a destination more closely related
to destiny than to business or sightseeing. Also, his aphorisms are
often succinct predictions of the future, as is, for instance, his observation (I, 473) that socialism is the younger brother of despotism
"whose heir it wants to be" and is, therefore, deeply "reactionary":
"For it aims at an abundance of state power such as only despots have
ever enjoyed." How, in 1878, did he know?

The distinctive gift that makes a master of aphorisms is an assured
sense of language, even a passion for words. In the most conspicuous
cases it is a word that begets a thought. Karl Kraus, the Austrian genius among writers of aphorisms, even said that language is the divin-
ing rod that leads him to hidden treasures of truth. This points to the
kind of relationship to language, the passionate love of it, that is of
the poet. One of them, Stefan George, even went so far as to utter the
"categorical imperative" that things acquire the right to exist only by
the jurisdiction of the words that express them: "*Kein Ding sei, wo das
Wort gebricht,*" meaning that there should be nothing where language
fails. This disposition of thinking is the very opposite of the attitude
taken up by almost all language theories of modernism or "postmodernism." ("Postmodernism" is the most unimaginative term of "per-
iodization" that was hit upon by an enfeebled age.) For "postmodern-
ists" take pride in not being proud of language. Language for them is,
after all, a method of all but random "signifiers": "In the beginning
was the signifier." Or was it the signified? Does a language, a more or
less arbitrary choice, as is held, of significations, owe its surprising
durability to the conservative laziness of man and his persuading himself that "in language he possessed knowledge of the world," as
Nietzsche puts it in I, 11, and elsewhere?* Some such skeptical observations on language in Nietzsche's works have been avidly used in the
course of "deconstruction," and, with special enthusiasm, his aphoristic pronouncement in this book (II, 2, 55) about the danger to which

---

*I discuss several such Nietzschean attacks upon the "metaphysics" of language in the
essay "Wittgnstein and Nietzsche," in *The Artist's Journey into the Interior* (New York,
1965, and London, 1966), reprinted in this volume.

intellectual freedom may be exposed by the belief in language: "Every word is a prejudice."

The trouble is that few of those who like to quote Nietzsche really know him, and many do not know him as the grand architect of an edifice that is not a "system" but is built from chiseled contradictions. They do not know him as the man who, in the Introduction to the second part of *Human, All Too Human,* says that, "sorely mistrustful" of himself as he had become, he took sides *against* himself and *for* anything that happened to hurt him and was hard for him—for instance, against Romantic music, above all Wagner; or against the trust in language, a faith that often was the target of his heretical utterances. Yet he was what every writer of aphorisms and certainly every poet is: a lover of words. But then, the thinker in him was often irresistibly driven to spite the poet in him: "In matters of knowledge, poets are always wrong," he once remarked.[11] Indeed, in *Zarathustra* he even called the poet an inveterate liar, and made Zarathustra himself woefully add that he, too, is a poet.[12] Is it, then, Zarathustra, the poet, the liar, or the lover of language, of words as the messengers of truth (yes, of truth, after all) who, in the solitude of his "Return Home," says: "Here the words and word-shrines of all Being open up before me: Here all Being wishes to become word, all Becoming wishes to learn from me how to speak."[13] Or is it Nietzsche himself, for once not siding with what hurts him?

# ZARATHUSTRA'S THREE
# METAMORPHOSES: FACETS OF
# NIETZSCHE'S INTELLECTUAL
# BIOGRAPHY AND THE
# APOTHEOSIS OF INNOCENCE

*Thus Spoke Zarathustra* (1883–1885) is, among Nietzsche's works, the book on which, for a long time, his fame rested most massively as if on a throne designed by some *art nouveaux* or *Jugendstil* artist; and if Nietzsche himself conceived of his bearded prophet in the image of Leonardo da Vinci's red chalk self-portrait in Turin, the likeness, as it turned out, was more in the manner of a Pre-Raphaelite painter. Yet Nietzsche looked upon his *Zarathustra* as the Fifth Gospel, the gospel to take back, indeed obliterate, the preceding four, and held it to be the truest child of his poetic-philosophical genius. In his autobiography of 1888, *Ecce Homo,* the very title of which betrays the incipient delusion of grandeur and which nonetheless, in the passionate brilliance and precision of its language, bears witness to his genius (a great mind's megalomania—what a catastrophic superfluity!)—in *Ecce Homo* he records the upheaval of the spirit which, five years earlier, accompanied the birth of the First Part of *Zarathustra.* Is there anyone, Nietzsche asks in his autobiography, who, living at the end of the nineteenth century, has a clear notion of that which poets of poetically more powerful epochs called inspiration? "Well, I shall describe it." It is such that if there were the slightest vestige of superstition in a man thus inspired, he would hardly be able to avoid believing that he was an incarnation, a mouthpiece, a medium of superior powers. "Revelation"—the word used to convey the sense of something suddenly becoming visible that had not been seen before—would, he writes, be no exaggerated name for what he experienced. For he suddenly found what he had not searched for, and took without asking whence it came, what offered itself. Luminous thoughts "struck like lightning, their form predetermined by necessity, leaving no room for hesitation—I had no choice."[1]

Although in reading and re-reading *Zarathustra* one wishes time and again that there had been less lightning and more hesitation, less necessity and more discretion, and above all less of that dialect of eternity which, like the eagle and the serpent and all the other evangelical, emblematic, and allegorical equipment, has sadly aged in excess of its years (while, to take only one example, the idiom of *Human, All Too Human* grows fresher with every reading), it is yet true to say that more often than not the radiance of Nietzsche's mind succeeds in penetrating its heavy prophetic attire, and sometimes even gains force by its parabolic presentation. Indeed, it happens that this or that tableau from *Zarathustra* does, despite those impediments, deliver its meaning with a directness unattainable by any discursive philosophizing. Take for instance Zarathustra's speech—it is his first—on "The Three Metamorphoses" (even if its beginning comes close to an allegorical disaster):

> Of three metamorphoses of the spirit I tell you: how the spirit becomes a camel; and the camel, a lion, and the lion, finally, a child. (P.N. 137)*

True, in trying to imagine these all-but unimaginable transformations it is hard to suppress a sense of extreme zoological and spiritual discomfort: Would, one wonders, the spirit not feel rather degraded by having to turn into a camel, and would the lion not resist the operation that incongruously forces him into so helpless a human shape? Still, the prophet's inspiration becomes more convincing in what follows, probably because of the inconsistent but less demanding "*like* a camel" now replacing the full presence of the beast's symbolic reality. There is, we read, a stage in the spirit's voyage when it desires nothing more than to test its ability to bear heavy burdens, "kneels down like a camel waiting to be well loaded" and asks for the most difficult** that "I may take it upon myself and exalt in my strength." But what is the most difficult, the spirit inquires—characteristically of "o heroes"? To humble oneself to wound one's pride? To let one's folly shine in order to mock one's wisdom? Abandoning one's cause in the hour of its triumph? "Climbing high mountains to tempt the tempter?"

---

*The reference here and throughout the essay is to Walter Kaufmann's translation of *Thus Spoke Zarathustra* in *The Portable Nietzsche* (New York: Viking Press, 1954) (abbreviated P. N.).

**The German word is *schwer*, which means both "heavy," the right adjective for the camel's load, and "difficult," the proper designation for the spirit's task. There is no English word that conveys the German double meaning.

Or is it this: feeding on the acorns and grass of knowledge and, for the sake of the truth, suffering hunger in one's soul?

Or is it this: being sick and sending home the comforters and making friends with the deaf, who never hear what you want?

Or is it this: stepping into filthy waters when they are the waters of truth, and not repulsing cold frogs and hot toads?

Or is it this: loving those who despise us and offering a hand to the ghost that would frighten us?*

All these most difficult things the spirit that would bear much takes upon itself: like the camel that, burdened, speeds into the desert, thus the spirit speeds into its desert. (P.N. 138)[2]

If the inspiration that produced this had been as successful in its literary effect as it was powerful in Nietzsche's experience; and if it had brought about, as Nietzsche obviously wished it should, the fusion of both thought and experience into a great poetic parable, it would be petty and mean to dissolve it again into the elements from which it was made. As it is, no impiety is involved if one disregards for a little the animalistic metamorphoses of the spirit and speaks of Nietzsche himself, of his personal and intellectual life—two biographical aspects that are, with him, more intimately related than in the case of many another philosopher. He knew this himself even though, as was his wont, he instantly translated the personal insight into a universal one: All philosophy, he said again and again, is in one sense or another autobiographical, for what distinguishes the philosopher from the "scholar" or scientist is that there is "nothing whatever impersonal about him," his thinking testifying at every point to "who he is."[3] (Could Aristotle have said this? St. Thomas Aquinas? Kant? Hardly. But Plato, yes; and possibly St. Augustine, and undoubtedly Pascal or Kierkegaard. This may well mark the point of departure for a typology of thought and thinkers.)

If *Zarathustra* is a philosophical work, then Nietzsche's equation of philosophy and autobiography is certainly applicable to this first speech of the philosopher-prophet; so much so that it would not be unthinkable to write a Life of Nietzsche as of one born under the sign of "the Camel." "Lonely and deeply suspicious of myself . . . , I took . . . sides *against* myself and *for* anything that happened to hurt me and was hard for me,"[5] he said, and it was the fundamental truth of his existence, from beginning to end and not only before Zarathustra assigned to the spirit a career that took it beyond the stage of the camel.

---

*Of such a ghost more will be said in the essay "Nietzsche's Terrors."

Indeed, we should be mistaken if we assumed that Nietzsche himself believed he had passed all the tests of Zarathustra's metamorphoses: camel, lion, child. Far from it, and if he wished to *show* Zarathustra as one who had done so, he did not succeed, for it is certainly neither a lion, rid of scruples, nor a child, free of self-consciousness, that, to give only one example, accuses the poets of lying too much and then, defeated by his self-knowledge, says: "But Zarathustra too is a poet. . . . *We* do lie too much."[6] (Should not the lion ask: "Why not lie?" He does not. On the contrary, the words convey, if not opprobrium, at least metaphysical discomfort or, worse still, Zarathustra's inability to believe in himself.)

Nor is it true to say that the thought of these metamorphoses "struck like lightning" or was found without search. It had been, as a note from the time before *Zarathustra* shows, conscientiously rehearsed. Nietzsche, in that posthumous note,[7] does not yet speak of three transformations, but of *"drei Gänge,"* three stages on the way, and does not clothe his meanings in symbols, but merely points to three different attitudes of mind and soul; and although the lines separating the three stages are not yet drawn as energetically as in Zarathustra's first speech, the sameness of the journey is yet discernible. To excel in admiring others, in obeying and learning, is the characteristic of the first stage, as well as to "assume heavy burdens," to allow oneself to be torn apart by contradictory devotions and to cultivate altogether a radical "asceticism of the spirit." The second stage, the "time of the desert"—"like the camel that, burdened, speeds into the desert . . ." was to be pronounced by Zarathustra in setting the scene for the spirit's second metamorphosis—this second stage demands of the admiring heart that it should, even if it breaks, deny what it had admired most, gain freedom and independence by "idealizing" what hitherto it had *not* loved and by attaching itself to "contrary values." And during the third stage it learns boundlessly to "affirm" and, knowing neither god nor man above itself, finally attains to that innocence of instinct— "the lion, finally, becomes a child" says Zarathustra—that is the condition of a new creativity.

"I took sides *against* myself and *for* everything that happened to hurt me . . ." It is amazing how much of Nietzsche's own mind and autobiography is depicted in Zarathustra's evocation of the spirit in its "camel" phase. "To humble oneself to wound one's pride"—he who has followed with fascination the eventful story of Nietzsche's relationship with Wagner has good reason to believe that, looked upon not only from the vantage-point of *Zarathustra,* there *always* was an element of self-humiliation even in the most enthusiastic services the young author of *The Birth of Tragedy* and, more conspicuously, of *Richard Wagner in Bayreuth* had rendered the composer. It is certainly true to say that in *The Birth of Tragedy* Nietzsche, with his own profound metaphysical intuition and classical learning, indeed his genius, "knelt down" before Wagner, just as if Dionysus and Apollo, the deities of the book, had come into their divine offices merely to pave the way for the musical return of Wotan. And is not that "questionable" book—as Nietzsche himself called it eighteen years after he had written it[8]— flawed by its issuing, not too smoothly, into a kind of metaphysical advertisement for the composer-dramatist? And if it is a correct reading of some of Nietzsche's ecstatic Dithyrambs to Dionysus to see in them his own love-songs for Cosima-Ariadne and indictments of Wagner-Theseus, then Tribschen, the place of Nietzsche's sojourns with Wagner and Cosima must have been for him the name for a labyrinthine state of the soul in which he was torn hither and thither by admiration, desire, jealousy, and self-effacement.

Moreover, putting side by side his essay *Wagner in Bayreuth,* still aglow with the fervor of the apostle, and the most skeptical, indeed hostile notebook entries about Wagner that he wrote at the same time—observations that anticipate much of the anti-Wagner diatribe *The Wagner Case* (1888)—we may guess what Zarathustra means by the camel-spirit's mocking his secret wisdom through publicly letting his folly shine—in praise of a man whose unquestionable artistic powers he had even then come close to judging disastrous. And he *did* break with him at a time when Wagner had indeed triumphed and was no longer in need of Nietzsche's espousing his "cause." On the contrary, had he maintained his friendship, he may have shared a little of the light that now so abundantly shone upon Wagner, the composer of whose work he said in a letter to Lou Salomé that he, Nietzsche, had "*erliebt*" it (a pun on "*erleben*"—to experience—and "*sich verlieben,*" to "fall in love.") That letter was written in the fall of 1882 when *Parsifal* was performed for the first time in Bayreuth, an event from which Nietzsche demonstratively stayed away. His letter went on to say that his love of Wagner's music had been a "long passion: I find no other word for it"; and then, that his break with Wagner was an act of renunciation which, although it was necessary if he was at last to find himself, was among the "hardest and most melancholy things" in his life.

2

Nietzsche had, or so it seemed to him, climbed his "high mountains" with the intent to challenge his enemy God—his hangman, as Zarathustra's magician calls Him in one of Nietzsche's most sinister ventriloquisms, his hangman, his agony, and yet his ultimate bliss.[9] Indeed, the desire to do so and thus to "tempt the tempter" Lucifer, the supreme challenger, is perhaps at the inmost core of his spiritual existence, the deepest secret of his psyche. Insofar as Thomas Mann's *Doctor Faustus* is a novel also about Nietzsche, it is Nietzschean above all in presenting its hero, the composer Adrian Leverkühn, as the victim, both triumphant and tragic, of such "tempting"; and surely Leverkühn might be found in the company of those men, most creative, lonely, and disturbed, in whose mouths Nietzsche put the words: "Oh grand madness, you heavenly powers! Madness that at last I may believe in myself . . . I am consumed by doubts, for I have destroyed the Law . . . If I am not more than the Law, then I am the most abject of all men."[10] For it was Leverkühn who had asked for the madness as well as the victorious self-assurance of genius, and was given both, although not by heavenly powers but by the Devil, the tempter whom he had tempted. The author of that prayer for madness, Nietzsche, had himself a perfect right to those words; and with even clearer autobiographical intent he once invented, alluding to the figure of the tempter's most notorious tempter, a character he called "the Don Juan of the Mind" who, having been disillusioned by every attainable knowledge, found himself in the end seeking "the knowledge which hurts most," and in the very end craved Hell itself, "the only knowledge which can still seduce him."[11]

Just as an unfathomable inner compulsion, both destructive and creative, made him "send home," in his lived life, those who might have comforted his tortured soul—Lou Salomé, for instance, whom he loved—, and allowed himself to be dominated by such "friends" as his sister was, stone-deaf to the voice of his true mind, so was he driven, in his intellectual existence, to abandon every pasture that sustained his spiritual nature (the metaphysical domains, for instance, of *The Birth of Tragedy* and *Thoughts out of Season*) in order to feed "for the sake of the truth," "on the acorn and grass of knowledge" that grew on the "god-forsaken" fields of *Human, All Too Human*. But *was* it "for the sake of the truth" that he wrote his antimetaphysical manifesto, the most brilliant and inspired document that mid-nineteenth century positivism has brought forth? To see it thus would be seeing it too simply. For *Human, All Too Human,* his great experiment in spiritual defiance, is already pervaded by the sense of there being *no truth* whatever, and certainly no spiritual truth, and by the suspicion that what is called truth is merely "the kind of error without which a certain type of animal finds it impossible to exist."[12] Once this intuition and powerful agent within the intellectual sensibility, as productive of wittily tragic paradoxes as it is impotent in logic, has taken possession of a mind, the demand for intellectual honesty—the demand Nietzsche constantly and insistently made upon himself "for the sake of the truth"—can only be met by irony, the kind of irony that looks like destiny rather than evasiveness, and with him often assumed the unironical appearance of extreme and extremely contradictory beliefs rehearsed simultaneously or in quick succession.

Where there is such a drought of truth, its waters will stagnate, and he who is nonetheless determined to step into them is likely to find himself in a morass, running after will-o'-the-wisps. "Will-o'-the-wisps of the morasses" that "simulate the stars": this is how Nietzsche, in the book that followed upon *Zarathustra,* in *Beyond Good and Evil*[13] calls "these great artists and altogether these higher beings." All of them have, he writes, something to conceal in their souls, something terrible, "some inner desecration"; and "lost in mud and almost in love with it," they rise from it, through the "forgeries" of their works, to those heights of sublimity to which naive and innocent spectators look up in pure adoration. Nietzsche, with his faculty to see great achievements as the compensatory maneuvers of wounded and humiliated souls, may well have been what he once claimed he was: the first psychologist of Europe, one who would not be shy of "frog or toad" or other creatures of the unclean waters if their habitats promised some "truth." But does intellectual honesty really demand that the seeker should seek the truth in muddy pools? A few pages after the swamp excursion, the author of *Beyond Good and Evil* is back on drier and cleaner ground: "From which follows that it is the sign of a finer humanity to respect 'the mask' and not, in the wrong places, indulge in psychology and psychological curiosity."[14] This is no longer spoken by the camel-spirit but by a mind who knows that "truth" is not the sole criterion of Truth. And yet he speaks of masks. But where there is no true face, there can be no mask either, or else *only* masks. And psychology "in the wrong places"? There are no wrong places where there is no right one. Or is the right place where, still in the vicinity of the "morasses," we read the eminently psychological dictum: "He who does not *wish* to see what is great in a man, has the sharpest eye for that which is low and superficial in him, and so gives away himself"?[15]

For every truth that departs from the world, there arrives a ghost. But there is one in particular whose acquaintance Nietzsche-Zarathustra has made, a demon-ghost who would frighten him and to whom he stretched out his hand in friendship as if it were the bearer of most joyful news. With this encounter ends the Fourth Book of *Joyous Science*. It is that strange, beautiful and still hesitant "What if" rehearsal of the Eternal Recurrence, the idea which, together with the prophecy of the *Übermensch,* was to become the most resounding of Zarathustra's messages. And as if to make quite sure that the connection between that passage and the prophetic book is not overlooked, it is followed, in *Joyous Science,* by the beginning—anticipated there word for word—of *Thus Spoke Zarathustra;* word for word, but with an added heading: "*incipit tragoedia*"; and the tragic, catastrophic potential of the Eternal Recurrence does indeed emerge most clearly from the passage. It is entitled "*Das grösste Schwergewicht*" which may—but only just—be rendered as "The greatest weight"; and what this translation loses of its original allusion to the integrating gravitational force, it gains by its closeness to the camel's heaviest burden. This is the text of "The greatest weight":

> What if one day or one night a demon secretly followed you into your loneliest solitude and said to you: "This life, as you are living it now and have been living it, you will have to live once more and an infinite number of times; and nothing will be new in it, but every pain and every joy, and all that has been trivial in your life or great must be repeated, and all in the same sequence; and also this spider here and the moonlight between the trees; and also this moment and I myself. The eternal hourglass will be turned again and again—and you with it, you tiny grain of sand among the sand!" Would you throw yourself down and, gnashing your teeth, curse the demon who spoke thus? Or have you ever experienced a moment so tremendous that you would reply: "You are a god and never have I heard anything more divine!" If that thought gained power over you, it would, as you are now, transform or perhaps crush you; the question: "Do you want this once again and an infinite number of times?" would lie as the greatest weight upon everything you do. Or else: how deeply would you have to fall in love with yourself and with life in order not to desire anything more than this ultimate confirmation and seal.[16]

Nothing that Zarathustra will have to say later in announcing, with blatant conviction and without "if" and "when," the Eternal Recurrence, will be as authentic as these poetic conditionals, and nothing will be as translucent. Indeed, what shines through this prose poem is the ground of tragic nihilism from which the annunciation springs, the frightening "or else" that stipulates ecstasy as the sole condition in which existence may be tolerable.* For between the "tremendous mo-

---

*In its crudest form, ecstasy is supplied by drugs.

ment" that wills itself again and again, and the cursing of the ghost, there stretches nothing but gloomy nothingness. Therefore the author of "The greatest weight" cannot but suspect that no one except the *Übermensch* would be able to press that seal of eternity upon an existence that knows only time and time and time: time and therefore only futility and death.

Certainly, Nietzsche, for himself, did not possess the power to transform his time into this eternity. He who wrote: "This life—it is your life eternal"[17] confessed "I do not wish to live *again*," and added: "How have I borne life? By creating. What has made me endure? The vision of the *Übermensch* who affirms life. I have tried to affirm life *myself*—but ah!"[18] And he said: "I perform the great experiment: Who can bear the idea of the Eternal Recurrence?—Those who cannot bear the sentence, There is no salvation, *ought* to perish."[19] This is how, in his notebook and, as it were, behind the back of the reader of *Zarathustra,* he explained why that demonic whisper of the Eternal Recurrence would crush him who receives it in his feeble nay-saying state. Or, even more frighteningly, he wrote: "Let us consider this idea in its most terrible form: existence as it is, without meaning or goal, but inescapably recurrent, without a finale into nothingness . . . ."[20] And surely it is not by mere accident that in the composition of *Joyous Science* the passage of "the greatest weight" is preceded by Nietzsche's scintillating reflection on the last words of Socrates; and "scintillating" is the *mot juste* if we consider the recklessly contradictory judgments Nietzsche has passed on Socrates throughout his writings. Here Socrates is called brave and wise in everything he did, said, and did not say; serene, balanced, ironical, mischievous, amorous, and above all, keeping discreetly silent on his ultimate knowledge. Yet his last words, spoken before he drank the hemlock, "ludicrous and terrifying" as they are, gave it away: "Crito, I owe a rooster to Asclepius"; and, Nietzsche writes, he who understands them aright suddenly discovers that Socrates, who had lived in public like a soldier of the truth, was surreptitiously a pessimist who was sick of life, looking upon it as a disease and upon death as the cure. (The sick of Athens who appealed to the spirit of the great healer Asclepius for recovery offered him a rooster in sacrifice.) Whereupon follows Nietzsche's final injunction: "Friends, we must overcome even the Greeks!" And this overcoming was to be accomplished by means of that total affirmation of individual existence demanded by the demon's message of the Eternal Recurrence.

What Nietzsche here says of Socrates is, of course, at the same time yet another fragment from his autobiography: "I do not wish to live *again*." For such a man to pronounce a Yea-saying as all-embracing, extreme and fanatical as is contained in the doctrine of the Eternal Recurrence, is indeed to "take sides *against*" himself and "*for* anything that happened to hurt and was hard" for him; is "to offer a hand to the ghost" that terrified him. "All these most difficult things the spirit that would bear much takes upon itself: like the camel that, burdened, speeds into the desert, thus the spirit speeds into its desert." And here, in its "loneliest desert," the "second metamorphosis occurs": "the spirit becomes a lion who would conquer his freedom and be master in its own desert." The external scene, be it noted, remains a desert, and, in a sense, the lion too remains a camel. It still carries a heavy burden: life. But in his soul he has accepted it so profoundly that what had been oppression has become lightness and feline grace, the "greatest weight" has turned into weightlessness, and the enslavement of the humble creature into the freedom of the unburdened lion who

> seeks out his last master: he wants to fight him and his last god; for ultimate victory he wants to fight with the great dragon.
>
> Who is the great dragon whom the spirit will no longer call lord and god? "Thou shalt" is the name of the great dragon. But the spirit of the lion says, "I will." "Thou shalt" lies in his way, sparkling like gold, an animal covered with scales; and on every scale shines a golden "thou shalt."
>
> Values, thousands of years old, shine on those scales; and thus speaks the mightiest of dragons: "All value of all things shine on me. All value has long been created, and I am all created value. Verily, there shall be no more 'I will.'" Thus speaks the dragon.
>
> My brothers, why is there a need in the spirit for the lion? Why is not the beast of burden, which renounces and is reverent, enough? (P.N. 138f.)[21]

The idiom is more garish and luxuriant than befits a desert, the pseudo-biblical tone is as hard to bear as the camel's burden, and the Wagnerian dragon is only waiting, with alarming obviousness, for a Siegfried to be killed by. Yet the meaning is clear, too clear to be much upset by its allegorical ornamentations: There is no moral law and therefore no moral duty. Dead is the old god from whom once issued both the law and the duty, and who was, in fact or rather in allegory, the maker of all the dragon's scales with their "Thou shalts." What, therefore, is needed is new tables, new values. To create them, so Nietzsche's parable continues, does not lie within the province of the lion. Certainly, it is not exactly a constructive animal; it may build lairs for itself, but no Mount Sinais for mankind. But what it can do—to stay within the terms of the anti-moral fable—is to conquer the sphere of freedom that the spirit needs for a new creativity. The first step towards such freedom is "a sacred No" where the camel had nodded its profane assent: in the face of Duty that now issues from nowhere, and of the unending "Thou shalt" that has been deprived of its lawgiver. This conquest of freedom is within the power of the beast of prey.

Here again, Zarathustra's first speech has succeeded, if in nothing else, at least in abbreviating, to the point of its appearing simple-minded, a long, complex, and tragic story. Its focal theme is: What is the nature of morality? Nietzsche, whose whole spiritual existence was dominated by this question, wrestled with it again and again—after the time of *Zarathustra* specifically in *Beyond Good and Evil* and *The Genealogy of Morals*—and failed. It is overwhelmingly true to say that this was a failure distinguished from most failures by the intellectual passion that went into the pursuit of the elusive goal—such passion as always, it would seem, is only another name for failures of grand dimensions. And has not the enterprise produced most brilliant insights? And does it not give the impression that it has been undertaken on the prompting of historical necessity itself? And yet . . .

Nietzsche was, with regard to a *certain* moral tradition, the Christian, his own, eminently perceptive in registering its decadence and thus its waning authenticity, its lagging vitality and thus its spiritual obstructiveness, its lack of genuine conviction and thus its culturally enfeebling effect; and goaded on by his spiritual discontent, he was inexhaustibly ingenious in analyzing the psychology of the Christian "camel-spirit": the pleasure it takes in carrying the burden of its cross, the excitements that are in ascetic renunciation, the erotic delights it finds in degrading Eros from a divine being to a vice, the sensation of power it enjoys in extolling the virtues of powerlessness and humility and thus afflicting the naively strong with a sense of guilt. Yet while he excelled in ever subtler, and towards the end, ever louder and more percussive variations on these themes, he left the question behind the themes untouched and unanswered: What is the meaning of the compulsion, deeply rooted in human beings and probably in being human, to make moral distinctions and to know good from evil—so that no "evil" is morally acceptable to man, no infamy, no deceit, no shamelessness, no hatred, without his "revaluing" it as good. If there is anything that deserves to be called "human nature," then it is moral in the sense that it is unthinkable without the faculty, indeed the innate need, of discriminating morally (and aesthetic judgments are, in their structure, so close to moral ones that sometimes they become indistinguishable from them). Even the great Christian injunction "Judge not, that ye be not judged" makes a moral judgment in condemning self-righteousness, and threatens the soul with the judge it will have to face eventually. And Nietzsche's vision of a sphere "beyond good and evil" is radiant with his hope of a radically new goodness. This is what he never quite acknowledged. Mostly he spoke like a physician who, diagnosing the harm done by a commonly indulged unwholesome diet, ignores the inescapable need for nourishment.

Or did he? Not quite when, for instance, he made his Zarathustra speak of the "creation of new values," values not in the slightest "a-moral" (there are no such values) but only different, *morally,* from those of the Christian inheritance; and certainly not at all when his prophet prophesies the *Übermensch.* For this paragon of a new and higher humanity, this hybrid of vision and contrivance, is, by implication, Nietzsche's acknowledgment of the death of man, bound to occur in the wake of the notorious death of God; and the strange cause of the human demise is that "absurdity" of man's nature which Nietzsche, although he was neither its discoverer nor inventor (within the Christian tradition he is, to be sure, preceded by Pascal and Kierkegaard), has yet explored and analyzed with obsessive persistence, intuition, and ingenuity. That "absurd" state of affairs lies in the incompatability, dramatized by the death of God, of the spiritual and moral needs of man and the character of the world into which he has come. Endowed with an insatiable appetite for "meaning," he is helplessly caught in the meaningless machinery of existence; ever anxious to justify his manner of living, he finds himself in a life devoid of judge or sanction; and desiring to make a little sense of his having been born and his having to die, he receives no sign or signal from the vast surrounding senselessness.

It is this absurd consciousness which after the death of God is both incurable and intolerable. Nietzsche looks upon it as the sensibility of nihilism, the condition of mind and soul which, for a while, will still be just supportable by means of the spiritual pittance left over from the past, but is bound to end catastrophically. For the ground gives, and "the wasteland grows" and "soon where we live, nobody will be able to exist."[22] Nobody, that is, before man's final metamorphosis into the *Übermensch* who, without being a god, will no longer be merely human; for he will have overcome the great nihilistic malaise, will have risen above the doom of absurdity, will, without going out in search for the waters of truth, strike the water of life itself from the dry sands of the desert, will lead the good life without needing the unattainable knowledge of the good, and will exist in glory without having to borrow it from that God who once let his light shine upon man and now is no more. Yet to come into this resplendent fortune, he will have to be more, unthinkably more, than the lion of Zarathustra's first speech and parable; for "to create new values—that even the lion cannot do." To do this, the spirit will have to be as a child. "Except ye . . . become like little children, ye shall not enter into the kingdom of heaven." Is it possible that Zarathustra speaks here with the voice of St. Matthew? It is; and here, amid all the biblical pastiche in which the book abounds, its speech touches with a measure of authenticity upon the biblical theme of grace:

> But . . . what can the child do that even the lion could not do? Why must the preying lion still become a child? The child is innocence and forgetting, a new beginning, a game, a self-propelled wheel, a first movement, a sacred Yes. For the game of creation . . . a sacred Yes is needed: the spirit now wills his own will and he who had been lost to the world now conquers his own world. (P.N. 139)[23]

This is how Zarathustra speaks of the lion's finally becoming a child. Even some ten years earlier—at that time Nietzsche was Professor of Classical Philology in Basel—he had spoken to his students, in a very unprofessorial and poetically self-willed interpretation of Heraclitus, of the child at play. There it served as the model image of the original force that has brought forth the world by playing its creator-game "in eternally unruffled innocence" and to no purpose other than the pleasure afforded by the pure aesthetic contemplation of the playfully created things.[24] In *The Birth of Tragedy,* written just before, it was this beholding of life as a pure "aesthetic phenomenon" that was the only "eternal justification" of the world.[25] But now it is lion into child, the parabolic and utopian definition of the *Übermensch.*

3

The problem involved defies every attempt to confine it historically. For it begins, if ever it began, far back in mythic time: with the parting of the human mind from Mind, from the domain of Plato's Ideas, and with its descent into the darkness that was to be only dimly illuminated by what little transpired of the Ideas' light. Man, from then on, has had merely a vague idea of himself and not, alas, his Reality. He has felt ill at ease ever since. Or in a different idiom, in the language of

Genesis: The curse fell upon him with his eating from the Tree of Knowledge, the curse that was believed, by St. Matthew and the other evangelists of salvation, to be removable only through the faith that is the child's. Without this faith there is only the affliction of self-consciousness, the grown man's shame and embarrassment at being his naked separate self, the particular punishment within the universal punishment that is called the Fall. Yet as long as God was, there was the hope of redemption. It was only when the malady came which, in Nietzsche's diagnosis, originated in the death of God, that human minds applied themselves to the huge task of designing a *historical* future as paradise regained: this would come about with the overcoming of self-consciousness and with the recovery, or a new creation, of innocence and naive spontaneity. When Rousseau demanded man's return to Nature, he meant such an Eden; and Hegel, who saw the "unhappy consciousness" plunged into sadness at every turn of its way by the ever-repeated discovery that "objective reality" was unyieldingly made of stuff different from Spirit, believed that finally the real would be so profusely irradiated by Mind, indeed transformed into it, that the suffering of consciousness would end in the final consummation of its oneness with the world, indeed its *being* the world. (It was this secular messianism of Hegel's that Marx turned around from mind, "the head," on to the material "feet" of the classless society, a society without contradictions and no longer offensive to the true mind of humanity.)

Endless and endlessly varied are the configurations of thought and vision produced by the intermingling of Rousseau's "Back to Nature" and Hegel's "Forward to Mind", but what all have in common is the longing for, indeed the expectation of, a state of being in which self-consciousness, the persistent obstacle in the soul's reaching out for its freedom, is done away with and dissolved in that "naivete" and "innocence" at last restored or attained. This restoration or attainment would be distinguished by the identity of what *is* and what *seems*, of *being* and *doing,* that identity of which Nature is the constant reminder and "the Child" the promise. In his great essay "On Naïve and Reflective Poetry," Schiller says of all things in Nature that they *are* what we *were* (again, as with Rousseau, the lost paradise of the natural state), but also what we ought to become by way of reason and freedom (again, as with Hegel, the natural undistracted rule of freedom and reason, paradise regained). This is why Nature "represents our lost childhood . . . and thus fills us with a certain melancholy" (for childhood is the only remnant of "unmutilated nature" to be met with in our civilized condition), but, in providing us at the same time with "the ideal of our highest perfection," also "sublimely elates us."[26]

It is this "sense sublime," the philosophy of the child's pure and unselfconscious being, that Wordsworth celebrates in "Intimations of Immortality," and to which Kleist has devoted his beautiful philosophical dialogue "On the Marionette Theater" where a dancer, a ballet master, in seeking out the perfect model of graceful movement, goes back beyond the child, even beyond the sphere of organic nature, to the mechanical contraption of the marionette. For in its absolute and unconscious obedience to natural laws, the laws of weight and counterweight, the marionette displays in its motions a grace that is wholly *unaffected*—unaffected, that is, by even the slightest trace of self-consciousness—, a grace that is not attainable by any man or woman: "Only a god could, in this respect, be its equal." Only a god, the child-god; this, adds the dancer, is the point where in our circular world the two extremes meet: the unconscious and the perfect consciousness. And as his partner responds with incredulous surprise to this lesson, he asks him whether he had ever read with attentiveness the third chapter of Genesis: only he who has grasped the meaning of this beginning of human history, will be able intelligently to speak of its end: ". . . that we shall have to eat once again from the Tree of Knowledge to fall back into the state of innocence"—the state of grace that an infinite consciousness would share with the unconscious marionette, or with the children of paradise before the serpent leads them into temptation, shame, and the awareness of their selfhood.

Kleist's dialogue on the marionettes has supplied the theatrical as well as the intellectual scenery of the most elegiac of Rilke's *Duino Elegies,* the fourth, where the stage—the stage of human inwardness—is set for the farewell enacted before the backdrop of the "well-known garden"; and there appears that dancer whom the spectator-poet angrily rejects: "No, not *this* one!" For however hard he tries to posture with grace and lightness, he is heavy with the consciousness of *not being* what he *acts*. He is nothing but a bourgeois in disguise, will soon remove his make-up and go home, "entering by the kitchen": "I do not want these half-filled masks. Let puppets dance! They at least are undivided." But the ultimate and at last *real* show will be enacted only when the Angel—Rilke's embodiment of "the fullness of being"—will hold in his hands the wires of the puppet. "Angel and puppet!"—only then will the seasons of our lives add up to the unbroken circle, to that integrity of existence of which childhood is the foreshadowing. The Fourth Elegy is Rilke's version of the last act played on Kleist's

Marionette Theater and the elegiac celebration of Nietzsche's Child-*Übermensch*.

What Kleist and Rilke personified in the bad dancer, Nietzsche again and again spoke of as "the problem of the *actor*": "the 'dissembling,' the typical ability to transform himself" was "a flaw in his character," as a jotting from the year 1888 disjointedly puts it.[27] But it was, of course, not only, indeed not at all, the professional actor that fascinated him; and not only the artist's consciously held and cultivated idea that he *is* an artist and has to conduct himself like one—a fact of the modern artistic consciousness that for Schiller made modern art "sentimental" (the word used in his particular sense, meaning "reflective" or "self-conscious"); that for Hegel signaled "the end of art"; and for Nietzsche made all art, for instance and above all the art of Richard Wagner, into a variant of the actor's craft.[28] No, what haunted Nietzsche in his later years like a malevolent ghost was the pervasive suspicion that the self-consciousness of the intelligence had grown to such a degree as to deprive *any* belief of its genuineness: to believe is now a form of self-deception, and to expound a conviction has become unthinkable without an ingredient of that rhetorical dishonesty that Zarathustra, equating it with lying, calls poetry, the poetry of poets and his own.[29] When madness had overtaken Nietzsche, he wrote (6 January 1889) that fantastic and uncannily revealing letter to Jacob Burckhardt, the professor of history in Basel, in which he, Nietzsche, the self-retired professor of classical philology from the same university, ironically and madly confessed that he too would have preferred to retain his Chair to having to be God, a god, moreover, who was condemned "to entertain the next eternity with bad witticisms." This is the last time that Nietzsche speaks of that "buffoonery," the "mask of despair," which had become his persistent characterization of much in the intellectual, artistic, and religious life of modernity—and insanely applies it to himself.

Twice in his notebooks he asked why everything in this civilization ends as a kind of histrionic display, as "acting"; and twice he states, by way of answering his own question, that insofar as anything is the product of the conscious will, it must needs lack perfection;[30] for everything that *is* perfect has at all times resulted from "the automatism," as he called it in his *Anti-Christ*,[31] of a deep and sure instinct. Such instinct is not to be found any more among modern men. Zarathustra's consciously willed *leonitas* must therefore fail in creating the new values of a new humanity. Within a world intellectually articulated by Nietzsche, the *Duino Elegies,* transcendental idealism, the Romantic expectations, will the Spirit ever succeed in accomplishing its third and final metamorphosis and become the child that, playing in self-forgetfulness, will give us the new law? Or must not in such a world the last word be the terrible prayer for the madness which would make the prophet at last believe in himself and his prophecy?

# RILKE AND NIETZSCHE
# WITH A DISCOURSE ON THOUGHT,
# BELIEF AND POETRY

"We came to speak of *Tasso,* and of the *idea* which Goethe sought to represent in it," reports Eckermann under the date of May 6th, 1827. "*Idea?*" said Goethe—"not that I know of!—I had the *life* of Tasso before me, and my own life, and by jumbling up two such peculiar figures . . . the picture of *Tasso* took shape within me. . . . The Germans are really peculiar people!—They make life more difficult for themselves than is necessary by seeking everywhere, and putting into everything, their profound thoughts and ideas.—Why not for once have the courage *to give yourselves up to impressions,* to allow yourselves to be amused, moved, edified, indeed taught and roused to something great; but don't believe all the time that everything must be vain if it is not some abstract thought or idea. . . . A poetic creation is the better for being incommensurable and rationally incomprehensible." A little later in the same year (July 5th, 1827), talking about inconsistencies in his treatment of the Helena scene in *Faust II,* Goethe says: "I only wonder what the German critics will think of it. Will they have the freedom and courage to ignore the inconsistencies? The French will be hampered by their reason and fail to recognize that imagination has to abide by laws of its own which reason neither can nor should comprehend. The imagination would hardly be worth bothering about, if it did not create things which will for ever remain problematical to reason. This is the difference between poetry and prose. In prose, reason is and may and should be at home."

For once T. S. Eliot* seems to agree with Goethe, of whom generally he thinks rather unkindly. In his essay on "Shakespeare and the Stoicism of Seneca"[1] he says about Shakespeare and his philosophical interpreters very much the same as what Goethe said about his *Tasso* and the German critics. Eliot quotes someone who wrote that "we

---

*My critical concentration on T. S. Eliot shows that this essay was written some time ago. But it also is a reminder of the speed with which authorities come and go. I wish to slow the stampede; not because of my dislike for such mindless forward-movements, but to honor T. S. Eliot's great critical intelligence. He devoted it to enduring problems.

possess a great deal of evidence as to what Shakespeare thought of military glory and martial events. "Do we?" asks Eliot, rather in the manner of Goethe's "Not that I know of," sure of the applause of anyone with even the slightest insight into the activities in a poet's workshop. For, indeed, what we possess of evidence goes to show conclusively that Shakespeare's imagination comprehended with the greatest precision every shade of difference between what, for instance, Anthony thought and felt about the significance of military events, both before and after he fell in love with Cleopatra, or what military glory meant to such varied characters as, say, Henry V, Ajax or Thersites. In fact, the politeness of good High Table manners, with everyone ready to see everyone's point of view except his own, is, on the highest level of imaginative achievement, the cardinal virtue of the dramatic writer; and the wider the scope of his imagination, the less evidence he will leave behind to show what he himself thought about this or that controversial issue. Having dwelt in so many divided minds and believed so many conflicting beliefs, he is likely to be slow in fulfilling the first commandment of all enlightened education: to form his own opinions. He may, alas, even begin *and* end by not knowing what he himself believes, or not believing what he himself knows.

So far, then, T. S. Eliot's "Do we?" justly commands that general consent which rhetorical questions take for granted. Yet some of it may be withdrawn when he continues "Or rather, did Shakespeare think anything at all? He was occupied with turning human actions into poetry"[2]—in precisely the same way, that is, in which Goethe, without concerning himself with ideas, made poetry out of Tasso's life and his own. Again, very much in keeping with Goethe's notorious dictum that all his works form part of a great confession, but with a striking shift of emphasis from earlier meditations on the subject in the essay "Tradition and the Individual Talent,"[3] Eliot now maintains that "every poet starts from his own emotions" and that "Shakespeare, too, was occupied with the struggle—which alone constitutes life for a poet—to transmute his personal and private agonies into something rich and strange, something universal and impersonal."[4] And in discussing whether the poet necessarily believes in such theories, theologies or philosophies as he may borrow for his poetic purposes— whether Dante actually believed in the theological system of Thomas Aquinas which he so magnificently used in the *Divina Commedia,* or whether Shakespeare, in poetically paraphrasing their thought, agreed with such thinkers as Machiavelli or Montaigne or Seneca—Eliot comes to a conclusion that seems to elaborate a Goethean image: "The poet makes poetry, the metaphysician makes metaphysics, the bee makes honey, the spider secretes a filament;[5] you can hardly say that any of these agents believes: he merely does." It is Goethe's Tasso who dismisses the advice that he should take a vacation from writing poetry, by exclaiming: Bid the silkworm stop spinning!

Clearly it all amounts to this: by drawing a parallel between Nietzsche, whose principal claim is to be a *thinker*, and Rilke, whose reputation rests on his *poetry*, the critic seems to commit the original sin of literary criticism. Yet I should be on safe ground if I now proceeded to show how Rilke used one or other of Nietzsche's ideas and, believing them or not, transformed them into poetry, as Goethe presumably drew on Spinoza, or Shakespeare on Seneca, Montaigne, and Machiavelli. This would be a literary exercise, respectable and time-honored, and on this occasion promising high entertainment as it is a *chercher la femme* that lurks behind the "and" connecting Rilke and Nietzsche: Frau Lou Andreas-Salomé, who played a not inconsiderable part in Nietzsche's life and certainly a very considerable one in Rilke's. The exercise would be still more rewarding if I could produce authentic records of conversations about Nietzsche which, of course, must have taken place between Lou and Rilke; or unearth a copy of *Also sprach Zarathustra* annotated in Rilke's hand. I might then go on to show what has happened to Nietzsche's thought in the process of its transmutation into Rilke's poetry, for, as Mr. Eliot says, the poet "is not necessarily interested in the thought itself" but merely in expressing "the emotional equivalent of thought." But, as it is precisely this theory of the relation between thought, belief and poetry which I should like to challenge, I am obliged to follow a different course, with the strictly scholarly road being barred in any case by the remarkable scarcity of testimony from those involved. Not even the publication of the correspondence between Rilke and Lou has yielded any useful information probably because Rilke was in the habit of suppressing any more elaborate acknowledgment of his intellectual debts, for he too believed that their assimilation and transformation in the unique medium of his art was the only thing that mattered.

## 2

The writings of the young Rilke show Nietzsche neither assimilated nor transformed, but rather imitated and sometimes vulgarized. In *Der Apostel* (1896),[6] *Ewald Tragy*,[7] and *Christus-Visionen* (1896–1897),[8] the effects of Nietzsche's hammering and dynamiting are unmistakable; yet there is not the slightest trace of the depth and complexity of

Nietzsche's thought and feeling. When, early in 1897, in Munich, Rilke met Lou Andreas-Salomé he must have still been in this "*Wie er sich räuspert und wie er spuckt*" stage of his Nietzsche fascination. We do not know whether he had read her book on Nietzsche, which was published in 1894,[9] and is, with all its inadequacies, profundity itself compared to the Nietzschean gesticulating of *Der Apostel* or *Ewald Tragy.* But even if Rilke did read it, the document he produced in the following spring and summer (1898), largely in Italy and entirely for Lou's eyes—his so-called *Tuscan Diary*[10]—is still quite innocently Young-Nietzschean in its rapturous vision of the Artist-Prophet. Yet in retrospect the reader of the *Tuscan Diary* can clearly discern in it almost all the threads that were to go into the rich texture of *Duino Elegies* and *Sonnets to Orpheus,* so very much more intimately related to Nietzsche (as I shall hope to show) than all the Nietzschean sound and fury lavishly displayed in Rilke's early writings. Much less noisy and more thoughtful are the glosses he wrote in 1900 on *The Birth of Tragedy.* Yet they contain hardly any critical comments on Nietzsche's book, being rather Rilke's own observations on the subject. In any case, these mark the point at which, to my knowledge, all relevant references to Nietzsche, or obvious borrowings from him, end. Up to 1904 the name of Nietzsche casually appears now and then in articles or letters, and sometimes, though very rarely, a faint echo of the earlier crude instrumentation of Nietzsche *motifs* can be heard, but certainly in no manner to command attention. Yet although the Zarathustra *opinions* and *gestures* vanish from Rilke's writings, the kinship between his own and Nietzsche's *ideas* and *inner attitudes* is steadily deepening, and is nowhere profounder than in *Duino Elegies,* and in *Sonnets to Orpheus,* so dramatically released at Castle Muzot as near the end of the poet's life as 1922.

We must not be deceived by appearances; there are, at first sight, as many striking differences between Rilke and Nietzsche as definite similarities. They were both uprooted and homeless. "*Wer jetzt kein Haus hat, baut sich keines mehr,*" writes the one, and the other: "*Weh dem, der keine Heimat hat!*" each lamenting his unhoused existence. They were lonely among men, driven by inner compulsion to shun all binding human relationships for the sake of an uninhibited indulgence of their one consuming passion: namely, to use Mr. Eliot's words about the poet in general, "to transmute their personal and private agonies into something rich and strange, something universal and impersonal." In their abhorrence of the plebian vulgarity of their time, they were both anxious to establish their own aristocratic descent. These are not mere biographical accidents. They have the same significance as their common dedication to beliefs that had never been uttered before, and to the adventure of willing what nobody has ever dared to will:

> *Ich glaube an alles noch nie Gesagte.*
> *Ich will meine frömmsten Gefühle befrein.*
> *Was noch keiner zu wollen wagte,*
> *wird mir einmal unwillkürlich sein.*[11]

I believe in everything that has never been said before. My most dedicated feelings I desire to set free, and one day there shall come to me spontaneously that which nobody has ever dared to will.

These verses of Rilke's spring from the very center of Zarathustra's message. And, to the point of a near-identity of images conveying the conquest of loneliness, the harmonizing of inner conflict in the feast of reconciliation, of the One becoming Two through the arrival of the divine guest, Rilke's lines

> *Wer seines Lebens viele Widersinne*
> *versöhnt und dankbar in ein Sinnbild fasst,*
> *der drängt*
> *die Lärmenden aus dem Palast,*
> *wird anders festlich, und du bist der Gast,*
> *den er an sanften Abenden empfängt.*
>
> *Du bist der Zweite seiner Einsamkeit,*
> *die ruhige Mitte seinen Monologen;*
> *und jeder Kreis, um dich gezogen,*
> *spannt ihm den Zirkel aus der Zeit.*[12]

He who succeeds in reconciling the many contradictions of his life, holding them all together in a symbol, pushes the noisy crowd from the palace and will be festive in a different sense, receiving you as his guest on mild evenings.

Then you will be the Other of his loneliness, the still center of his monologues; and every circle drawn around you takes his compasses right outside time.

sound like the *adagio* treatment of a theme which gets rather out of hand in the *fortissimo* passage of Nietzsche's Zarathustra poem:

> *um Mittag war's, da wurde Eins zu zwei. . . .*
> *Nun feiern wir, vereinten Siegs gewiss,*
> *    das Fest der Feste:*
> *Freund Zarathustra kam, der Gast der Gäste!*

> *Nun lacht die Welt, der grause Vorhang riss,*
> *die Hochzeit kam für Licht und Finsternis. . . .*[13]

It was at midday when One became Two. . . . Together now and sure
of our triumph, we celebrate the feast of feasts: friend *Zarathustra* has
arrived, the guest of guests! The world is overjoyed, the weird curtain is
torn apart, the wedding day has come for light and darkness.

It is on evenings, calm and gentle, when the great Other of Rilke's
loneliness comes to his only disciple who, in all his gentleness, has
already managed to drive the noisy crowd from the temple. Zarathustra, on the other hand, arrives in the glaring midday hour. Midday and
evening—this example will have to stand for the most striking difference, obvious throughout their works, between Rilke and Nietzsche.
Nietzsche's tone is imperial. He has received the great commandment,
has once faced his God, and henceforward he will speak out. Rilke's
orders are of a more cumulative nature. His head is bent in the attitude
of one who listens intently to *"das Wehende,"* the continual lesson
formed out of stillness. But is this necessarily a difference in substance?
Not if the whispered news amounts in the end to the same as the revelation which Nietzsche receives with the dramatic incisiveness of the
thunderbolt. Some, however, believe that it is altogether other news,
and are, I think, misled by their belief; for they do not seem to know
that one theme may be sustained through many variations, and one
soul preserve its identity through many a season; and while Nietzsche
and Rilke may merely be two moods of the same heart, they are often
held to be possessed by fundamentally different certainties. It may be
difficult to see the one garden for its very varied flowers. But only if
we are inclined to take the transports produced by night-scented stock
for a distinct spiritual initiation shall we be convinced of the profound
difference between Rilke's religion and Zarathustra's, proclaimed in
the proudest of daylights with "the crown of roses on the prophet's
brow." Yet we should perhaps remember that St. Paul served with
prophetic zeal the same God whom others loved in humbler dedica-
tions. We shall come to see Rilke as the St. Francis of the Will to Power.
This assertion will seem extravagant only to those who are victims
of the popular misapprehension which suggests that the Will to Power
is a kind of moral teaching sanctioning violence and ruthlessness, and
not the metaphysical inspiration which in fact it is, comprehending, or
at least attempting to comprehend, the meaning behind the representative beliefs and unbeliefs, activities and philosophies of Europe in war
and peace throughout its more recent history. Rilke may be to Nietz-

sche what Orpheus is to Dionysus; and Rilke's Orpheus and Nietzsche's Dionysus are brothers, by virtue of that peculiar adjustment to more modern attitudes of the soul which was forced upon Greek mythology by the spiritual need and hunger of modernity. But before we establish this equation, we shall have to attend to what else they have in common.

They are both initiates in the alchemy of loneliness and suffering. Rilke as well as Nietzsche discovers the fountainhead of joy in the very heart of the land of sorrow. Happiness for them is not, as it was for Schopenhauer, in the absence of pain; it is the fruit of so radical an acceptance of suffering that abundant delight springs from its very affirmation. For the denial of pain means the denial of existence. Existence is pain, and joy lies not in non-existence, as Schopenhauer would have it, but in its tragic transfiguration. This is the theme of Nietzsche's *Birth of Tragedy* as well as of *Zarathustra,* where it is treated with ever growing assurance by a man, it is well to remember, who wrote to a friend: "The terrible and all but incessant torture of my life makes me thirst for the end. . . . As far as agony and renunciation are concerned, my life during these last years is a match for that of any ascetic at any time. . . . Yet no pain has been able or shall be able to tempt me into giving false testimony about life as I recognize it."[14] And this recognition is praise. From the darkest night of the soul rises Zarathustra's "*Trunkenes Lied,*" his Dionysian song of the deep suffering of the world, which is yet surpassed in depth by that rapture of delight, willing not that the world with its pain should pass away, but that it should last for ever:

> *doch alle Lust will Ewigkeit—,*
> *—will tiefe, tiefe Ewigkeit!—*

an eternity not of joy (as Nietzsche is so often misunderstood to mean) but of the world *with* all its sorrow, transfigured in the act of willing it.

If we bear in mind what has been said about the difference in tone and gesture between Rilke and Nietzsche, there remains hardly a single element in Nietzsche's acceptance and transformation of suffering that could not also be found in Rilke. Indeed, the parallels appear to be exact. As early as his *Tuscan Diary* he writes: "To think that I myself was once among those who suspect life and distrust its power. Now I would love it at all events. . . . Whatever of it is mine . . . , I would love with tenderness, and would bring to ripeness within myself all possibilities that its possession offers to me."[15] And much later, in the Tenth Elegy, we encounter what is an elegiac version of the theme of *The Birth of Tragedy:* Rilke's *Klage*, the embodiment of Lamentation, guiding the dead youth through the country of her ancestors with its mines of sorrow, until they reach the terminus where *Klage* and youth must part, that gorge

> *wo es schimmert im Mondschein:*
> *die Quelle der Freude. In Ehrfurcht*
> *nennt sie sie, sagt: "Bei den Menschen*
> *ist sie ein tragender Strom."**

> where it gleams in the moonlight:
> the source of Joy. With awe
> she names it, says "Among men
> it is a carrying stream."

And not even an intonation alien to Nietzsche's, but *merely* the presence of the Angels seems (and merely *seems*) to render the beginning of Rilke's Tenth Elegy unsuitable as an epitaph for Nietzsche:

> *Dass ich dereinst, an dem Ausgang der grimmigen Einsicht,*
> *Jubel und Ruhm aufsinge zustimmenden Engeln.*
> *Dass von den klargeschlagenen Hämmern des Herzens,*
> *keiner versage an weichen, zweifelnden oder*
> *reissenden Saiten.*

> Some day, emerging at last from the vision of terror,
> may I burst into jubilant praise to assenting Angels.
> May no one of the clear-struck keys of the heart
> fail to respond through alighting on slack or doubtful
> or rending strings!

Nietzsche, who for a while believed that he was a musician as well as a philosopher, once composed a "Hymn to Life," the text of which is—strangest of biographical coincidences—by Lou Salomé. In *Ecce Homo* he says that he chose it because its last lines possess greatness; their meaning is that suffering is no argument against life: "*Hast du kein Glück mehr übrig mir zu geben, wohlan! noch hast du deine Pein. . . .*"[16] It is a bad poem. The future lover of the poetess would have

---

*With a number of separate editions of *Duino Elegies* and *Sonnets to Orpheus* available, I shall refer to these poems by their numbers only. The translations are, with some modifications of my own, by J. B. Leishman and Stephen Spender (*Duino Elegies*, London, 1948) and J. B. Leishman (*Sonnets to Orpheus*, London, 1946). This, perhaps, dates the writing of this essay at 1973.

done better. If Nietzsche discovered some greatness in those verses, persuaded no doubt by the theme of praise, the great persuasion of the *Sonnets to Orpheus* would have overwhelmed him.

For instance, the sonnet "*Singe die Gärten, mein Herz, die du nicht kennst.*" It almost sounds like Lou's "Hymn to Life" set to music by Rilke (though perhaps in this sonnet the music is actually not very much better than Nietzsche's):

> *Meide den Irrtum, dass es Entbehrungen gebe*
> *für den geschehnen Entschluss, diesen: zu sein!*
> *Seidener Faden, kamst du hinein ins Gewebe.*
>
> *Welchem der Bilder du auch im Innern geeint bist*
> *(sei es selbst ein Moment aus dem Leben der Pein),*
> *fühl, dass der ganze, der rühmliche Teppich gemeint ist.*

> Do not believe you will be deprived
> of something by your resolution: to *be*.
> Silken thread, you have entered the weaving.
>
> With whatever pattern you are inwardly blended
> (and be it a scene from the story of Agony),
> feel that the whole, the praiseworthy carpet is meant.

And the sonnet which begins with the beautiful lines:

> *Nur in Raum der Rühmung darf die Klage*
> *gehn, die Nymphe des geweinten Quells*

Only in the realm of Praise may Lamentation move, naiad of the wept fountain

is indeed Rilke's "*Trunkenes Lied,*" the lyrical echo of Zarathustra's Dionysian song. For in this song too sorrow transcends itself in the *knowing* certainty of jubilation, raising to the skies a constellation of immaculate joy:

> *Jubel weiss, und Sehnsucht ist geständig,—*
> *nur die Klage lernt noch; mädchenhändig*
> *zählt sie nächtelang das alte Schlimme.*
>
> *Aber plötzlich, schräg und ungeübt,*
> *hält sie doch ein Sternbild unsrer Stimme*
> *in den Himmel, den ihr Hauch nicht trübt.*
>
> (I, VIII)

> Triumph knows, and Longing makes confession,—
> Lamentation learns: in nightly session
> counts, with maiden-hands, old tribulation.

Then, however inexpertly limned,
lifts our voices in a constellation
to the sky her breathing has not dimmed.

Delighted as Nietzsche would have been by these sonnets, would he necessarily have recognized Orpheus as their inspiration? He himself was preoccupied with gods of fuller status: with Dionysus and Apollo. His early *Birth of Tragedy* interpreted the Attic drama as the outcome of an age-old struggle which these two gods waged within the Greek soul. In tragedy, at last, the two hostile gods came together and concluded peace: Dionysus, the god of chaotic ecstasy, rapturously abandoning all claims to form and shape, all individuality, to the amorphous oneness of life; and Apollo, the god with the lyre at whose call all things were arrested within their own contours and their own articulate order. Would Europe, after the end of the "tragic" period of Greece, ever again know such reconciliation, and achieve so profound a harmony between the deepest and most conflicting impulses of the human soul? Shall we ever create an order which is not, as all our orders are, at the expense of the fullness of life, but its richest unfolding; a pattern which is not imposed upon chaos, but overreaching and surpassing it, its beauty still tremulous with the ancient terror? Or is the ancient god of ecstasy doomed to an ignominious existence in the murky corners of sin and depravity, and the god of order to be imprisoned in the petrified structure of classicism and morality? Or *shall* Dionysus and Apollo be united again, as they were in Attic tragedy?

Such were the youthfully enthusiastic questions which Nietzsche asked in his *Birth of Tragedy*. At the time his equally enthusiastic answer was: the old gods have risen again; they live in the work of Richard Wagner. It was to prove an agonizingly provisional answer. Perhaps Rilke's Orpheus would have made good the promise that Wagner's Parsifal broke.

The attempt of scholars to unravel the complex of historical reminiscences, images, insights, feelings that make up the story of Dionysus, Apollo and Orpheus in modern German literature and thought, and then to relate it to what may be the Greek reality of these divine creatures, is as heroic as it is doomed to failure. For a scholar's guarded steps cannot possibly keep pace with the rush and dance of the passions of the mind swirling around those names and arrested only for brief moments in innumerable figurations. Nietzsche, from *The Birth of Tragedy* onwards, is seeking spiritual employment in the service of a god who is a synthesis of Dionysus and Apollo. In this composite Nietzschean deity, Apollo, it is true, loses his name more and more to the other god, but by no means loses the power of his artistic creativeness, forever articulating the Dionysian chaos in distinct shapes, sounds and images, which are Dionysian only because they are still aglow with the heat of the primeval fire. In some of his latest notes, that is, at the end of the life of his mind, Nietzsche once more returned to the antagonism within the Greek soul between the Dionysian and Apolline, and once more celebrated the triumph of a god who wrests the utmost of glorifying beauty from the monstrous terror of chaotic passions. This triumphant god, far from suffering the chill of classicism, has, as it were, Apollo's eyes and the heart of Dionysus. In Nietzsche's mature years the real opposition is not Dionysus versus Apollo, but the Apolline Dionysus versus Christ.[17]

And Rilke? In a letter from Rome, written probably in the spring of 1904, eighteen years before the *Sonnets to Orpheus* Rilke indulges in a kind of eschatological vision of Apollo's ultimate triumph over the chaotic dominion of Dionysus. The phrases of this letter have not only the ring, but almost the precise wording of Nietzsche's evocations of Apollo-Dionysus. It is chaos itself, says Rilke, which, at the end of days, will stand transformed into "a million ripe, fine and golden forms," an "Apolline product, fermented into maturity and still radiant with its inner glow." And nothing could be more Nietzschean than "the wakeful, lucid enthusiasm" of Rilke's Apolline world.[18]*

This is the eschatology of an artist; of an artist, at that, whose business is not merely to heighten by his own creations the beauty of a world, beautiful and significant in itself, but to *create* himself the only beautiful and significant world that there is or can be. It is astonishing and instructive to see how long an idea, present right at the beginning of a poet's career, takes to mature into poetry. We may also observe how this same idea, originally part of a quasi-historical or Darwinian theory about the development of man, becomes in the end the timeless assertion, not of a future state, but of existence itself. In 1898 Rilke notes in the *Tuscan Diary:* "Not for all time will the artist live side by side with ordinary men. As soon as the artist—the more flexible and deeper type among them—becomes rich and virile, as soon as he *lives* what now he merely *dreams,* man will degenerate and gradually die out. The artist is eternity protruding into time."[19] In the *Sonnets to Orpheus* this eternity not merely protrudes, it has arrived. It *is* the world itself; a world which exists in and through song alone. Song is

---

*The authentic wording of this letter was established with considerable effort and great scholarly care by Eudo C. Mason. (Cf. his *Der Zopf des Münchhausen,* Einsiedeln, 1949, 77.)

existence—"*Gesang ist Dasein.*" A god could easily achieve it: "*Für den Gott ein Leichtes.*" But if there are no gods? Then we must become gods ourselves. We? We who hardly *are*? "*Wann aber sind wir?*" Indeed, man must transform and transfigure himself; and in transfiguring himself he will be the redeemer and transfigurer of all existence: "*der Verklärer des Daseins.*"[20]

This dialogue, made up of verbatim quotations from Rilke and Nietzsche, is about the Orpheus of the sonnets. The other name of this "*Verklärer des Daseins*"—the formula is Nietzsche's—is Dionysus Apollo:

> *Du aber, Göttlicher, du, bis zuletzt noch Ertöner,*
> *da ihn der Schwarm der verschmähten Mänaden befiel,*
> *hast ihr Geschrei übertönt mit Ordnung, du Schöner,*
> *aus den Zerstörenden stieg dein erbauendes Spiel.*
>
> . . . . . .
>
> *O du verlorener Gott! Du unendliche Spur!*
> *Nur weil dich reissend zuletzt die Feindschaft verteilte,*
> *sind wir die Hörenden jetzt und ein Mund der Natur.*

(1, XXVI)

You that could sound till the end, though, immortal accorder
seized by the scorn-maddened Maenads' intemperate throng,
wholly outsounded their cries when in musical order
soared from the swarm of deformers your formative song.

. . . . . .

O you god that has vanished! You infinite track!
Only because dismembering hatred dispersed you
are we hearers to-day and a mouth which else Nature would lack.

This composite deity is still more obviously present in the following sonnet, in which allusions to Rilke's imagined family tree, repeated in the Third Elegy, are merged in a kind of Dionyso-Apolline anthropology of universal significance:

> *Zu unterst der Alte, verworrn,*
> *all der Erbauten*
> *Wurzel, verborgener Born,*
> *den sie nie schauten.*
>
> *Sturmhelm und Jägerhorn,*
> *Spruch von Ergrauten,*
> *Männer im Bruderzorn,*
> *Frauen wie Lauten. . . .*
>
> *Drängender Zweig an Zweig,*
> *nirgends ein freier. . . .*
> *Einer! o steig . . . o steig. . . .*

*Aber sie brechen noch.*
*Dieser erst oben doch*
*biegt sich zur Leier.*

(I, XVII)

Undermost he, the earth-bound
root of uprearing
multitudes, source underground,
never appearing.

Helmet and hunting-horn,
words of the aging,
rage between brothers-born,
women assuaging.

Branch on branch, time on time,
vainly they spire. . . .
One free! Oh, climb . . . oh, climb. . . .

One, though the others drop,
curves, as it scales the top,
into a lyre.

There are also sonnets in which the image of Orpheus could, without imposing the slightest strain on either the poem or our imagination, fade out altogether, making room for Zarathustra himself; for instance, the sonnet which begins

*Rühmen, das ist's! Ein zum Rühmen Bestellter,*
*ging er hervor wie das Erz aus des Steins*
*Schweigen. Sein Herz, o vergängliche Kelter*
*eines den Menschen unendlichen Weins.*

(I, VII)

Praising, that's it! As a praiser and blesser
he came like the ore from the taciturn mine.
Came with his heart, oh, transient presser,
for men, of a never-exhaustible wine.

and, still more so, the sonnet

*Wolle die Wandlung. O sei für die Flamme begeistert*
(2, XII)

Choose to be changed. With the flame be enraptured

in which almost every word—*"Wandlung," "Flamme," "jener entwerfende Geist, welcher das Irdische meistert," "Was sich ins Bleiben verschliesst, schon ists das Erstarrte," "Hammer"* and *"Härtestes"*—belongs as its unmistakable property to Zarathustra's prophetic household, although there can be no doubt that they have come into Rilke's possession through perfectly legitimate channels. The seal on the deed is authentic. It shows a lonely priest in a ruined cathedral. The roof is off. Through the vast opening comes down what looks a little like the traditional image of the Holy Ghost. But as it is blurred and indistinct, this may be too hasty an interpretation, merely suggested by the cathedral. It may also be rain. As it descends through the open roof of a ruin, we might perhaps just call it "openness," *"das Offene."* This seems to be confirmed by the words which are printed around the circumference of the seal. They say: *"Denn offen ist es bei dir und hell,"* "Where you are at home, everything is open and light," and *"Mit allen Augen sieht die Kreatur das Offene,"* "With all its eyes the creature-world beholds the open."

The last sentence is the beginning of Rilke's Eighth Elegy; but the first was spoken by Zarathustra on coming home to his lonely cave.* Once more he has left the noisy town—one is irresistibly tempted to say, the *"Leid-Stadt"* of Rilke's Tenth Elegy:

> wo in der falschen, aus Übertönung gemachten
> Stille, stark, aus der Gussform des Leeren der Ausguss,
> prahlt, der vergoldete Lärm, das platzende Denkmal.
> O wie spurlos zerträte ein Engel ihnen den Trostmarkt,
> den die Kirche begrenzt, ihre fertig gekaufte:
> reinlich und zu und enttäuscht wie ein Postamt am Sonntag

> where, in the seeming stillness of uproar outroared,
> stoutly, a thing cast out from the mold of vacuity,
> swaggers that gilded fuss, the bursting memorial.
> How an Angel would tread beyond trace their market of comfort,
> with the church alongside, bought ready for use: as tidy
> and disappointed and shut as the Post on a Sunday

for Rilke's is as exact a description as Nietzsche gives of the town that Zarathustra has left behind in order to converse with his own solitude:

> "Here you are in your own home and house. . . . Here all things come caressingly to your discourse and flatter you, for they want to ride on your back. On every symbol you ride to every truth. . . ."
>     Here the words and word-shrines open up before me: here all Being wishes to become word, all becoming wishes to learn from you how to speak." [21]

---

*Cf. also Zarathustra's words: "Only when a clear sky looks down through broken ceilings . . . will my heart turn again towards the places of God." (M.A., XIII, 116, *Zarathustra* II, "On the Virtuous.")

Rilke too was to travel on many a symbol, yielded by the word-shrines of things, towards many of Zarathustra's truths. Rilke's youthful *Tuscan Diary* version of Zarathustra's secret sessions with "*die Dinge*" is as follows: ". . . I feel that more and more I am becoming the disciple of things (not merely their listener), a disciple who adds, through comprehending questions, intensity to their answers and confessions, and who, enticing them to spend their advice and wisdom, learns how to reward their generous love with the disciple's humility."[22]

The aspect of things changes in the new "openneses" of Nietzsche's, of Rilke's solitude. Within the perspective of this expanded, and yet, as we shall see, more radically confined space, it appears that neither things nor names have ever been really known. With a new consciousness and perception gained, they must be christened anew, baptized, as it were, into a new Church. For another dimension of speech has been thrown open, and all things desire to hear their names once more, uttered in a voice resonant enough to fill the new spaces. Said as they used to be said, words fall flat in these changed acoustical conditions.

What happened to the *form* and *shape* of things at the beginning of the Renaissance seems now to happen to their *names*. With the third dimension *consciously* perceived as an essential aspect of vision, all objects demanded to be seen and painted afresh, and indeed quite new ones called out for recognition. Zarathustra's words of the things that "come caressingly to your discourse and flatter you, for they want to ride on your back," would, with a change from speech to canvas, have made good sense to the first of the great Renaissance painters. If the medieval madonnas and angels seemed to complain that they cut poor figures in their two-dimensional flatness, at the same time an abundance of other images pressed upon the painters' imaginations, claiming their right to significance in the new field of vision. Pillars, towers, gates, trees, jugs and windows demanded to be *seen* with an intensity as never before—"*wie selber die Dinge niemals innig meinten zu sein.*"

Rilke's new dimension is inwardness. As they came to Zarathustra with their novel claims, so the things approach Rilke, asking to be taught how to become words and how to make themselves truly felt in the widened space; and in return they show him that this is precisely his real task in the world: to assimilate them into the new inward dimension:

> —*Sind wir vielleicht hier, um zu sagen: Haus,*
> *Brücke, Brunnen, Tor, Krug, Obstbaum, Fenster,—*
> *höchstens: Säule, Turm . . . aber zu sagen, verstehs,*

*oh zu sagen so, wie selber die Dinge niemals*
*innig meinten zu sein. . . .*

(Ninth Elegy)

—Are we, perhaps, *here* in order to say: House,
Bridge, Fountain, Gate, Jug, Peartree, Window,—
at most: Pillar, Tower? . . . but to *say*, remember,
oh, to say this so as never the things themselves
meant so intensely to be. . . .

It has often been said of both Nietzsche and Rilke that they were
masters of new nuances, the one of thought, and the other of feeling.
True, they both felt that their souls and minds were at the mercy of
sensations and revelations so subtle as had never been received before;
that they were instruments on which the wind of unsuspected spaces
played its first tentative tunes. In this unexplored space, which is, as it
were, made up of the "empty distances" *between* and *around* our normal
concepts of thought and feeling, lies our "*wirklicher Bezug*," our *real*
"relatedness" to what really *is*. Like a hymn of spiritual friendship,
addressed to Nietzsche, sounds Rilke's sonnet:

*Heil dem Geist, der uns verbinden mag;*
*denn wir leben wahrhaft in Figuren.*
*Und mit kleinen Schritten gehn die Uhren*
*neben unserm eigentlichen Tag.*

*Ohne unsern wahren Platz zu kennen,*
*handeln wir aus wirklichem Bezug.*
*Die Antennen fühlen die Antennen,*
*und die leere Ferne trug. . . .*

(I, XII)

Hail, the spirit able to unite us!
For we truly live our lives in symbols,
and with tiny steps move our clocks,
beside our real, actual day.

Without knowing our true place,
we yet act from real relatedness.
Antennae feel antennae,
and the empty distance carries. . . .

And Nietzsche's response:

*Jenseits des Nordens, des Eises, des Heute,*
*jenseits des Todes,*
*abseits:*

unser *Leben,* unser *Glück!*
*Weder zu Lande*
*noch zu Wasser*
*kannst du den Weg*
*zu den Hyperboreren finden:*
*von* uns *wahrsagte so ein weiser Mund.*[23]

Beyond the North, the ice, the present day,
beyond death,
away from it:
*our* life, *our* bliss!
Neither by land nor by sea
can you find the way
to the Hyperboreans:
it was of *us* that the mouth of wisdom thus prophesied.

And the solitary figure of Rilke in the Piccola Marina of Capri, feeling the

*uraltes Wehn vom Meer,*
*welches weht*
*nur wie für Urgestein,*
*lauter Raum*
*reissend von weit herein. . . .*[24]

primeval waft from the sea,
that wafts
only as if for primeval stone,
pure space rushing
in from afar. . . .

easily merges with that of Nietzsche, leaning over a bridge in the Venetian evening:

*Meine Seele, ein Saitenspiel,*
*. . . unsichtbar berührt*[25]

My soul, a play of strings
. . . touched by an invisible hand

words which might be followed by Rilke's

*Und welcher Geiger hat uns in der Hand?*
*O süsses Lied.*[26]

And who is the minstrel that holds us in his hand?
O sweet song.

Yet these are only lyrical prolegomena or accompaniments to the great theme: the radical revision of all frontiers within human experience. The full realization of this theme comes to both of them in ecstatic states of inspiration. Both Nietzsche and Rilke knew they were inspired, irresistibly commanded to write, the one *Zarathustra* and the other *Duino Elegies*. Theirs are the only personal accounts we possess in modern literature of states of inspiration. The reports are almost interchangeable, except that Nietzsche's, written at some distance from the experience itself, is more sober than are Rilke's breathless announcements of victory upon having completed, after ten years of waiting, the cycle of the *Elegies* in 1922. "Has anyone, at the end of the nineteenth century, any clear idea of what poets of more vigorous ages called *inspiration?*" asks Nietzsche in the *Zarathustra* chapter of his autobiography *Ecce Homo,* and continues: "If one were in the least superstitious, one would not know how to reject the suggestion that one is merely an incarnation, merely a mouthpiece, merely a medium of superior powers."²⁷ Rilke speaks of "days of enormous obedience," of "a storm of the spirit" which threatened to annihilate the body. "O that I was allowed to survive to this day, through everything. Wonder. Grace."²⁸ Both Nietzsche and Rilke felt that the very physical surroundings which were the chosen scenes of these Pentecosts were hallowed places. The tenderness with which Nietzsche describes his walks on the hillsides of Genoa and through the Mediterranean pinewoods along the Bay of Santa Margherita, where Zarathustra accompanied him, is equalled by Rilke's stepping out into the cold moonlight, when he had survived the onrush of the Elegies, and stroking the walls of the "little castle Muzot" as if it were "an old animal."

This is not the way mere nuances are discovered. The word nuance presupposes an order of firmly established ideas and objects between which an indefinite number of subtly-colored shades may playfully mediate, whereas Nietzsche's and Rilke's sensibilities tend towards a radical denial of that very principle of separation—philosophically speaking, the *principium individuationis,* within a world perceived under the dual aspects of immanence and transcendence—on which our intellectual perception has been based throughout the centuries. Nietzsche denounces its results with regard to our thought as that "barbarism of concepts" which we are still far from fully recognizing, and Rilke deplores its effects on our feeling as that pauperism of the heart which makes us outcasts among angels, men and beasts alike, distressed vagabonds of the crudely interpreted world—

*dass wir nicht sehr verlässlich zu Haus sind*
*in der gedeuteten Welt.*

For all men make the mistake of *distinguishing* too sharply—

. . . *Aber Lebendige machen*
*alle den Fehler, dass sie zu stark unterscheiden.*
(First Elegy)

But this is an elegiac understatement of the real denunciation implicit in Rilke's mature work, which is that our traditional way of distinguishing is false throughout the whole range of our fundamental distinctions between transcendence and immanence, God and man, man and things, external reality and inwardness, joy and suffering, communion of love and separation, life and death—a list to which Nietzsche's main contribution is: good and evil. "To presuppose the *oneness* of life and death," Rilke writes, one year after *Duino Elegies* and *Sonnets to Orpheus,* and again, "to know the *identity* of terror and bliss . . . is the essential meaning and idea of my two books."[29]

3

We seem to have travelled a fair distance without being perturbed by our initial scruples which ought to have cast a shadow over the whole enterprise of relating the *poet* Rilke to the *thinker* Nietzsche. It appears that we had neither the courage nor the wisdom to act on Goethe's advice and "give ourselves up to impressions," to allow ourselves freely "to be amused, moved, and edified" by Rilke's poetry; nor did we share, or work on, Mr. Eliot's belief that "the poet who 'thinks' is merely the poet who can express the emotional equivalent of thought. But he is not necessarily interested in the thought itself."[30] For the conviction informing this essay is that Rilke *as a poet* is interested "in the thought itself," and Nietzsche *as a thinker* also expresses "the emotional equivalent of thought"; and yet Nietzsche remains a thinker throughout, and is not, as he himself sometimes believed and his philosophical critics often assert, "merely a poet," nor does Rilke ever cease to be a poet, even if some complain that he is "too speculative" in his mature phase. On the contrary, I believe that Nietzsche's and Rilke's opposition to traditional or even *valid* ways of distinguishing is rooted in their antagonism to one profoundly *invalid* distinction to which their age clung with almost religious passion: the distinction between thought and feeling. It is the distinction on which both rationalism and romanticism throve, spending their forces in an ultimately futile struggle to establish the superiority of the one or the other. Yet it is no good trying to choose between two misfits. Both Goethe and T. S. Eliot, in the quoted instances, attempt to clear up a confusion by using tools of thought manufactured in the very workshop that is responsible for the muddle.

This becomes quite obvious if we look at the concepts to which both Goethe and Eliot oppose poetry. Goethe says that it has nothing to do with "ideas." "Ideas" always were the *bête noire* as well as the weak point of Goethe. Once, as he tells us, he was on the verge of being very angry with Schiller, who accused his *Urpflanze* of belonging to that oppressive and oppressed class. But of course Schiller was right and Goethe was offended only because the word "idea" suggested to him something "abstract," something "thought out" by what he was in the habit of calling "*Verstand*": discursive and analytical reason. And throughout the conversation with Eckermann, quoted at the beginning of this essay, it is this analytical reason that is set against poetry, this "*Verstand*" which Goethe disliked so much as the prosaic enemy of poetry—and, indeed, of science too. For him it assumed mythological shape in the figure of Newton.*

T. S. Eliot, on the other hand, knows that the meaning of "thought" does not permit so lighthearted and restrictive a definition. He deplores the difficulty of "having to use the same words for different things."[31] But when it actually comes to using "thought" in *his* sense, this is what happens: "Champions of Shakespeare as a great philosopher have a great deal to say about Shakespeare's power of thought, but they fail to show that he *thought to any purpose,* that he *had any coherent view of life,* or that he *recommended any procedure to follow.*"[32] In other words, "thought" in this sense appears to be the preoccupation of a group of men among whom the professional bores are in the majority. The three criteria amount to a definition of a certain type of rationalism. It is a definition that excludes, first, the thinker for whom

---

*A dictionary of Goethe's vacillating use of the word "idea" would reveal the full measure of ambiguity that besets the problem of "thought and poetry" in the age of rationalism and romanticism, and the difficulties of a man who is opposed to both. The essay "Goethe and the Idea of Scientific Truth" in my book *The Disinherited Mind* contains a number of quotations from Goethe that show a much more positive attitude towards "ideas" than his conversation about *Tasso* would suggest. About *Faust* he said to Luden on August 19th, 1806, that its "higher interest" lies in "the idea which has inspired the poet and which is capable of knitting all the details of the poem into a whole, providing norm and significance for its individual elements."

thinking is not a means to an end, but a passion; secondly, the thinker who knows that no system of thought can ever be completely coherent without the knowledge of the inescapable measure of incoherence worked into the whole structure of the system; and thirdly, the thinker whose thought does not issue in recipes for action, but in invitations to think. In short, it excludes the thinker.

To make poetry is to think. Of course, it is not *merely* thinking. But there is no such activity as "merely thinking," unless we confine the term to purely logical or mathematical operations. Language is not quite so stupid as some of our linguistic philosophers seem to assume. It knows what it does when it allows us to say that we "think of someone," and when it calls actions deficient in kindness or imagination "thoughtless." "Thinking" and "thought" in these phrases are words that mean what they say: thought and thinking. And if we have it on authority still higher than Goethe's or Eliot's that in the beginning was *logos,* the word, the thought, the meaning, we should think twice before we answer the question whether or not a poet thinks. It is a happy coincidence in German that *"Dichter und Denker,"* poet and thinker, form an alliterative pair.

T. S. Eliot suggests that Shakespeare, in making Hamlet think sometimes in the manner of Montaigne, did not think himself, but merely "used" thought for dramatic ends. This sounds true enough, and would be even truer if it were possible to "use" thought without thinking in the process of using it. For thought is not an object, but an activity, and it is impossible to "use" an activity without becoming active. One can use a table without contributing to its manufacture; but one cannot use thinking or feeling without thinking or feeling. Of course, one can use the results of thought in a thoughtless fashion. In this case, however, one does not use thought but merely words which will, more likely than not, fail to make sense.

In so far as Hamlet's thought makes sense, Shakespeare must have been thinking it, although not necessarily as the first to do so and certainly in a manner of thinking which is more imaginative and intuitive than rationally deliberate. To define "thinking" in such a way that the activity which Shakespeare pursued in composing the speeches of Hamlet, or Ulysses, or Lear has to be dismissed as "non-thought" is to let thinking fall into the rationalist trap from which it is likely to emerge as a cripple, full of animosity against that other deformed creature, mutilated in the same operation: the Romantic emotion. If thought, stripped of imaginative feeling, and emotion, stripped of imaginative thought, become the dominant modes both of thinking and feeling, the outcome is the "*Leid-Stadt,*" that insufferable city of sorrows, or the Waste Land, in which the spirits of Nietzsche and Rilke and Eliot feel ill at ease. Paradoxically enough, it is precisely this neat separation between thought and feeling which has forced, on the one hand, "the Absurd" upon modern philosophy as one of its principal themes, and, on the other hand, an excessive degree of *intellectual* complexity upon modern poetry.

Poetry is not, as Goethe would suggest in that conversation with Eckermann, in opposition to "ideas," nor does it, as Eliot says, merely give the "emotional equivalent" of thought. Dante, Shakespeare, Goethe, Rilke and Eliot, in making poetry, have ideas; and they think. Only in the "pure" lyric and the "pure" epic may ideas and thought be so negligible as to be irrelevant to aesthetic or critical appreciation. If Dante's thought is Thomas Aquinas's, it is yet Dante's: not only by virtue of imaginative sympathy and assimilation, and certainly not as a reward for the supply of an "emotional equivalent." It is Dante's property by birthright. He has recreated it within himself—poetically. For poetry is not a garment around thought, nor is it its shadowy aesthetic reflection. It is a certain kind of thought, hopelessly uncertain of itself at a time when thought is "merely" thought and poetry "merely" poetry and therefore, to quote Eliot's *East Coker,* "does not matter:"

> Because one has only learnt to get the better of words
> For the thing one no longer has to say, or the way in which
> One is no longer disposed to say it.

If this happens, the problem of thought and poetry takes on an altogether new complexion. For happy is the poet whose only job is to learn how to get the better of words for things which he *has* to say. He is the poet who thinks with the thought of his age, as Dante thought with the thought of St. Thomas. Whether or not the poet thinks in the thought-mold of his time does not necessarily depend on the goodness or profundity of its thought, and certainly not on its systematic coherence. The question is, rather, whether this thought springs from the same level of spiritual experience on which poetry is formed; and whether it is linked to that reservoir of fundamental intellectual certainties (and be it the certainty of doubt, skepticism or stoicism) from which the poetic impulse must be sustained if it is not to be in danger of breaking under a burden too heavy for its delicate constitution. This danger will arise when the poet, compelled by the peculiar spiritual barrenness of his age, has to struggle for the poetic expression of unheard-of and unthought-of experiences. It is then that he will have to do *all* the thinking himself, because the experiences for which, as a poet, he has to find the adequate *poetic* thought have not yet become articulate even in *intellectual* thought.

What has become articulate in intellectual thought is experience so prosaic that its mere contemplation paralyzes the poetic imagination. It is the situation that Hegel had in mind when in his *Aesthetics* he wrote: "If the mode of prose has absorbed all the concepts of the mind and impressed them with its prosaic stamp, then poetry has to take on the business of so thorough a recasting and remodelling that, faced with the unyielding mass of the prosaic, it finds itself involved everywhere in manifold difficulties"; and which led him to the pessimistic dictum that therefore "art . . . is and will remain for us a thing of the past."[33] In such conditions a kind of poetry will be produced for which, anomalously enough, the *intellectual* thinking has to be done after the event. Whole gangs of interpreters will rush in, to prepare the ground intellectually for what has already grown—ploughboys of the sparse harvest.

Yet T. S. Eliot is not, I suspect, concerned as much with the question of thought in poetry as with the problem of belief. For the assumption underlying his essay is that the thinker is interested in the *truth* of thought, but the poet merely in its fitting expression. In other words, the thinker invites us to *believe* what he says, whereas the poet aims only at our being *moved* or *pleased* by the way he puts it. This is indeed a very relevant problem at a time when more and more people try to believe in poetry as in a religion. Around Rilke, for instance, a vast body of literature has grown up that appears to aim not at gaining comprehending readers for the poet, but at making proselytes.

The question, then, is: is the poet a trustworthy counselor? Does he himself believe what he says? Without going into the endless intricacies of this problem, I would say that it has nothing to do with the nature of either poetry or thought as such, but with the character of any particular poet or thinker, or with the character of any particular poetry or thought. There *are* poetic creations which bear the unmistakable stamp of convictions deeply held by the poet; and the *aesthetic* success of this kind of poetry is inextricably bound up with the sincerity of the personal beliefs expressed in them. This applies, for instance, to the poetry of St. John of the Cross. But it applies, also, on varying levels and in different degrees, to less extreme examples: to George Herbert, John Donne, Milton, Andreas Gryphius, Claudius, Hölderlin—and T. S. Eliot. It does not matter in the slightest whether such a poet is, while writing, *preoccupied* with his beliefs. Of course, in the act of writing he is preoccupied with the business of writing as well as possible. But what does matter is the fact that such poets could not produce good poetry if they were prepared to betray their beliefs for the sake of occasional heresies offering a more felicitous phrase. On a profounder level it would even be true to say that a poet, in writing his poetry, *discovers* the precise nature of these beliefs. Whether he is a believer all the time, realizing what he believes through his actions, is another matter, again wholly irrelevant to the specific problem of poetry. Few men are like Pascal, and even he had to remind himself continually, by a sheet of paper sewn into his jacket, of what he had on one sacred occasion recognized as wholly true.

Naturally, the beliefs of such a poet, as proclaimed in his poetry, may be of so subtle, esoteric and even eccentric a sort that it would be unwise to try to live by them. But he is not necessarily less "trustworthy" as a prophet of truths than any other type of prophet. The difficulty does not lie in the fact that he is a poet, but is of a universal nature. It is the difficulty of translating spiritual convictions into living convictions. If this were an easy matter, the Christian Church would have no "history." Its practices would be as unchanging and unchangeable as the core of its spiritual beliefs. The reasons why one should, or should not, accept the beliefs inherent in Rilke's later poetry are not different in kind from the reasons why one should, or should not, accept the beliefs of Marxism, or of the Oxford Group, or of anthroposophy. To say, "but he is merely a poet" (and not, I suppose, a sectarian hawker, an ideologist or a political propagandist) is to suggest that, by his profession, he is less capable of perceiving truth than others; to say, "but his poetry is too beautiful to be true" is to insinuate that the closer the poetry is to truth, the less successful it will be as art, because all truth is necessarily ungainly. This is a point extremely important to the later Nietzsche. We shall return to it in the essay "Nietzsche's Last Words about Art versus Truth."

I am not concerned with advocating Rilke's beliefs. But I am concerned with a bizarre type of aesthetic fallacy: that Rilke's ideas do not matter because they are a poet's ideas. If I could see a choice where, in fact, I believe there is none, between the ideas and the poetry, I think I should rather be inclined to say with Eliot that it is the poetry which "does not matter." But there is no such choice. In *Duino Elegies* the poetry is the ideas, and the ideas are the poetry. If the ideas were all humbug, or if, as the German critic H. E. Holthusen suggests in his book on Rilke, they were all "wrong," in the sense of contradicting that "intuitive logic" which tells us what is a true and what is a false picture of man,[34] then the poetry would have little chance of being what he believes it to be: *great* poetry.

The appreciation of poetry is not like looking at a beautiful apple; it is rather like looking and eating. If the core is rotten, the outside beauty will soon be felt to be a mockery. Holthusen's way out of the dilemma between his Christian beliefs, which make him condemn Rilke's ideas, and the pagan enchantment that impels him to acknowledge the greatness of Rilke's poetry, is, I think, the way of spiritual timidity. Its coarser symbols are the fig-leaves of the Vatican museum. Let us enjoy the pagan beauty, but not go too far. How far? Not as far as the *whole* poetry. For the poetry of the *Duino Elegies* is indivisible. There is no poetry left if we *feel* that the "ideas" are false to the point of being a distortion of the true image of man. If, on the other hand, we merely *know* this, not by that "intuitive logic" of which Holthusen speaks, but by theological deliberations, we are by no means immune from sharing the beliefs of the *Duino Elegies*. Why not accept a situation which for most Christians in Europe is at least as old as the Renaissance? The characteristic spiritual quality of that long period of history of which we are the bewildered heirs was not only a dissociation of faith from knowledge; this was a comparatively harmless episode, lasting from the seventeenth century to the age of Victoria, a mere surface repercussion of that mightier earthquake which severed faith from sensibility. It is this rift which has made it impossible for most Christians not to *feel,* or at least not to feel *also,* as true many "truths" which are imcompatible with the truth of their accepted and proclaimed faith. If this is agony, it must be borne by those who are incapable of Keats's "Negative Capability, that is, when a man is capable of being in uncertainties, mysteries, doubts, without any irritable reaching after fact and reason." Such an "irritable reaching" is the all too facile distinction between the "truth" of a poem and its "aesthetic appeal," between the "idea" and the "poetry," a separation which can only do damage to the resources, meager as they are, with which we have to carry on in our modest efforts to get a little nearer the spiritual integrity within which, in Nietzsche's words, "the religious, aesthetic and moral perceptions are at one." For the time being, which does not seem to be God's good time:

> *Jede dumpfe Umkehr der Welt hat solche Enterbte,*
> *denen das Frühere nicht und noch nicht das Nächste gehört.*
> (Seventh Elegy)

> Each torpid turn of the world has such disinherited children,
> to whom no longer what's been, and not yet what's coming, belongs.

This again is spoken, not only from the heart of Nietzsche, but almost with his tongue, suggesting that we should resume the discussion of the particular poet and the particular philosopher.*

## 4

We observed them, each in his own way, working, thinking and feeling towards a radical revision of the frontiers between traditionally articulated concepts of thought and, as it were, "units" of feeling. There remains the question of how and why they came to undertake such a stupendous labor of thought and feeling—"*Herzwerk,*" "work of heart," as Rilke called it. The answer was given for both of them by Nietzsche: because God is dead. And God was so powerful, efficient and secretive a landlord that to look after His Estate all by ourselves

*In his essay on Dante, written in 1929, two years after "Shakespeare and the Stoicism of Seneca," T. S. Eliot discusses once more the question of belief and poetry. "There is a difference," he says, "between philosophical *belief* and poetic *assent*" (*Collected Essays*, p. 257). This is undoubtedly true in an age in which "the religious, aesthetic and moral perceptions" are *not* at one. We may, however, disregard the word "philosophical" in Eliot's phrase, for his context is more strictly a religious or theological one. An agnostic can give his poetic assent to Dante and a Christian withhold it from every single hymn sung on a Sunday in his church. Yet there will be a certain strain in such a situation. The more *serious* becomes a reader's love for Dante's poetry, the more will he be tempted to accept his beliefs, or else be exasperated by the poet's wrongheadedness in holding them or his own inability to share them; and exasperation detracts from enjoyment. Differences of opinion are more worrying between lovers than between superficial acquaintances; in fact, they tend to become or reveal something else: flaws in mutual understanding. And because this is so, T. S. Eliot's discussion of this particular problem comes to nothing. His statement on page 258: "You are not called upon to believe what Dante believed, for your belief will not give you a groat's worth more of understanding and appreciation" is, after its more forceful reiteration in a postscript (p. 269), crossed out again by "So I cannot, in practice, wholly separate my poetic appreciation from my personal beliefs" (p. 271). The question is extremely difficult, so difficult that both assertions, blatantly contradictory, are in some measure true. It seems to me that two points could be added to make them a few degrees truer and less incompatible: 1. Where beliefs embodied in poetry are as important as they are in what one may call confessional poetry, we cannot fully appreciate the poetry without being at least *tempted* to accept the beliefs as well. The measure of our appreciation will be the degree to which we experience the poem's persuasiveness and our weakness in the face of the challenge. With such poetry before us, complete immunity from infection would prove either the bluntness of our perception or the worthlessness of the poetry; 2. There are ideas and beliefs so prosaic, outlandish or perverse at their core that no great or good poetry can come from them: for instance, Hitler's racialism. It is this *negative* consideration that to me finally proves the intimate *positive* relation between belief, thought and poetry. If there were no relation, there would be no reason either why the most perverse or idiotic beliefs should not be convertible into *great* poetry. They are not.

involves us in great difficulties. What under His management used to be clearly defined spheres are now objects of confused and conflicting claims. Much that we were powerfully persuaded to accept as true dissolves into sheer illusion. For all the land appears to have been heavily mortgaged. We have lived in splendor, but the splendor was merely loaned. Payment was due on the death of God, and the unknown transcendental creditor lost little time in claiming it. A tremendous effort has to be exacted to restore the glory.

Both Nietzsche and Rilke have made themselves administrators of the impoverished estate. The enormous complexity of their works must not deceive us; the design behind it is consistently simple; it has the simplicity of that immense single-mindedness with which they, consciously or intuitively, dedicated their lives to the one task: to reassess and redefine all experience in thought and feeling; to show that the traditional modes of thought and feeling, in so far as they were determined, or decisively modified, by Christian transcendental beliefs—and to which of them does this not apply?—had been rendered invalid by the divine demise; to replace them; to overcome the great spiritual depression, caused by the death of God, through new and ever greater powers of glory and praise; to adjust, indeed to revolutionize, thought and feeling in accordance with the reality of a world of absolute immanence; and to achieve this without any loss of spiritual grandeur. "Indeed," writes Nietzsche (to Overbeck, May 21st, 1884), "who can feel with me what it means to feel with every shred of one's being that the weight of all things must be defined anew," and Rilke (to Ilse Jahr, February 22nd, 1923): "God, the no longer sayable, is being stripped of his attributes; they return to his creation;"[35] and in "The Letter from the Young Workman" (reversing the debtor-creditor relationship and presenting the bill to Heaven): "It is high time for the impoverished earth to claim back all those loans which have been raised at the expense of her own bliss for the equipment of some superfuture."[36] Nietzsche spoke for himself as well as for Rilke when at the time of writing *Zarathustra* he made the following entry in his notebook: "He who no longer finds what is great in God will find it nowhere—he must either deny or create it."[37] It is the most precise formula for the religiously disinherited religious mind.

Nietzsche and Rilke experienced and explored this situation with the utmost consistency, courageously facing the paradox to which it leads: the paradox of affirming from negation, and creating from denial. For the denial of God involves for both Nietzsche and Rilke the denial of man *as he is*. Even before Zarathustra proclaimed the rule of the *Übermensch*, Nietzsche, knowing that man has become "impossible" after doing away with God, "the holiest and mightiest that the world possessed," asked: "Is not the greatness of this deed too great for us? To prove worthy of it, must not we ourselves become gods?"[38] And Rilke said of his *Malte Laurids Brigge* that it almost "proved that this life, suspended in a bottomless pit, is impossible."[39]

How is this impossible life to become possible again? How is the vanished glory issuing from a transcendental god to be recreated by a world gloomily imprisoned in its own immanence? At this point both Nietzsche and Rilke indulge in the same alchemy that we have seen employed in their transmutation of pain and suffering. The idea of even heightening the agony of existence in order to increase the resources from which ultimate bliss will be sustained is familiar to both of them. Nietzsche once quoted Cardanus as having said that one ought to seek out as much suffering as possible in order to intensify the joy springing from its conquest;[40] and Rilke wrote of the "holy cunning of the martyrs," taking "the most concentrated dose of pain" to acquire the immunity of continual bliss.[41] Now again they seek in the greatest possible intensification of immanence salvation from the inglorious prison. They almost invent more and more deprivations of transcendence to heighten the pressure within the hermetic vessel. In that, Nietzsche's Eternal Recurrence and Rilke's "*Ein*mal and nicht-mehr," "*once* and no more," are contrasts merely in verbal expression, but identical in meaning. This identity lies in the emphasis both these symbols place on the *eternity* of the moment here and now, the *irrevocability* of the one and unique opportunity and test of living.

The idea of Eternal Recurrence seeks to bestow the paradox of an eternity of finite time on the transient moment, which Rilke, in his turn, eternalizes in the hermetical flame of inner experience, consuming all that is merely corruptible matter and concreteness in our world and leaving us with an essence as imperishable as it is invisible. Rilke states this theme of his mature work with explicit precision as early as his *Tuscan Diary:* "We need *eternity;* for only eternity can provide space for our gestures. Yet we know that we live in narrow finiteness. Thus it is our task to create infinity within these boundaries, for we no longer believe in the unbounded."[42] And the imaginations of both Nietzsche and Rilke have given birth to symbolic creatures moving with perfect grace and ease in a sphere to which man can attain only in the utmost realization of his spiritual powers. These creatures of immanence, transcending immanence in the achievement of a yet profounder immanence, are Nietzsche's *Übermensch* and Rilke's Angel.

Both are terrible to man, threatening with annihilation the image that, fondly and lazily, he has built up of himself, an image resting on the illusion of transcendence and now shattered in the great undeceiving: "To create the *Übermensch* after we have thought, indeed rendered thinkable, the whole of nature in terms of man himself" and then "to *break all your images of man* with the image of the *Übermensch*—this is Zarathustra's will . . ."[43] says one of Nietzsche's notebooks from the time of *Zarathustra;* and Rilke's *Duino Elegies* begin with the invocation of the angelic terror:

> *Wer, wenn ich schriee, hörte mich denn aus der Engel*
> *Ordnungen? und gesetzt selbst, es nähme*
> *einer mich plötzlich ans Herz: ich verginge von seinem*
> *stärkeren Dasein . . .*
>
> (First Elegy)
>
> Who, if I cried, would hear me among the angelic
> orders? And even if one of them suddenly
> pressed me against his heart, I should fade in the strength of his
> stronger existence . . .

and

> *Jeder Engel ist schrecklich. Und dennoch, weh mir,*
> *ansing ich euch, fast tödliche Vögel der Seele,*
> *wissend um euch. . . .*
>
> (Second Elegy)
>
> Every angel is terrible. Still, though, alas!
> I invoke you, almost deadly birds of the soul,
> knowing of you. . . .

The supreme realization of immanence and its metamorphosis into everlasting inwardness is man's task in a world dominated by Rilke's Angel, in the same way in which Nietzsche conceives Eternal Recurrence as the terrifying discipline which must break man and make the *Übermensch.* Only he, in the glory of his own strength, joy and power of praise, can *will* again and again a life which, even if lived only once, must be all but unendurable to man as soon as he is exposed to the full impact of its absolute godlessness and senselessness, and no longer sheltered from it by the ruins of Christianity among which he exists. "I perform the great experiment: who can bear the idea of Eternal Recurrence? He who cannot endure the sentence, 'There is no redemption,' ought to die out."[44] The *Übermensch* is for Nietzsche what Orpheus is for Rilke: the transfigurer of unredeemable existence, with the "mystery of its unending repetition issuing from superhuman delight."[45]

> *Und so drängen wir uns und wollen es leisten,*
> *wollens enthalten in unseren einfachen Händen,*
> *im überfülteren Blick und im sprachlosen Herzen.*
> *Wollen es werden. . . .*
>
> (Ninth Elegy)

And so we press on and try to achieve it,
try to contain it within our simple hands,
in the gaze ever more overcrowded and in the speechless heart.
Try to become it. . . .

But what we try to achieve here and what overcrowds our gaze and heart—with *"uberzähliges Dasein,"* "Supernumerary existence"—is not the vision of Eternal Recurrence, but, on the contrary, of

> Einmal
> *jedes, nur einmal. Einmal und nichtmehr. Und wir auch*
> *einmal. Nie wieder. Aber dieses*
> *einmal gewesen zu sein, wenn auch nur einmal:*
> *irdisch gewesen zu sein, scheint nicht widerrufbar.*
>
> (Ninth Elegy)

Just *once*,
everything only for once. *Once* and no more. And we, too,
once. And never again. But this
having been once, thought only once,
having been once on earth—can it ever be canceled?

Nietzsche's Eternal Recurrence and Rilke's eternally reiterated "Once" are both the extreme symbols of the determination to wrest the utmost of spiritual significance from a life that, in traditional terms, has ceased to be spiritually significant. How to cast eternity from the new mold of absolute transience, and how to achieve the mode of transcendence within the consciousness of pure immanence, is one of the main concerns of Nietzsche as well as of Rilke. This problem links Rilke (and, of course, Nietzsche) with the philosophers of Existence or "Being." Heidegger, for instance, is said to have remarked that his philosophy is merely the unfolding in thought of what Rilke has expressed poetically;[46] but even without this confession the affinity would be obvious. What, above all, Rilke and the existentialists have in common is the experience of the utter exposure and defenselessness of the frontiers of human existence against the neighboring void, that area which was once established as the divine home of souls and is now the unassailable fortress of the *nihil,* defeating for ever every new and heroic attempt of man to assert himself in that region: hence Jaspers's *Scheitern,* Heidegger's *Geworfensein* and, long before them, Kierkegaard's—and even Pascal's—*Angst.* The focal point of all existentialist philosophies is this "marginal situation" of man in the border-districts of immanence and the realization of the existence of a sphere which seems to invite and yet relentlessly beat back every attempt at transcendence.

It is this impenetrable void against which Zarathustra hurls his armies of men, knowing that they will not be victorious, but utterly routed; yet a few will return in triumph, having gained the strength of *Übermenschen* in the purifying defeat. For life is a *"Wagnis,"* a perpetual staking of existence, man a mere "essay in existence" and lovable only because he is *"ein Übergang und ein Untergang,"*[47] at once transition and perdition. The same frontier is the defeat of Malte Laurids Brigge, until the mature Rilke succeeds in concluding an everlasting truce with the anonymous powers on the other side—by appropriating their territory "inwardly." Where man knew merely the terror of the monstrous emptiness beyond, there is now the peace of *"reiner Bezug,"* "pure relatedness," which is so pure because no real "otherness" enters into it. In this *"reiner Bezug"* life and death are one. As soon as it is achieved,

> *entsteht*
> *aus unsern Jahreszeiten erst der Umkreis*
> *des ganzen Wandelns. Über uns hinüber*
> *spielt dann der Engel. . . .*
> (Fourth Elegy)

> arises
> from our seasons the cycle
> of the entire motion. Over and above us,
> then, there is the Angel's play. . . .

Or, one is tempted to add, the *Übermensch's* dance, the joy of the creatures who have gained eternity in the resigned and yet victorious return to themselves. Rilke, in the Super-Narcissus image of his Angels, at the same time expresses the essence of Nietzsche's race of *Übermenschen* who assert their power and beauty in the cycle of Eternal Recurrence:

> *. . . die die entströmte eigene Schönheit*
> *wiederschöpfen zurück in das eigene Antlitz.*
> (Second Elegy)

. . . drawing up their own
outstreamed beauty into their faces again.

It is not correct to say that after the *Duino Elegies* Rilke returned, as
some critics suggest, to a "simpler" and "purely lyrical" mode of
expression. The apparent simplicity and pure lyricism of the final
phase are not different in kind from the *Sonnets to Orpheus*. There is,
indeed, repose; but it is the repose of a poetry that appears to have
settled peacefully on the very pastures which had for so long been the
goal of the struggle. If the *Duino Elegies* are the invocation of the Angel, some of the poems that come afterwards sound like the Angel's
own poetry; and it is hardly surprising that it could also be said: like
the poetry of the *Übermensch*. This, indeed, does not make them easier
to understand. There is little gain in it for those who find the "ideas"
of the preceding period disturbing. The ideas are not abandoned, but
realized; for instance, in the poem written in 1924:

> *Da dich das geflügelte Entzücken*
> *über manchen frühen Abgrund trug,*
> *baue jetzt der unerhörten Brüken*
> *kühn berechenbaren Bug.*
>
> *Wunder ist nicht nur im unerklärten*
> *Überstehen der Gefahr;*
> *erst in einer klaren reingewährten*
> *Leistung wird das Wunder wunderbar.*
>
> *Mitzuwirken ist nicht Überhebung*
> *an dem unbeschreiblichen Bezug,*
> *immer inniger wird die Verwebung,*
> *nur Getragensein ist nicht genug.*
>
> *Deine ausgeübten Kräfte spanne,*
> *bis sie reichen, zwischen zwein*
> *Widersprüchen. . . .Denn im Manne*
> *Will der Gott beraten sein.*[48]

All the winged ecstasy
has borne you over many an early abyss,
now, with mathematical audacity
build the arches of unheard-of bridges.

Wonder is not merely in the inexplicable
surviving of danger;
only in the clear and purely granted
achievement is the miracle miraculous.

To participate in the indescribable
relating, is not presumption,

ever more intense becomes the pattern,
only being borne along will not suffice.

Stretch your practiced powers till they span
the distance between two contradictions,
for the god must find
counsel in man.

Or in Rilke's last known poem in German, which, if it is simple, has the inexhaustibly complex simplicity of a sphere so esoteric that it renders it untranslatable, defeating even the attempt to give a prose version of it in English. Yet all that has been said here about Rilke and Nietzsche could easily be based on this one poem alone and would need no further support. It is dated August 24th, 1926, four months before Rilke's death, and is dedicated to Erika Mitterer "for the feast of praise:"

> *Taube, die draussen blieb,    ausser dem Taubenschlag,*
> *wieder in Kreis and Haus,    einig der Nacht, dem Tag,*
> *weiss sie die Heimlichkeit,    wenn sich der Einbezug*
> *fremdester Schrecken schmiegt    in den gefühlten Flug.*
>
> *Unter den Tauben, die    allergeschonteste,*
> *niemals gefährdetste,    kennt nicht die Zärtlichkeit;*
> *wiedererholtes Herz    ist das bewohnteste:*
> *freier durch Widerruf    freut sich die Fähigkeit.*
>
> *Über dem Nirgendssein    spannt sich das Überall!*
> *Ach der geworfene,    ach der gewagte Ball,*
> *füllt er die Hände nicht    anders mit Wiederkehr:*
> *rein um sein Heimgewicht    ist er mehr.*[49]*

## 5

Both Nietzsche and Rilke, experiencing life as wholly immanent, irrevocable in its transience and unredeemable in its imperfection, stake

---

*In a later essay of mine, "The Hazard of Modern Poetry," I attempted, after all, a paraphrase: The first stanza speaks of a dove that stayed outside the dovecot, an adventurous and "creative" dove; but now the dove is back in the dovecot, united with the rest of its fellows in the routine of day and night, and only now, after all its exploits, has it come to know what it means to be at home, for only now is the movement of its wings truly felt, enriched as it is by the assimilation of strangest terrors. Among doves, the second stanza continues, the most protected creature, never exposed to terrible dangers, knows not what gentleness is—as it is the recovered heart that is richest in feeling, and as power rejoices at its greater freedom won through renunciation. Above Being Nowhere, says the third stanza, extends the Everywhere (and the German word "*Überall*"—everywhere—also carries the associations of "above everything"). The ball, jeopardized in the most daring throw—does it not fill your hands with a new sensation of return? Has it not increased by the pure weight of its homecoming?

it on the supreme "*Wagnis,*" the daring experiment: man himself must become the redeemer of existence. This is the ultimate consequence of the Will to Power, or of humanism thought out and felt to its radical conclusion by the *anima naturaliter religiosa.* Nietzsche replaces the mystery of the Incarnation by the *Übermensch,* the Will to Power incarnate; and Rilke by the angelic vision of a world disembodied in human inwardness. "We must transform our prayers into blessings,"[50] says Nietzsche; and Rilke:

> *Erde, ist es nicht dies, was du willst:* unsichtbar
> *in uns erstehen?—Ist es dein Traum nicht,*
> *einmal unsichtbar zu sein?—Erde! unsichtbar!*
> *Was, wenn Verwandlung nicht, ist dein drängender Auftrag?*
> (Ninth Elegy)

> Earth, isn't this what you want: an *invisible*
> re-arising in us? Is it not your dream
> to be one day invisible? Earth! invisible!
> What is your urgent command, if not transformation?

Only on the discovery of this redeeming mission follows Rilke's final affirmation: "*Erde, du liebe, ich will.*"

Interpreting the Elegies to his Polish translator, Rilke wrote: "*There is neither a Here and Now nor Beyond, but only the great Oneness,* in which the creatures surpassing us, the Angels, are at home. . . . *We are the bees of the Invisible. Nous butinons éperdument le miel du visible, pour l'accumuler dans la grande ruche d'or de l'Invisible.*" And after denouncing the ceaselessly progressing depreciation of the spiritual value of all "things," he continues: "The earth has no other refuge except to become invisible: *in us* . . . only *in us* can this intimate and enduring transformation of the Visible into the Invisible . . . be accomplished. . . . The Angel of the *Elegies* has nothing to do with the angel of the Christian Heaven. . . . He is the creature in whom the transformation of the Visible into the Invisible, which is our task, appears already accomplished. . . ."[51] But for all this, the most illuminating part of Rilke's much-quoted letter is the statement that the ultimate affirmation of life, achieved in the *Elegies,* is sustained by precisely the same awareness that persuaded Malte Laurids Brigge of life's "impossibility." Malte's disgust and the Ninth Elegy's praise spring from an identical source. In other words, the Angel did for Rilke what the *Übermensch* did for Nietzsche: he supplied the philosophers' stone with which to make gold from base matter. Yet it appears that of the two Rilke was the more successful alchemist. The letters he wrote after the

*Duino Elegies* lavished the precious stuff from the poet's workshop on as many needy as cared to apply for it. Nietzsche, on the other hand, while writing *Zarathustra* and expounding the doctrines of Eternal Recurrence, praise and affirmation, made the following entry in his notebook: "I do not wish to live *again*. How have I borne life? By creating. What has made me endure? The vision of the *Übermensch* who *affirms* life. I have tried to affirm it *myself*—but ah![52]

These two confessions of Rilke and Nietzsche clinch the whole excruciating problem that besets the spritually disinherited mind of Europe, and raise anew the question of poetry and truth in an age dispossessed of all spiritual certainties. Without that all-pervasive sense of truth which bestows upon happier cultures their intuition of order and reality, poetry—in company with all the other arts—will be faced with ever increasing demands for ever greater "creativeness." For the "real order" has to be "created" where there is no intuitive conviction that it exists. The story of the rise of the poet from the humble position of a teller of tales and a singer of songs to the heights of creation, from a lover of fancies to a slave of the imagination, from the mouthpiece of divine wisdom to the begetter of new gods, is a story as glorious as it is agonizing. For with every new gain in poetic creativity the world as it is, the world as created without the poet's intervention, becomes poorer; and every new impoverishment of the world is a new incentive to poetic creativeness. In the end the world as it is is nothing but a slum to the spirit and an offense to the artist. Leaving its vapors behind in audacious flight, his genius settles in a world wholly created by the creator-poet: "*Gesang ist Dasein.*"

"Only after the death of religion will the imagination be able to luxuriate again in divine spheres,"[53] said Nietzsche, perhaps not knowing that in saying it he was merely echoing one of the favorite ideas of the Romantics whom he usually disliked. For it was Friedrich Schlegel who wrote: "Only he can be an artist who has a religion of his own, an original view of infinity,"[54] and it was Novalis who added to this dictum the marginal note "The artist is thoroughly irreligious. Hence he can work in the medium of religion as though it were bronze."[55] But the original views of infinity cannot for ever remain unaffected by the spiritual destitution of the finite. There must come a time when owing to excessive mining bronze is devalued and the soil becomes too dry for anything to grow luxuriantly, except in artificial conditions.

Neither Rilke nor Nietzsche praises the praiseworthy. They praise. They do not believe the believable. They believe. And it is their praising and believing itself that becomes praiseworthy and believable in the act of worship. Theirs is a *religio intransitiva*. Future anthropologists may see in it the distinctive religious achievement of modern Europe, the theological equivalent of *l'art pour l'art*. For the time being, it may help us to assess the rank of Rilke as a poet, and to clear up some of the confusion into which we are plunged by dissociating his "great poetry" from his "false ideas."

In a sense Rilke's poetry is as "false" as his ideas are. This sense, however, is not simply derogatory. There is a kind of falseness which, quite legitimately, affords the most refined aesthetic pleasure: at the point, that is, at which consistently sustained artificiality assumes the semblance of spontaneity, and the most elaborate magical procedure the appearance of the naïvely miraculous. In this sense both Rilke's poetry and his ideas show the intrinsic falseness of a self-created reality and a self-induced love for it. In defending a sense and vision of reality different from Rilke's, the critic implicitly upholds, often against his explicit intentions, standards of poetry by which the poetic work of Rilke's mature years stands judged as too eccentric to be really great. Rilke poetically exploits a marginal position, precariously maintained on the brink of catastrophe. The catastrophe, perpetually threatening and only just warded off by the most dazzling acrobatics of soul and mind, is the loss of significant external reality. In the great poetry of the European tradition the emotions do not interpret; they respond to the interpreted world. In Rilke's mature poetry the emotions do the interpreting and then respond to their own interpretation.

All great art (and, for that matter, every human order stabilized by tradition) rests on a fundamentally fixed correspondence between the impact of external experience on man and man's articulate answers. These answers may be given on varying levels of profundity and with varying degrees of precision, but they are all recognizable by, as it were, their basic color as the more or less right answers. Indeed, the imagination, this kingfisher after new experiences and new articulations, may discover new waters in lands which have long remained inaccessible and unexplored. But there will be a place for them, hitherto left blank, on the maps of the familiar world.

Rilke, however, is the poet of a world of which the philosopher is Nietzsche. Its formations evade all traditional systems of cartography. Doubt has dislodged all certainties. The unnameable is christened and the unsayable uttered. It is a world in which the order of correspondences is violently disturbed. We can no longer be sure that we love the lovable and abhor the detestable. Good does no good and evil no harm. Terror and bliss are one. Life and death are the same. Lovers seek separation, not union. All the sweetness of the visible world is stored in invisible hives.

Unembarrassed greatness is not to be expected from the poetry of such a world.* Yet Rilke is uniquely successful in evoking the traditional responses of the emotions to fundamentally new impacts. At his bidding the soul travels as though through familiar land; but on arrival it finds itself in a place where it never meant to be. It is not for nothing that the central position in the *Duino Elegies*—the fifth among the ten—is occupied by *Les Saltimbanques,* the acrobats. There is, despite the Fifth Elegy's wonderfully sustained attack upon their soul-less "doing," an acrobatic element in Rilke's poetry itself which tinges its successes with the hue of the abstruse. For his most superb accomplishment is the *salto mortale* of despair which lands the soul in a "*Raum der Rühmung,*" a sphere of praise, where all the praise is sung in honor of the singer while the voiceless world, deranged and dizzy, is left behind to face the music.

"What was it that Zarathustra once told you? That poets lie too much?—But Zarathustra too is a poet. . . . *We* lie too much."[56] These words of Nietzsche's sound like an anticipated motto to Rilke's letters. For the utter precariousness of Rilke's vision is exposed most painfully in endless prose variations which form a large part of his correspon-

---

*T. S. Eliot, in discussing the question of whether a poet "thinks," says: "We talk as if thought was precise and emotion was vague. In reality there is precise emotion and there is vague emotion. To express precise emotion requires as great intellectual power as to express precise thought." This is an important point admirably put, although it would be difficult to find a word other than "thought" for the *intellectual* power required to express precise emotion. Yet the passage continues: "But by 'thinking' I mean something different from anything that I find in Shakespeare"—namely, as we saw, "thinking to a purpose," etc. (*Selected Essays,* p. 135).

Asked for a definition of the "unembarrassed greatness of poetry" I should accept Eliot's sentence and say that, among other things, it is "the precise expression of precise emotion." But I should add that precise emotion is a mode of response or even of comprehension, closely linked to thought. Their common medium is language. Indeed, precise emotion is the result of that sustained and refining interaction between thought and emotion to which we give the name of culture. The only measure for the precision of emotion is in its articulation. Inarticulate emotion is vague and thoughtless. And precise emotional articulation in language is possible only within a definite "system of correspondences" between thought, feeling and external impacts. This, however, is hardly provided by the situation in which modern poetry finds itself involved. Its situation is inimical to such precision partly because by "thought," according to T. S. Eliot, we have come to "mean something different from anything" we may find in Shakespeare or Dante.

dence. Only a generation of recipients and readers benumbed and be-
fogged by every conceivable spiritual deprivation, and insensitive to
the intimate relation between language and authenticity, could accept
as genuine spiritual guidance pronouncements which more often than
not show the unmistakable stylistic imprint of untruth; of that most
dangerous kind of untruth which does not spring from fraudulent intent, but from a self-deception so profound that nothing less powerful
than a false inflection, a hollow adjective or a synthetic noun can un-
deceive us of its hypnotic persuasion. Rilke takes the unending curtain
calls which acknowledge his poetic achievement, in the *costume* of his
inspiration. Then the prophecy turns to performance, and the vision-
ary glance seems produced by makeup. But it was Nietzsche, the
thinker, not Rilke, the poet, who was obsessed with the problem of
the actor-artist, as it was Nietzsche who wrote the lines:

> *Dass ich verbannt sei*
> *von aller Wahrheit!*
> *Nur* Narr! *Nur* Dichter! . . . [57]

> Oh, that I am banished
> from all Truth!
> Mere *fool*! Mere *poet*! . . .

This brings to its paradoxical conclusion an argument that took its
bearings from a theory expounding that the poet merely makes poetry
while the thinker is unequivocally bound to his thought.

My earliest serious concern was with the relationship between Art
and Truth," wrote Nietzsche in 1888, just at the end of his conscious
life, in a renewed attempt to understand the mind that in 1870 conceived *The Birth of Tragedy*. "And even now," the meditation continues,
"I am seized with holy terror in the face of that dilemma. The belief
that informs *The Birth of Tragedy* is a belief in Art, against the background of yet another belief: that it is *impossible to live with Truth*. . . .
The will to *illusion* . . . is profounder, more 'metaphysical,' than the
will to Truth, Reality and Being." [58] Thus the essential function of art
is, according to Nietzsche, to think and feel existence to that conclusion which convinces us of its perfection, "to create perfection and the
fullness of life," to "*affirm, bless* and *deify* existence." [59]

This is the perfect definition of Rilke's poetic project. It also marks
the summit reached by art and poetry in its steep ascent to the heights
of absolute creativeness. At this point the separation between art and
reality appears to be complete. Reality is the death of the spirit and art
its salvation. Where does truth reside? Is it in the deadly real world

or in the saving vision of the artist? The question lingers on the all but imperceptible borderline between delusion and lunacy, between Nietzsche's madness and Rilke's prophetic pose, tenaciously maintained even beyond the confines of poetic inspiration. Nietzsche, believing that truth was insufferable and that poetry was an illusion, continually suspected that at least some of his thought was "merely poetry." Rilke, on the other hand, succeeded most of the time in convincing himself that the thought behind his poetry was the mind of truth. Illusion or truth, *Übermensch* or Angel, Will to Power or the Will to Inwardness—in both Nietzsche and Rilke the human mind and imagination are engaged in the ultimate task of creating a world to take the place of the spiritually useless productions of God.

"Indeed, the whole book acknowledges only an artist's meaning behind everything that happens—a 'god' if you like, but certainly only an artist-god . . . desirous of achieving his delight and sovereignty through making things and unmaking them . . . and who, in creating worlds, frees himself from the agony . . . of his inner conflicts. The world . . . seen as the successful salvation of god, as a vision . . . of one who suffers most, one who is the richest in conflicts and contradictions and can only save himself by creating illusion. . . ." [60] The book in question is *The Birth of Tragedy,* thus described by Nietzsche himself in 1886, sixteen years after it was written. A critic could hardly do better in the case of *Duino Elegies* and *Sonnets to Orpheus.*

In January, 1889, Nietzsche, then in Turin, became clinically insane. On the fourth of that month the uncanniest of all calls to Orpheus was posted at the Turin railway station. The note was addressed to Nietzsche's friend, the composer Peter Gast. It ran: "To my maestro Pietro. Sing a new song for me: the world is transfigured and all the heavens rejoice." It was signed "The Crucified."

Sharing with each other the fruits of defeat, inflicted upon all besiegers of the Absolute in a world without Truth, thought ceases to be merely thought and poetry is no longer merely poetry. Song, trying to prove the glory, and thought, determined to dispel the illusion, are adventurers in the same heroic saga. It tells the story of one Tantalus who has deprived the gods of their seats at the banquet. Sitting all by himself at the divinely laid table, he yet cannot eat without letting them into his own secret: that he does not think well enough of himself to believe in the reality of his triumph. This is their curse, which he cannot escape. Intoxicated with their wine, he glories in their absence; but with the sobriety of his thought returning, he sees the water of life receding before the hollow of his outstretched hand.

It is the redeeming achievement of Nietzsche and Rilke that they have raised, the one in the intensely felt plight of his thought, the other in his intensely meditated poetry, the abysmal contradictions of their age to a plane where doubt and confusion once more dissolve into the certainty of mystery.

# YEATS AND NIETZSCHE:

# REFLECTIONS ON AESTHETICISM

# AND A POET'S MARGINAL NOTES

William Butler Yeats most probably came into contact with Nietzsche's thought in 1902. It was only two years after the philosopher's death, but fourteen years after his mind had died in that catastrophe which is recorded in one of the last pieces of coherent, if mad, prose written by him: a postcard mailed at Turin railway station on the 4th of January 1889 and addressed to his friend Peter Gast. "To my maestro Pietro," it began, and then came the Orphic injunction: "Sing a new song for me: the world is transfigured and all the heavens rejoice." It was signed "The Crucified."

This note carried to the young composer not only that strange exalted commission but also, implicitly, the terrible news of Nietzsche's mental collapse. Brief and mad though it is, it is all but a résumé of his early masterpiece *The Birth of Tragedy,* a work which so intriguingly blends the learning and intuition of the classical philologist with the dithyrambic confession of a soul singularly initiated, as he believed, into the secret of beauty; that it emerges from pain and suffering, that Apollo's command of surpassingly beautiful forms derives its power from the frenzy of Dionysus's dismemberment. Thinking of Greek tragedy and Greek art, Nietzsche was inspired by Schopenhauer's metaphysical pessimism and aesthetic exultancy as well as by the Romantic trinity of love, death, and music upon which Wagner's *Tristan und Isolde* is founded. Treating in so Romantic a manner even so Classical a subject, he pronounced with the utmost lucidity the central dogma of the new philosophy of art: "Only as an aesthetic phenomenon is the world for ever justified." How unimaginably must those Greeks have been wounded by life, Nietzsche exclaimed, to redeem its horrors in such epiphany of the Beautiful! Nietzsche, this Christian of the aesthetic passion, believed—as early as *The Birth of Tragedy* of 1871–72, and not only when he sent that insane message to his friend the composer—that it was the crucified spirit which in its agony acquired the power to transfigure the world through beauty so that all the heavens rejoiced. "Sing a new song for me. . . ."

There is no other poet of the twentieth century who *sang* so greatly even of his agonies as did Yeats:

> An aged man is but a paltry thing,
> A tattered coat upon a stick, unless
> Soul clap its hands and sing, and louder sing
> For every tatter in its mortal dress. . . .

And further:

> Once out of nature I shall never take
> My bodily form from any natural thing,
> But such a form as Grecian goldsmiths make
> Of hammered gold and gold enamelling
> To keep a drowsy Emperor awake;
> Or set upon a golden bough to sing
> To lords and ladies of Byzantium
> Of what is past, or passing, or to come.
>
> ('Sailing to Byzantium')

This song of the Irish sailor would suffice to show the affinity between Yeats's sensibility and Nietzsche's aesthetic philosophy. Of course, Yeats had not "learned" it; but he discovered that Nietzsche was the great anatomist of the epoch's body of art. This is how Nietzsche nearly became one of the "singing masters" of the poet's soul, that soul which, "fastened to a dying animal," desired to be gathered "into the artifice of eternity"—desired (in Nietzsche's words) to attain to that redeeming vision of world and existence in which world and existence are for ever justified: namely, as something "out of nature" and "beyond the dying animal," as an "aesthetic phenomenon" or an "artifice of eternity."

Of course, such wisdom and such desire entail, just as the Christian vision and desire for eternity once did, the distress the spirit suffers in the *world as it is,* that is, the world before the arrival of the saving grace; or (in the nineteenth and twentieth centuries) the aesthetic metamorphosis. Yeats's "artifice of eternity" and Nietzsche's "aesthetic phenomenon" are, in all their apparent artificiality and "aestheticism," blood relations of the Apocalypse. They spring from the same source as the Christian belief that the world is doomed unless it be transfigured in a final act of salvation. Neither the meaning of Nietzsche's "aesthetic phenomenon" nor of his supremely "aesthetic" *Übermensch* is comprehensible without the story which (as he once said) his philosophy tells, namely "the history of the next two centuries":

For a long time now our whole civilization has been driving, with a tortured intensity that increases from decade to decade, as if towards a catastrophe: restlessly, violently, tempestuously, like a mighty river craving the end of its journey without pausing to reflect, indeed fearful of reflection. . . . Where we live, soon nobody will be able to exist.[1]

Or elsewhere:

I foresee something terrible. Chaos everywhere; nothing left which is of any value; nothing which commands: Thou shalt[2]

And just as Nietzsche's aesthetic philosophy eludes our grasp if we do not see it as the aesthetic refuge from his apocalyptic diagnosis of our "reality," so Yeats's aesthetic "Byzantinism," so important in his education as a poet, cannot be fathomed to the depth of its impulse if we do not relate its apotheosis of art to his poem "The Second Coming." For it is indeed Nietzsche's prophecy of "what is to come" that in this poem assumes the form of grand verse:

> Turning and turning in the widening gyre
> The falcon cannot hear the falconer;
> Things fall apart; the centre cannot hold;
> Mere anarchy is loosed upon the world,
> The blood-dimmed tide is loosed, and everywhere
> The ceremony of innocence is drowned;
> The best lack all conviction, while the worst
> Are full of passionate intensity.

I apologize for quoting these lines of Yeats, worn as they are by constant use, but they succinctly make my point. For it is my contention that the religion of Art, the deification of the "artifice of eternity" or the "aesthetic phenomenon," which for many great and good minds of the last hundred years had taken the place once held by a different gospel of salvation, is supported—as, at its origin, the Christian religion was—by the sense of a condemned "real word." This is certainly true of such *religiosi* of Art as Baudelaire, Rimbaud, and Mallarmé; of Nietzsche, Rilke, and Stefan George; and it is true of the Yeats of "The Second Coming":

> The darkness drops again; but now I know
> That twenty centuries of stony sleep
> Were vexed to nightmare by a rocking cradle,
> And what rough beast, its hour come round at last,
> Slouches towards Bethlehem to be born?

Although such rhetorical questions do not require any answers, this one was answered by Nietzsche long before Yeats asked it. The beast to be born was the Anti-Christ; and this is what, when he was already close to insanity, Nietzsche called himself. He did so at about the time he wrote, "We have *Art* in order *not to perish of Truth.*"[3]

2

About 1902, then, Yeats discovered Nietzsche, very likely through a little volume ambitiously entitled *Nietzsche as Critic, Philosopher, Poet and Prophet,* described more modestly in the subtitle as "Choice Selections from his Works" (and compiled by a man who most humbly and, considering the aristocratic doctrines that anthology contains, somewhat inappropriately was called Thomas Common). The book was published in 1901 in London, and is now (such are the vagaries of our travelsome scholarship) kept under lock and key in the Deering Library of Northwestern University. The poet read the book with an active and capricious pencil in his hand. He heavily underlined sentences, scribbled queries, arguments, and even little discourses in the margins, and thus, very differently from what in the assessment of librarians the scribblings of lesser readers would do to a book, considerably raised its value.

A comparison between Nietzsche's text and Yeats's marginal entries may supply the student with many insights into the troublesome problem of "influence," that is, the effect one creative mind has upon another. T. S. Eliot, in his essay "Tradition and the Individual Talent," compared the receptive mind of the poet to a catalyst, an "impersonal" chemical presence that, a little in the manner of the philosopher Don Alfonso in Mozart's *Cosi fan tutte,* contrives the union of elements, hitherto otherwise engaged, and then discreetly withdraws from the newly compounded and sometimes confounded scene. (There is indeed no trace of Don Alfonso's agency discernible in the music that wittily and sublimely voices the fresh and faithless enchantments drawing the exchanged lovers towards one another.) Whether the poetic mind acts on all occasions like Don Alfonso, the philosophical catalyst, is doubtful. In our instance it is certainly not the "subjectivity" of the *poet* but rather the mind of the *thinker* that tends to vanish as soon as Yeats becomes entangled, in the margin, with Nietzsche's ideas. There are, for instance, in Thomas Common's anthology a number of passages from Nietzsche's *Genealogy of Morals;* they denounce the "Christian infamy" of promising the virtuously weak and meek, deprived of many pleasures here and now, the compensations of an afterlife when they will be privileged to watch the hellish torments of those who were strong and wicked on earth. Dante—so we read in Nietzsche's lines—committed a spiritual *faux pas* of the first order when he put above the gates of Hell the inscription, "*I too have been created by Love Eternal.*" For if we accept the opinion of Dante's theological teacher, St. Thomas Aquinas, the Love Eternal that created Hell made it for the purpose of perversely rewarding its darlings. Thomas, "the great teacher and saint," we learn from Nietzsche's text that lay open before Yeats, promised, "with the gentleness of a lamb," that "the Blessed in Heaven will see how the Damned are punished, and thus will enjoy their own beatitude even more." And Nietzsche reflects that, whatever might be a suitable text for the gates of Hell, at the entrance door of a Paradise with such a profitable view of the tormented could be inscribed with greater justice: "*I too have been created by Eternal Hatred.*"

One might expect that this would have been of some interest to Yeats, the Irish renegade Protestant with (as he put it) "a wicked theology" of his own, who at about that time had his first meeting with the ill-mannered James Joyce and mistakenly tried to ascribe the young man's intellectual arrogance to his Thomist indoctrination:

> He is from the Royal [the Catholic Dublin] University, I thought, and he thinks that everything has been settled by Thomas Aquinas, so we need not trouble about it.

But all that Yeats says in the margin of Nietzsche's anti-Christian and anti-Thomist diatribe is:

> Does Christianity create commerce by teaching men to live not in the continual present of self-revelation but to deny self and present for future gain, first heaven and then wealth?

It sounds as if it had been written by the Fabian R. H. Tawney after a first reading of Max Weber and in preparation of his book on *Religion and the Rise of Capitalism*. Strange, very strange. But even stranger is the question that Yeats asks immediately afterwards:

> But why does Nietzsche think that the night has no stars, nothing but bats and owls and the insane moon?

Now, Nietzsche does not think anything of the sort, and besides, nowhere near this Yeatsian query does Nietzsche's text mention any such nocturnal apparitions. Yet while these are entirely foreign to the text

on which they appear to comment, they are germane to some poems
Yeats wrote at the time:

> Because of something told under the famished horn
> Of the hunter's moon, that hung between the night and the day. . . .
>
> ("Under the Moon")

Or, most strikingly, this:

> I cried when the moon was murmuring to the birds:
> "Let peewit call and curlew cry where they will,
> I long for your merry and tender and pitiful words,
> For the roads are unending, and there is no place to my mind."
>
> ("The Withering of the Boughs")

Whatever may be the intellectual, translatably sane meaning of that
insane moon (perhaps the moon of the *Vision* in her "famished horn"
phase?) or of those marginal bats and owls (perhaps poetry's second
cousins to the peewits and curlews?), only a mind, kept very busy by
its own poetic affairs, would read another writer's writing with such
imaginative impatience. Or to put the matter more frivolously: he
who has bees in his bonnet reads not so much for the love of what he
reads as for the honey to be made from it; and not since Blake has there
been, in the history of great English poetry, a bonnet like Yeats's, buzz-
ing with so many agile bees.

Clearly, we have to guard against misinterpreting the nature of the
"influence" Nietzsche had upon Yeats, indeed the kind of intellectual
reception one creative spirit can possibly give to another. True, the
examples shown constitute an extreme case of what in university syl-
labuses is called "independent reading"; at other times Yeats has dealt
less extravagantly with Nietzsche's possessions. Yet when mind comes
to mind, what happens is never like the printing of words upon an
empty sheet. It is more—to keep within Yeats's symbols—like Jupiter
visiting Leda; and this visitation, surely, did not result in the lady's
becoming more "jovial"; nor "did she put on his knowledge with his
power." No, she became pregnant with her own mythology.

When Yeats read Nietzsche for the first time, he probably read more
of him than is collected in Thomas Common's *Choice Selections*. For
the "strong enchanter" (as Yeats called Nietzsche in a letter he wrote
in August 1902 to Lady Gregory) made him neglect his friends, wors-
ened his eyesight by making him read to excess, and filled him with a
"curious astringent joy," three words that could be lifted from the letter and put down again in a line of Yeatsian poetry. About twenty years

later Yeats published *A Vision,* a book that not only owes something to Nietzsche's vision of both the Eternal Recurrence and the *Übermensch* but also elevates Nietzsche to the highest office ever assigned to him in the varied history of his reputation:

> . . .Eleven pass, and then
> Athena takes Achilles by the hair,
> Hector is in the dust, Nietzsche is born,
> Because the hero's crescent is the twelfth.
> ("The Phases of the Moon")

Not even in his most euphoric moments would Nietzsche have dreamt of such a career: from Thomas Common's *Choice Selections* to this most uncommon succession. It needed Ireland, it needed Yeats, the last great poet who—after Blake, after Hölderlin—dared aspire to a systematic mythology (and this mythological ambition is inseparable from the particular quality of his poetic greatness)—it needed Yeats so dramatically to make good the neglect Nietzsche had suffered in his lifetime.

### 3

Like much in Nietzsche's writings, Yeats's *Vision* ought to embarrass us, aesthetic educators that we claim to be, much more painfully than it appears to have done. It should compel us to ponder more seriously the questions it raises—not by what it says but by what it is: a disturbing mixture of obsessive mythologizing, pseudo-cosmological meticulousness, acute critical observations, and most outlandish beliefs. At least one of the questions that it thus invites is of the greatest urgency—and it is a question also suggested again and again by the reading of Nietzsche. It concerns the eccentricity of thought, the strains of the fancy, the self-conscious mysticism, and even the monstrosities of political ideas that, with disquieting regularity, came to the fore when sallies into "life" were made by the life-starved inhabitants of the ivory towers. Nasty creatures lay in wait where the philosophy of French symbolism (a philosophy that was an essential part of Yeats's inheritance) met with German or even Italian appetites for political realities that were to be charged with the same wild, quivering, ruthless, "terrible" beauty a perfect Symbolist poem possessed; where the exodus of art, from "life" reached, at the end of its circular journey, the border of the "real" world again, determined now to invade it with barbaric ecstasies, knights in shining armor, and flags flying in the wind like so many birds of paradise; and where even Yeats, using Nietzsche's Dionysian and Apollonian vocabulary, confessed (as he did in a letter to George Russell, May 14, 1903) that the time for pursuing through poetry "some kind of disembodied beauty" had passed: "I feel about me and in me," he wrote, "an impulse to . . . carry the realisation of beauty as far as possible." Consciously, he may have meant only his desire "to create form" through poetry of a more Apollonian kind than ever before. But the very words "to carry the realisation of beauty as far as possible" do point in the direction of the poet D'Annunzio's march on Fiume, or put one in mind of the disturbing ambiguities of Stefan George's poem "The Burning of the Temple," not to mention Yeats's own flirtations with the Blue Shirts of Dublin.

It was all very well for that sophisticated cold-and-hot-gospeler of unbridled aestheticism, Villiers de l'Isle-Adam, whose *Axël* Yeats once called his "sacred book," to say that nothing counted in life but the cultivation and contemplation of beauty: "As for living, our servants will do that for us. . . ." Yeats was fond of quoting this (and quoted it even in one of those stories that, very oddly, preface his *Vision*). Of course, the French writer's "cultivation of beauty"—with nothing else "counting"—is his version of Nietzsche's doctrine from *The Birth of Tragedy* (note well: of tragedy!): "Only as an aesthetic phenomenon are world and existence for ever justified," or "The purpose of life is . . . the pure aesthetic delight." It is Nietzsche transposed into the lighter idiom of *Axël*. "As for living, our servants will do that for us"—yet there came a time (the First World War was its beginning) when the servants did the living and, for that matter, the dying with such violent intensity that it seemed to acquire a perverse beauty of its own in the eyes of some pure aesthetic beholders, so much so that the swans and herons and albatrosses and flamingos and peacocks and all the rest of the aristocratic Symbolist poultry had to give way to more "real" raw material of the creative imagination: destroy the cities of man so that, perhaps, they might be rebuilt after the images of pure aesthetic delight. (There was once a man who thought of himself as an artist. He wanted to be a painter and failed. But he succeeded in using his country, his continent, as the canvas on which he set out to realize his sick, megalomaniac vision of an ideal world, blotting out with insane intensity the mistakes made, he believed, by the previous creator, History.)*

One day *this* story of aestheticism will have to be written. It might take its cue from Thomas Mann's *Doctor Faustus,* the story of the artist

---

*Cf. the end of the essay "Nietzsche's Last Words about Art versus Truth."

who (like his forerunner, Gustav Aschenbach in *Death in Venice*) came to know the swampy, sultry estuaries in which the cold, pearly, translucent streams of the land wholly dedicated to Art may reach their destination. Or it might take as its point of departure Yeats himself who, in the *Autobiography,* concludes the chapter on "The Tragic Generation" in a manner more Nietzschean than he himself is likely to have known: "After Stéphane Malarmé, after Paul Verlaine, after Gustave Moreau, after Puvis de Chavannes, after our own verse, after all our subtle colour and nervous rhythm, after the faint mixed tints of Conder, what more is possible? After us the Savage God," or the beast of the final lines of "The Second Coming":

> And what rough beast, its hour come round at last,
> Slouches towards Bethlehem to be born?

Nietzsche had diagnosed such pregnancy in the aesthetic absolutism of earlier artists: Baudelaire and Flaubert. He indeed was acquainted with the Furies of annihilation into which the Muses of aestheticism might one day transform themselves. Beauty into Beast—this is, if not *the* last scene, undoubtedly one of the concluding scenes in the drama of aestheticism, a scene evoked once again in Yeats's late poem "Meru" (which is Nietzschean in a more thorough sense than the first obviousness reveals):

> Civilisation is hooped together, brought
> Under a rule, under the semblance of peace
> By manifold illusion; but man's life is thought,
> And he, despite his terror, cannot cease
> Ravening, raging, and uprooting that he may come
> Into the desolation of reality:
> Egypt and Greece, good-bye, and good-bye, Rome!

4

This is not the occasion for an exercise in "close reading." Yet the terrible meaning of "Meru" ought not to be allowed to escape us, the less so as these lines take up back from 1935 (the time when they were written) to 1902, the time of Yeats's first reading of Nietzsche. "But man's life is thought"—that is, the uniquely human faculty which in Yeats's much earlier poem "Michael Robartes and the Dancer" (1921) had assumed the funny shape of a half-dead dragon, at least in so far as it was a beautiful lady who did the thinking and thus puritanically interfered with her suitor's desire:

> Opinion is not worth a rush;
> In this altar-piece the knight
> Who grips his long spear so to push
> That dragon through the fading light,
> Loved the lady; and it's plain
> The half-dead dragon was her thought,
> That every morning rose again
> And dug its claws and shrieked and fought.
> Could the impossible come to pass
> She would have time to turn her eyes,
> Her lover thought, upon the glass
> And on the instant would grow wise.

In other words—even Yeats's other words—she should forgo thinking and submit instead to "the heroic discipline of the looking-glass." Critics of Yeats have acquired the habit of calling this poem "witty and charming." Yes, it is quite witty, but it is not charming. As it progresses, it becomes blasphemous and abysmal. There is, perhaps, not much to be said against either blasphemies or abysses; yet whatever adjectives we may choose for abysses, "charming" is the wrong one. Now, if this witty poem presents "Thought" in the guise of a grotesque thing, a half-dead dragon, in the much later poem "Meru" the dragon has become truly formidable. "Thought," in "Michael Robartes and the Dancer," was just powerful enough to make women ignore the wisdom of the mirror, obstruct the natural intelligence and "uncomposite blessedness" of their beautiful bodies, frustrate their lovers, and grow perplexed at the amorously and blasphemously theological question:

> Did God in portioning wine and bread
> Give man His thought or His mere body?—

In "Meru," however, "thought" has consequences still weightier than the erotic disappointment of the ardent knight. It causes man to rave and rage and desolate his reality. Why? The question is important, and the answer given within the poem "Meru" itself is: because thought makes man recognize as sham a civilization hooped together by manifold illusion; and clearly there can be nothing very objectionable about thought that shows illusions for what they are, namely illusory. In "Michael Robartes and the Dancer," then, "thought" is wrong and erroneous; it prevents the woman from seeing what truly is: the joy (joyous beyond all thoughtful questions and disputes) of erotic abandonment. In "Meru," on the contrary, "thought" is right: it compels man to recognize the essential falsity of his civilized arrangements: these *are,* it is implied, "hooped together by manifold illusion." But in either case, whether it be true or false, "thought" is disastrous. In both cases it is thought that has *and* reveals such deplorable results.

The sad story is a very old one: the Tree of Knowledge does not stand for the good life. Again and again, and with increasing urgency in his later years, Yeats returned to the grand theme. The question, taken up, varied, and variously answered by his poetry, is: Why does man seem to have to choose between the perfection of life and that perfection which resides in the works of the mind, a mind trained "in a learned school" with such intensity that body and blood are condemned to "slow decay" and "dull decrepitude"? Or is there, will there ever be, a "spiritual intellect" capable of that serene profundity which gives to its thought a "dance-like" glory? Or would "life" and "mind" one day be reconciled in that "lasting song," the singing of which is utterly beyond the power of men thinking "in the mind alone," but is sung with splendid ease by him who "thinks in a marrow-bone"? Of course, the theme has not been invented by Yeats, and not by Nietzsche either—although Zarathustra is among prophets the keenest in extolling the marriage between thought and dance, the keenest too in aspiring to that Yeatsian realm of the spirit where

> The body is not bruised to pleasure soul,
> Nor beauty born out of its own despair,
> Nor blear-eyed wisdom out of midnight oil,

but where, on the contrary, the body is the soul's delight, where all nay-saying is given the lie by the advent of the Beautiful, and where the joyous sage gives of his wisdom in the light of noonday. Yet this may have been before the birth of tragedy, before the "harsh reproof," the "trivial event" that changed the "childish day to tragedy," or after the fulfillment of that persistent Romantic hope that longs for the healing of the wound from which man has suffered ever since the Fall. This hope has been voiced by innumerable voices, and with particular poetic emphasis throughout the Romantic age, but by no one, I believe, more poignantly or more enticingly than by Yeats in the eighth stanza of his "Among School Children," a stanza that by itself is one of his best poems, untired yet and surely not to be exhausted by being used and quoted so profusely. For that chestnut-tree and great-rooted blossomer has grown from the richest soil of Romantic poetry. It embodies the Romantic vision of the Tree of Life that has the power to cure the disease man has contracted through so greedily reaching for the Tree of Knowledge:

> O chestnut-tree, great-rooted blossomer,
> Are you the leaf, the blossom or the bole?
> O body swayed to music, O brightning glance,
> How can we know the dancer from the dance?

Alas, once out of the delicious light and shade of the great tree, we can know and we do know. Nietzsche has much to tell of dancers who wear their dance like a mask of innocence. And Rilke (another remarkable poet who had read Nietzsche, had a Tower in which to write poetry, an even more aristocratic Lady Gregory to help and encourage him, and in the end even a mythology which, though less astrological and more poetic than Yeats's, is not altogether lacking in parallels to his)—Rilke, in the Fourth of the *Duino Elegies,* angrily dismisses *his* dancer, the dancer who theatrically dances before the backdrop of "the well-known garden." He dismisses him because he *is* not what he *does,* but is disguised, "a mask half-filled with life," and will be a mediocrity as soon as the performance is over and the makeup removed.

The figure of that dancer came to Rilke from Kleist's essayistic story about the Marionette Theatre, a story in which this most Romantic theme is treated with the lucidity of genius. The theme is, of course, that of the Fall and the story that of modern man: his painfully growing awareness of the lost unity between the dancer and the dance. Consciousness, self-consciousness, thought—the thought of Yeats's "Michael Robartes and the Dancer" and "Meru"—stands between man and his desire for the spontaneity of innocence and the integrity of being. Schiller, Kleist, and above all Hegel, believed that the Paradise, once lost, could only be regained *by thought,* by thought reaching that apex where consciousness itself becomes the crystallizing force of a new and higher unity. Later sufferers of the metaphysical discomfort—Nietzsche, for example, D. H. Lawrence, or Yeats—were more impatient. Long before D. H. Lawrence discovered the liberating powers of Priapus, Nietzsche enthroned and celebrated Dionysus, the god of intoxication and ecstasy, in whose revels the conscious and self-conscious self vanishes, merging as it does with that universal dance that is not so much danced by the dancers as it *is* the dancers in their orgiastic self-forgetfulness. Nietzsche, Lawrence, Yeats—it would indeed be a great comfort if the world in which they wrote had afterwards embarked upon a different history. As it is, it is impossible to be sure that its recent terrors have nothing whatever to do with the fascinations the dark river gods of the blood and the soil, Dionysus, Priapus, or Pan, have held for those minds.

5

When Yeats first read Thomas Common's anthology, he came upon some passages from the *Anti-Christ,* written by Nietzsche during the last months before his mental breakdown. It is likely that neither the compilator nor the reader recognized their vertiginous ambivalence, the ambivalence of the Romantic mind, the modern mind, at that pitch to which it rose with and through Nietzsche. In one of those passages Nietzsche speaks, with the violent brilliance his style assumed at that time, of the need for a new instinctive unreflectiveness in man's dealings with the aristocratic values by which he ought to live; of the need for an "automatism of instinct" to be achieved by the new élite; the achievement indeed of the oneness of dance and dancer. At that point Yeats noted in the margin:

Were bodily functions like that of the pulse once conscious?

This is an absurd yet most revealing marginal gloss, and one that certainly does not ride roughshod over Nietzsche's meanings as other Yeatsian glosses in the margins of that anthology had done. The history of the world, it implies, is not what (among others) Hegel imagined it to be: a constant progress from "natural" functions towards consciousness. The opposite may be true: consciousness may be the primitive beginning, the unconsciousness the end. While Hegel thought that art, the product of the imagination, would have no place in the domain of absolute consciousness, Yeats's query reads, on the contrary, like a promise given to the artist that his "spontaneous creativity" would inherit the earth. Dance and dancer would once again be one. What is in the making in that margin is the anachronism of an artistic eschatology. The Day of Judgment will be the Day of Art. Such was the grand superstition of aestheticism.

It was, perhaps, this vestigially sustained anachronism that gave to Yeats's poetry the uninhibited poetic eloquence that is not likely to find its equal in whatever the future may hold for the art of language. If in Nietzsche's last message to his composer friend the earth was transfigured and all the heavens rejoiced, then it was Yeats's aim to allow the earth, even without its transfiguration, to rejoice with the joys of the old heavens. We are indeed the poorer, if less anachronistic, for not being able to believe in so happy an ending. Nietzsche, again and again, rehearsed such a blissful consummation. It was of no avail. In his beginning as well as in his end he knew that whosoever has built a new Heaven has gathered the strength for it in his own Hell; and this Hell, although he was certainly no Hegelian, was not altogether different from what Hegel meant by the unhappy consciousness. If there is to be Heaven again, it will be at the end of the mind's journey, not somewhere in the middle of it, brought to a halt there by the force of some dream of the imagination. Perhaps this is what T. S. Eliot meant when, *in a poem,* he wrote: "The poetry does not matter."

Oh yes, it matters, it matters very much. But there is no salvation through consciously induced spontaneities, and there is no salvation through Art.

# WITTGENSTEIN AND NIETZSCHE

What manner of man was Ludwig Wittgenstein? One answer which is easy to come by, vague, large, and true, is: a man of rarest genius. Of all words that defy definition—which may be, simply, all words—genius is the most defiant. But how else describe a man who was a logician of the first order; a writer of German prose abundant in intellectual passion and disciplined clarity (perhaps only talent is needed for writing such prose in any other language, but certainly genius for writing it in German); an engineer of great promise and some achievement; the architect of a modern mansion; a gifted sculptor; a musician who very probably would have become, had he chosen this career, a remarkable conductor; a hermit capable of enduring for long periods the utmost rigors of mind and loneliness; a rich man who chose poverty; a Cambridge professor who thought and taught but neither lectured nor dined?

He was also an Austrian who conquered British philosophy; but this, as befits Austrian conquests, was due to a misunderstanding. At least he himself believed that it was so. When the pages of the journal *Mind* were filled with variations on his philosophical themes, he praised a certain American magazine of detective stories, and wondered how, with the offer of such reading matter, "anyone can read

The original occasion of this essay was the appearance of Ludwig Wittgenstein's *The Blue and Brown Books* (Oxford: Basil Blackwell, 1958. New York: Harper, 1958), and Norman Malcolm's *Ludwig Wittgenstein, A Memoir*, with a biographical sketch by Georg Henrik von Wright (London and New York: Oxford University Press, 1958). *The Blue and Brown Books*, prefaced by Rush Rhees, were dictated by Wittgenstein to some of his pupils between 1933 and 1935. They are indispensable for any study of the intellectual history that led, within the lifetime of a whole generation of Anglo-Saxon philosophers, to a change in philosophical opinion—a break outwardly less dramatic but probably more significant than that which occurred when Bertrand Russell and G. E. Moore banished the very much post-Hegelian metaphysics of F. H. Bradley and Bernard Bosanquet from the academic scene; and it was the most strange characteristic of that new "revolution" that it was the same man, Ludwig Wittgenstein, who both perfected the "old system" (in the *Tractatus Logico-Philosophicus*, finished by 1918, first published in 1921) *and* initiated its destruction (with *Philosophical Investigations*, completed by 1949, posthumously published in 1953). Malcolm's *Memoir*, greatly assisted by Professor Wright's informative sketch, is a noble biographical document, the more moving by virtue of its simplicity and affectionate restraint. It is from this book that the biographical references of my notes are taken.

*Mind* with all its impotence and bankruptcy";[1] and when his influence at Oxford was at its height, he referred to the place as "a philosophical desert" and as "the influenza area."[2] These were ironical exaggerations, but undoubtedly serious expressions of Wittgenstein's discontent.

Why should he have been so displeased with the role his thought played in contemporary philosophical circles? What was the source of his suspicion that a misunderstanding was viciously at work in the proliferation of his views and methods throughout the departments of philosophy? And if it was a misunderstanding, was it avoidable? These questions raise a bigger one: What is the nature of philosophical opinion?

There are philosophies which, however difficult they may be, are in principle easy to teach and to learn. Of course, not everyone can teach or learn philosophy—any more than higher mathematics; but the philosophies of certain philosophers have this in common with higher mathematics: they present the simple alternative of being either understood or not understood. It is, in the last analysis, impossible to *mis*understand them. This is true of Aristotle, or St. Thomas Aquinas, or Descartes, or Locke, or Kant. Such philosophies are like mountains: you climb to their tops or you give up; or like weights: you lift them or they are too heavy for you. In either case you will know what has happened and "where you are." But this is not so with the thought of Plato, or St. Augustine, or Pascal, or Kierkegaard, or Nietzsche. Their philosophies are like human faces on the features of which are inscribed, disquietingly, the destinies of souls; or like cities rich in history. "Do you understand Kant?" is like asking "Have you been to the summit of Mont Blanc?" The answer is *yes* or *no*. "Do you understand Nietzsche?" is like asking "Do you know Rome?" The answer is simple only if you have never been there. The trouble with Wittgenstein's thinking is that it sometimes looks like Descartes's: you believe you can learn it as you learn logic or mathematics; but it almost always is more like Pascal's: you may be quite sure you cannot. For to understand it on its own level is as much a matter of imagination and character as it is one of "thinking." Its temperature is of its essence, in its passion lies its seriousness, the rhythm of the sentences that express it is as telling as is that which they tell, and sometimes a semicolon marks the frontier between a thought and a triviality. How can this be? Are we speaking of an artist or a philosopher? We are speaking of Ludwig Wittgenstein. "*Der Philosoph behandelt eine Frage; wie eine Krankheit.*" It is a profound semicolon, and not even a philosophically initiated translator could save the profundity: "The philosopher's treatment of a question is like the treatment of an illness" is, by comparison, a flat *aperçu*.[3]

Philosophy, for Wittgenstein, was not a profession; it was a consuming passion; and not just "a" passion, but the only possible form of his existence: the thought of losing his gift for philosophy made him feel suicidal. He could not but have contempt for philosophers who "did" philosophy and, having done it, thought of other things: money, lists of publications, academic advancements, university intrigues, love affairs, or the Athenaeum—and thought of these things in a manner which showed even more clearly than the products of their philosophical thought that they had philosophized with much less than their whole person. Wittgenstein had no difficulty in detecting in their style of thinking, debating, or writing the corruption of the divided life, the painless jugglery with words and meanings, the shallow flirtation with depth, and the ear deaf to the command of authenticity. Thinking for him was as much a moral as an intellectual concern. In this lay his affinity with Otto Weininger, for whom he had great respect. The sight of a thought that was detachable from a man filled him with loathing and with an anger very much like that with which Rilke in the Fourth of the *Duino Elegies* denounced, through the image of the dancer, the cursed non-identity between performer and performance:

> . . . How gracefully he moves!
> And yet he is disguised, a dressed-up philistine,
> who will come home soon, entering through the kitchen.
> I cannot bear these masks, half-filled with life.

Had Wittgenstein ever cared to write about himself, this apparently most "intellectual" of philosophers might have said:

> I have at all times thought with my whole body and my whole life. I do not know what purely intellectual problems are. . . . You know these things by way of thinking, yet your thought is not your experience but the reverberation of the experience of others; as your room trembles when a carriage passes. I am sitting in that carriage, and often am the carriage itself.

This, however, was written by Nietzsche.[4] And it was Nietzsche whom he resembled in many other ways: in his homelessness, his restless wanderings, his perpetual search for the exactly right conditions in which to work, his loneliness, his asceticism, his need for affection and his shyness in giving it, his intellectual extremism which drove thought to the border of insanity, the elasticity of his style, and (as we shall see) in one philosophically most important respect. Like Nietzsche, then, he knew that philosophical opinion was not merely a matter of logically demonstrable right or wrong. This most rigorous logician was convinced that it was above all a matter of authenticity—and thus, in a sense, not at all of negotiable opinions. What assumed with him so often the semblance of intolerable intellectual pride, was the demand, which he made upon himself still more than upon others, that all utterances should be absolutely authentic. The question was not only "Is this opinion right or wrong?" but also "Is this or that person *entitled* to this or that opinion?" At times this lent to his manner of debating the harsh tone of the Old Testament prophets: he would suddenly be seized by an uncontrollable desire to mete out intellectual punishment. He reacted to errors of judgment as if they were sins of the heart, and vehemently rejected opinions, which in themselves—if this distinction were possible—might have been harmless enough or even "correct," and rejected them because they were untrue in the self that uttered them: they lacked the sanction of the moral and intellectual pain suffered on behalf of truth.

Wittgenstein once said, using a comparison with swimming, that "just as one's body has a natural tendency towards the surface and one has to make an exertion to get to the bottom—so it is with thinking." And in talking about the stature of a philosopher, he remarked "that the measure of a man's greatness would be in terms of what his work *cost* him."[5] This is Kantian ethics applied to the realm of thought: true moral goodness was for Kant a victory over natural inclination, the costlier the better. By character and insight, Nietzsche too was such a Kantian moralist of the intellectual life. yet he, who was never more ingenious than in producing the devastating argument against himself, could also say this:

> The labor involved in climbing a mountain is no measure of its height. But where knowledge is concerned, it is to be different; at least this is what we are told by some who consider themselves initiates: the effort which a truth costs, is to decide its value! This crazy morality is founded upon the idea that "truths" are like the installations in a Swedish gymnasium, designed to tire one out—a morality of the mind's athletics and gymnastic displays.[6]

Perhaps it is a pity that Wittgenstein was not the man to say things of this kind. It might have lightened the burden of earnest irritability carried by many a philosophical debate.

2

The appreciation of Wittgenstein as a person and thinker (and how misleading is this "and"!) is bedeviled by a persistent optical delusion: the high moral pathos of his life (in which his "legend" has already taken firm roots) *seems* at first glance to be unconnected with the drift and trend, the content and method of his philosophical thought. Every page of Pascal, or Kierkegaard, or Nietzsche, at once conveys, however impersonal may be the subject matter, a sense of urgent personal involvement; but it is possible for anyone but the most sensitively predisposed to read many pages of Wittgenstein's without suspecting that the ruthless precision and often apparently eccentric virtuosity of this thinking, which has neither models nor parallels in the history of philosophy, is anything but the result of the utmost intellectual detachment. Its first emotional effect upon the reader may well be one of exasperation or melancholia—the effect which Robert Musil (not for nothing an Austrian contemporary of Wittgenstein's) ascribes in *The Man without Qualities* to a certain thinker:

> He had drawn the curtains and worked in the subdued light of his room like an acrobat who, in an only half-illuminated circus tent and before the public is admitted, shows to a select audience of experts his latest break-neck leaps.[7]

Yet Wittgenstein's work is none the less suffused with authentic pathos, and it will one day be seen as an integral part of the tragically self-destructive design of European thought.

If by some miracle both European history and thought continue, then the future historians of thought will be not a little puzzled by Wittgenstein. For nothing could be less predictable than that a work which more deeply than any other affected Anglo-Saxon philosophy, Wittgenstein's *Philosophical Investigations,* should have as its motto a sentence from the classical comic playwright of Austria, Nestroy, or that its philosophical author should have experienced a kind of religious awakening thanks to a performance of *Die Kreuzelscheiber* by Anzengruber, a considerably lesser Austrian dramatist.[8] However, these will be minor surprises, less important, certainly, than the discovery of the affinities between Wittgenstein's manner of thinking and writing and that of the great eighteenth-century German aphorist Lichtenberg.* But of greater weight still would be the realization that

---

*Professor Wright was, to my knowledge, the first to draw attention to this; a fuller discussion of this intellectual kinship can; be found in J. P. Stern's book on Lichtenberg: *A Doctrine of Occasions* (Bloomington, Ind., 1959).

the name of Wittgenstein marks the historical point at which, most unexpectedly, the cool analytical intellect of British philosophy meets with those passions of mind and imagination which we associate first with Nietzsche and then, in manifold crystallizations, with such Austrians as Otto Weininger, Adolf Loos, Karl Kraus, Franz Kafka, and Robert Musil.

Like Otto Weininger, Wittgenstein believed in the surpassing ethical significance of thinking, and in thought as both a deeply personal and almost religiously supra-personal dedication; with Adolf Loos he shared the rejection of all ornamental comforts and decorative relaxations of the mind, and the concentration on the purest lines of intellectual architecture; with Karl Kraus, he had in common the conviction that there is an inescapable bond between the forms of living, thinking, feeling, and the forms of language (Wittgenstein's dictum "Ethics and aesthetics are one and the same"[9] may serve as a perfect characterization of Karl Kraus's artistic *credo*). As far as Kafka and Musil are concerned, a comparison between their styles of writing (and therefore their modes of perception) and Wittgenstein's would certainly be as fruitful as that between his and Lichtenberg's, and the more revealing because there can be no question of influence beyond the anonymous and peculiarly Austrian dispensations of the *Zeitgeist*. There even is a family resemblance between the logical structures, motives, and intentions of Wittgenstein's *Tractatus* and those of Schönberg's musical theory: for Schönberg too is guided by the conviction that the "language" of his medium, music, has to be raised to that level of logical necessity which would eliminate all subjective accidents. It is in such a constellation of minds that Wittgenstein is truly at home, whereas in the history of British philosophy he may merely "hold an important position." This, at least, is one way of accounting for the discomforts he suffered from the British philosophical climate and from a philosophical company which so deceptively appeared to consist largely of his own disciples.

What are the motives and intentions behind Wittgenstein's philosophy? What is, beyond and above its own philosophical declarations, the historical meaning of that "revolution" which changed the face of Anglo-Saxon philosophy in the course of Wittgenstein's gradual modification and final abandonment of the fundamental principle laid down in his *Tractatus Logico-Philosophicus?*

In his book *My Philosophical Development*, Bertrand Russell engages in a bitter attack on the author of *Philosophical Investigations*, a broadside which, if it is not damaging, is yet illuminating. The man who was one of the first to recognize Wittgenstein's *Tractatus* as a work of philosophical genius (even if he interpreted it too exclusively as the culmination of his own doctrine of Logical Atomism) says of the *Philosophical Investigations* that he has not found in it "anything interesting": "I cannot understand why a whole school finds important wisdom in its pages." He abhors the suggestion, which he believes to be implied in Wittgenstein's later work, "that the world of language can be quite divorced from the world of fact," and suspects that such a view must render philosophical activity trivial ("at best, a slight help to lexicographers, and at worst, an idle tea-table amusement") by insidiously giving to "language an untrammelled freedom which it has never hitherto enjoyed." He disagrees most emphatically with the disciples of Wittgenstein when they tend to regard "as an outdated folly the desire to understand the world"—a desire, it would seem, very different from their own to understand the workings of language. (This would have been, even angrier and more cogent, Russell's argument against Deconstructivism.) If incomprehension can ever be significant, then this can be said of Lord Russell's estimate of Wittgenstein's *Philosophical Investigations.* For he certainly knew what he attacked when once upon a time he victoriously fought the domineering influence of Bradley's Idealism, and also knew what *he* welcomed when Wittgenstein first sent him the *Tractatus;* but the later Wittgenstein is to him, he confesses, "completely unintelligible." [10] This might clearly show which of the two recent changes in philosophical outlook—Russell's dislodging of Bradley, or Wittgenstein's superseding of Wittgenstein—is the more profound.

Bertrand Russell was at ease intellectually with Bradley as well as with the Wittgenstein of the *Tractatus* because both were, like himself, philosophers thinking *within* the metaphysical tradition of European philosophy. This goes without saying in the case of Bradley; in the case of the *Tractatus* it may sound alarming. But it is true to say that in its own way—and an exceedingly subtle way it is!—the *Tractatus* participates in a pre-Kantian metaphysical faith: there is, in however small an area of human understanding, a pre-established correspondence between the cognitive faculties of man and the nature of the world. In other words: what man thinks and feels—and therefore *says*—about the world, has a chance of being true in a *metaphysical* sense. At a time when philosophers were still on intimate terms with God, this metaphysical faith found its luminously comprehensive dogma: God is no deceiver; He has created the world and planted in man the desire to understand it; He has also endowed him with perception and rationality, faculties which man cannot help taking for the servants of this desire. Could it have been God's intention to frustrate it from the outset by giving man nothing but the *illusion* of understanding? Is the creature made in His own image to be the eternal dupe of the universe? The simple faith that this cannot be lies at the heart of the complex metaphysical systems of the seventeenth century that have profoundly affected European thought. This faith is discernible behind the scholastic apparatus of Leibniz's Pre-established Harmony and Descartes's *Cogito ergo sum,* those grandiose attempts to demonstrate logically the integral accord between human thought and the true nature of Being. And it is the same faith in reason's power to "comprehend the wondrous architecture of the world," which inspires the great cosmic discoveries of that age; or as Kepler puts it at the end of the ninth chapter of the fifth book of his *Harmonices mundi:* "Thanks be unto you, my Lord Creator! . . . To those men who will read my demonstrations, I have revealed the glory of your creation . . ."

It is a far cry from Descartes to Wittgenstein's *Tractatus;* and yet there is an angle of vision from which the *Tractatus* looks like a last victory of the traditional metaphysical faith: a Pyrrhic victory. Compared to the vast dominions that metaphysical thought had claimed in the past for its settlements of truth, there is now hardly more than a little province of "significant" speech in a vast area of silence. But within this catastrophically narrowed space, man can still confidently assert some truths about the world, utter words whose meanings are not imprisoned within themselves, and speak sentences whose significance is not wholly embedded within the flux of linguistic commerce and convention. No, there are still words and sentences which are true in an absolute sense, reflect what "is the case," and *picture Reality.* Of course, this ideal correspondence between picture and model, thought and world, language and reality, is not easily attained. Its condition is the observance of the strictest logical rules. Thus it will hardly ever occur in the actuality of human speech. Yet it is realized, nevertheless, in the *essence* of language: indeed, it is its *real meaning.* True, in order to speak "essentially" and "significantly," we must leave much unsaid; but once we respond to the "atomic facts"—the bricks of the intelligible world—with "atomic propositions" or their "truth-functional compounds"—concepts which Wittgenstein, considerably modifying and refining them, took over from Russell—our speech, and therefore our thought, is perfectly attuned to Reality: for "Logic is not a body of doctrine, but a mirror-image of the world."[11] And although Wittgenstein courageously insisted that in proposing this relationship between language and fact he himself broke the law governing meaningful propositions,[12] his *Tractatus* is yet built upon a site salvaged from the metaphysical estate of the Pre-established Harmony. The ground, however, was soon to give; and as it gave, Bertrand Russell, for one, saw nothing but total collapse. And it is true to say that from the *Blue Books* onward Wittgenstein immersed himself in a philosophical enterprise which, if set up against the traditional hopes of philosophers, looks desperate indeed. For its intention is to cure philosophers of a sickness the name of which may well be—philosophy. His aphorism of the philosopher's treating questions as if they were patients has more than epigrammatic relevance.

3

The break between *Tractatus* and *Philosophical Investigations* is of the same kind as that between Nietzsche's *The Birth of Tragedy* (1871) and his *Human, All Too Human* (1879). In both cases it was brought about by the abnegation of metaphysics, the loss of faith in any pre-established correspondence between, on the one hand, the logic of our thought and language, and, on the other hand, the "logic" of Reality. In the course of those eight years stretching from *The Birth of Tragedy to Human, All Too Human,* Nietzsche came to believe that he had freed himself of this "philosophical prejudice"—which he diagnosed as the prejudice vitiating the whole history of thought—by turning (to use Wittgenstein's obviously autobiographical words from *Investigations*) his "whole examination round. (One might say: the axis of reference of our examination must be rotated, but about the fixed point of our real need.)"[13] It is no exaggeration to say that Nietzsche could have written this. Indeed, it might serve as an exact description of what he claimed as his great achievement: to have turned our whole horizon 180 degrees around the point of our "real need," which was radically different from that

> which had been satisfied in forming the . . . [traditional] categories of thought; namely the need not to "recognize" but to subsume, to schematize, and, for the sake of communication and calculation, to manipulate and fabricate similarities and sameness . . . No, this was not the work of a pre-existent "Idea"; it happened under the persuasion of usefulness: it was profitable to coarsen and level down things; for only then were they calculable and comfortable . . . Our categories are "truths" only in so far as they make life possible for us: Euclidean space is also such a purposeful "truth" . . . The inner compulsion not to contradict these "truths," the instinct to reach our kind of useful conclusions is inbred in us, we almost *are* this instinct. But how naive to take this as proof of a "truth *per se.*" Our inability to contradict proves impotence and not "truth."[14]

It was Nietzsche's declared intention not to follow any longer this "instinct" and thus to cure the philosophical sickness of centuries, just as it was Wittgenstein's to "solve the philosophical problems" by recognizing their source in "the functioning of our language": "*in spite* of an instinct to misunderstand it."[15] For Nietzsche the truth about man was that he must live without Truth. This was the "real need." The creature that would satisfy it Nietzsche called *Übermensch*—and never mind the offensive word, poetically begotten in a great mind by a Darwinian age. In his letters he often used less grandiose, if not less ambitious, words in speaking of his philosophical goal, words to the effect that "he felt as though he were writing for people who would think in a quite different way, breathe a different air of life from that of present-day men: for people of a different culture . . ." But this is reported by Professor von Wright as a saying of Wittgenstein's.[16]

It would of course be absurd to represent Wittgenstein as a latter-day Nietzsche, and the comparison is certainly not meant to "manipulate and fabricate similarities and samenesses." The two philosophers could hardly be more different in the scope and object, the approach and humor, the key and tempo of their thought; and yet they have in common something which is of the greatest importance: the creative distrust of *all* those categorical certainties that, as if they were an inherited anatomy, have been allowed to determine the body of traditional thought. Nietzsche and Wittgenstein share a genius for directing doubt into the most unsuspected hiding places of error and fallacy: namely where, as Wittgenstein puts it, "everything lies open to view," where everything is simple and familiar, where, day in day out, man takes things for granted—until suddenly one day the fact that he has habitually ignored the most important aspects of things, strikes him as the most striking and most powerful."[17] This may happen on the day when suspicion reaches the notion of "meaning," that is, the idea, held however vaguely, that through some kind of cosmic arrangement, maybe by God, or logic, or the spirit of language, a definite meaning had become attached to the world, to life, to facts, or to words. When Nietzsche discovered the "death of God," the universe of meanings collapsed—everything, that is, that was founded upon the transcendent faith, or was leaning against it, or was intertwined with it: in fact, *everything,* as Nietzsche believed; and henceforward everything was in need of re-valuation.

With Wittgenstein the decisive change of vision, which occurred between *Tractatus* and *Investigations,* seemed centered upon an event less dramatic than the death of God; namely, the vanishing of the belief in a categorical logic of language, and hence in a categorically harmonious relationship between words and world. But the event behind the event was of the same magnitude as the Nietzschean demise of the divinity; it entailed the same crisis of metaphysical confidence that, through the metaphysical audacity of certain German and French thinkers, led to the great perversion of metaphysics: the loss of the belief in any metaphysically dependable dealings with Reality was made up by the notion that a Pre-established *Absurdity* determined the relationship between the intellectual constitution of man and whatever may be the true constitution of the world. Nietzsche was the first to conceive of such a possibility, and after him European art and literature excelled in showing man and world laboring under the tragic, or melancholy, or grotesque, or hilarious compulsion to make nonsense of one another. And there is a historical sense in which the two extremes of contemporary philosophizing, Heidegger's tortuous metaphysical probings into language and Wittgenstein's absorption in language-games (and some of the examples he chooses reveal an almost Thurber-like talent for absurd and grotesque inventions) can be seen as two aspects of the same intention: to track down to their source in language, and there to correct, the absurdities resulting from the human endeavor to speak the truth. It is an intention which was by no means alien to Nietzsche. Certainly his universal suspicion did not spare language, and some of his utterances on the subject are virtually indistinguishable from those of Wittgenstein.

Very early in his philosophical life, Nietzsche knew that he "who finds language interesting in itself has a mind different from him who only regards it as a medium of thought," and he left no doubt which of the two he regarded as the more *philosophical* mind: "Language is something all-too-familiar to us; therefore it needs a philosopher to be struck by it."[18] This is Nietzsche's way of saying what Wittgenstein said when he discovered that "the most important aspects of things are hidden from us by virtue of their simplicity and familiarity."[19] And when Nietzsche said that "the philosopher is caught in the net of *language,*"[20] he meant much the same as Wittgenstein when, referring to his own *Tractatus,* he wrote: "A *picture* held us captive. and we could not get outside it, for it lay in our language and language seemed to repeat it to us inexorably."[21] Indeed, Nietzsche sounds as if he had in mind the metaphysics of the *Tractatus* when he speaks of the conclusion of a primitive metaphysical peace which once upon a time fixed "what henceforward is to be called truth": "A universally valid and compelling notation of facts is invented and the legislation of language fixes the principal rules for truth." This would seem to come close to what Wittgenstein attempted in the *Tractatus:* "To give the essence of a proposition means to give the essence of all description, and thus the essence of the world."[22] *But,* Nietzsche asked, "is language the adequate expression for all realities?"[23] And soon he was to be quite sure that it was not. On the contrary, the grammatical and syntactical order of language, its subjects, predicates, objects, causal and conditional connections, were "the petrified fallacies of reason" which continued to exercise their "seductive spell" upon our intelligence.[24]

> Philosophy is a battle against the bewitchment of our intelligence by means of language.

This last aphorism is by Wittgenstein;[25] but it would be impossible to guess where Nietzsche ends and Wittgenstein begins.

4

One of Wittgenstein's aphorisms runs as follows:

> Philosophy results in the discovery of one or another piece of simple nonsense, and in bruises which the understanding has suffered by bumping its head against the limits of language. They, the bruises, make us see the value of that discovery.*[26]

And in one of the jottings of his late years Nietzsche wrote under the heading "Fundamental solution":

> Language is founded upon the most naive prejudices . . . We read contradictions and problems into everything because we *think only* within the forms of language . . . *We have to cease to think if we refuse to do it in the prisonhouse of language;* for we cannot reach further than the doubt which asks whether the limit we see is really a limit . . . *All rational thought is interpretation in accordance with a scheme which we cannot throw off.*[27]

Yet neither Nietzsche nor Wittgenstein "ceased to think." In Nietzsche's thought, the persistent misgiving that the established conventions of philosophical language did not cater for our "real" intellectual needs was only one facet of his central thesis: With the death of God, with the silencing of that Word which was in the beginning, *all* certainties of faith, belief, metaphysics, morality, and knowledge had come to an end, and henceforward man was under the terrible com-

*This is one of Karl Kraus's aphorisms on language: "If I cannot get further, this is because I have banged my head against the wall of language. Then, with my head bleeding, I withdraw. And want to go on." (*Beim Wort genommen* [Munich, 1955], 326)

pulsion of absolute freedom of thought, the threat of unlimited intellectual license. His choice was that of either creating, with the surpassing creativity of the Creator, his own world, or of spiritually perishing. For the world *as it is* has neither meaning nor value. Meaning and value must be *given* to it: by God or by man himself. If God is dead and man fails, then nothing in this world has any value and our own language deceives us with all its ancient intimations of higher meanings.

> In the world everything is as it is, and everything happens as it does happen: *in* it no value exists—and if it did, it would have no value.

These sentences from Wittgenstein's *Tractatus*[28] might have been invented by Nietzsche—and many like these were in fact invented by him in the notes, published as *The Will to Power,* where, as an inspired actor, indeed as an initiate, he defined the mind of European nihilism which he so urgently desired to overcome.

Wittgenstein's *Investigations* would be as trivial as Bertrand Russell thinks they are, were they not, in their infinite intellectual patience, informed with a sense of urgency not altogether unlike that which inspired Nietzsche's prophetic impetuosity. To bring some light into "the darkness of this time"—this was the hesitant hope of the author of *Philosophical Investigations.* This hope, like all true hope, was founded upon the paradox of faith: faith despite doubt. It was, for Wittgenstein, a faith in language; and language remained all-important for him even after it had ceased to be the mirror of Reality, the function Wittgenstein assigned to it in the *Tractatus.* Having exposed all its dangers, shown how our minds are held captive by its metaphors, denounced the witchcraft with which it assails our intelligence, he was still left with the ineradicable trust in its ultimate wisdom and its power to heal our disease.

Nothing in Wittgenstein's work is more vulnerable to further questioning than this trust; indeed, its very intellectual vulnerability confirms it as his faith. Often he speaks of language with utmost vagueness:

> When philosophers use a word—"knowledge," "being," "object," "I," "proposition," "name,"—and try to grasp the *essence* of the thing, one must always ask oneself: is the word ever actually used in this way in the langauge in which it has its home?*[29]

---

*Was it the vagueness of this which induced the translator to use "language-game" where the German has simply "*Sprache*"?

One may well ask: who, with language speaking in a hundred tongues through our literatures, dialects, social classes, journals, and newspapers, establishes this actual use? Shakespeare? Donne? James Joyce? The *Oxford English Dictionary?* The College Porter? The habitual reader of the daily gazettes? And when Wittgenstein says, "What *we* do is to bring words back from their metaphysical to their everyday usage,"[30] or "When I talk about language, . . . I must speak the language of every day,"[31] one is struck by the homely imprecision of this program and wonders why he does not wish to bring language back to Lichtenberg's or Gottfried Keller's usage, or speak the language of Karl Kraus, which is in fact much closer to Wittgenstein's than is the speech of a Vienna or London "every day"?

Wittgenstein said:

> Philosophy may in no way interfere with the actual use of language; it can in the end only describe it . . . It leaves everything as it is.[32]
>
> We must do away with all explanation, and description alone must take its place.[33]

But might we not be "held captive" by a picture "actually used" in language, and can we be sure that "actual usage" will never "bewitch our intelligence"? And if it does, how are we to loosen its grip without "explaining" its nature? (And I am using "explain" here as it is "actually used.") Or is Schopenhauer, who so indignantly "interfered" with the corrupt use made of language by those who thoughtlessly speak or print it day in day out, guilty of errors of judgment *because* he wrote a prose inspired by a literary tradition which indeed he believed was being more and more betrayed by the everyday traffic in words? And what is the "everything" that philosophy "leaves as it is"? Not, surely, the manner of thinking and uttering thoughts. Many philosophers, like all great poets, have deeply affected our perception, and therefore our language, and thus have changed our world: Plato, for instance, or Descartes, or Rousseau, or Kant, or Nietzsche, or indeed Wittgenstein.

When Wittgenstein speaks of the language of every day, he does not mean what "actual usage" suggests he means. In fact, he means Language—means something that is of surpassing importance as the repository of our common humanity, of understanding, knowledge, and wisdom. Why then does he describe what he means with the words "actual usage" or "the language of every day"? Is this merely an uneasy concession made by a believer to an empiricist? Or a way of denouncing the violations of language of which many a philosopher has been guilty in his pursuit of spurious heights and depths? This may be so. But Wittgenstein may have been prompted even more by a Tolstoyan belief in the virtue of the simple life, a belief that he applied to the life of language. Tolstoy indeed was one of the very few writers of the nineteenth century who deeply interested him; and thus it was perhaps a kind of linguistic Rousseau-Tolstoyism that led Wittgenstein to insist upon "natural" language, a language unspoiled by the dubious refinements of a philosophical "civilization" which, having uprooted words from the ground of their origin, had made them serve "unnatural" demands.

In *Investigations* there are, above all, two aphorisms that allow the reader to observe how Wittgenstein avoids, in the manner of an empiricist fighting shy of metaphysics, the open declaration of his all-but-metaphysical faith in Language. This is the first:

> The problems arising through a misinterpretation of our forms of language have the character of *depth*. They are deep disquietudes; their roots are as deep in us as the forms of our language, and their significance is as great as the importance of our language.[34]

How true! And yet how disquieting is the word "misinterpretation"! It seems to suggest that there is, or can be, an absolutely reliable "rule" for deciding, philosophically or philologically, what is a correct and what is an incorrect "interpretation" of every particular "form of language." But no such standard can apply. For to a higher degree than is dreamt of in linguistic philosophy, language has this in common with other forms of human expression that it often evades unambiguous "interpretation": it can be as purely allusive as dance and gesture, as evanescent in meaning as music, as ungrammatically extravagant as life itself. No sooner have we left the field of logic, grammar, and syntax, than we have entered the sphere of aesthetics where we do not ask whether a writer "interprets"[35] words correctly, but whether he uses them well or badly: and whether or not he uses them well, depends not upon his ability to "interpret" them, but upon something more adequately described as a feeling for language, as sensibility, or as genius. However original such genius may be, tradition has helped to form it—tradition or, to use Wittgenstein's words, the particular "form of life" within which alone, according to him, language has its meaning: "to imagine a language means to imagine a form of life."[36] That this is so, is one of Wittgenstein's most striking realizations; and indeed it not only renders the "rules of language," as he well knew, logically unmanageable but also makes their "description," which he hoped for, a task that could not be fulfilled by even a legion of Prousts or Wittgensteins: for what is *the* "form of life" which, in one language, is shared by Goethe and Hitler, or, in another, by Keats and the *National Enquirer?*

With the "deep disquietudes" caused by a "misinterpretation of our forms of language," the quoted aphorism suggests something even more misleading than the word "misinterpretation" itself. For the suggestion is that depth is a by-product of error, and this is precisely what Nietzsche, from *The Birth of Tragedy* onward, maintained and repeated again and again: that the will to create illusion—art—is profounder than the will to keep faith with what "really" and "truly" is.[37] But if words like "depth" or "truth" or "error" are meaningful at all, then truth is deeper than falsehood; and indeed Wittgenstein's suggestion is, as it were, withdrawn by the aphorism's very form and rhythm, which unmistakably intimate that language itself, not only its misinterpretation, has the character of depth, and that the disquietudes which arise from it are as deep as is the peace it may bring: through a great writer and even, rarely, through a philosopher whose thought is rooted in the mystery of words—or, to use the terms of the second aphorism we have had in mind, "in the ground of language." This second aphorism does indeed come close to revealing Wittgenstein's metaphysical secret. "What is it that gives to our investigation its importance," he asks with the voice of an imaginary interlocutor, "since it seems only to destroy everything interesting? (As it were all the buildings, leaving behind only bits of stone and rubble.)" And he replies: "What we are destroying is nothing but houses of cards and we are clearing up the ground of language on which they stand."[38] The ground of language—it is a transparent metaphor; and what shines through it is a mystical light, even if there is nothing left for it to illuminate but a philosophical landscape most thoughtfully cleared of all the fragile and disfiguring edifices built throughout the ages by the victims of linguistic delusion, such as Plato, St. Thomas Aquinas, Spinoza, or Immanuel Kant, those "ancient thinkers" who, wherever they "placed a word," believed

> they had made a discovery. Yet the truth about it is quite different!—
> they had touched upon a problem and, deluding themselves that they
> had solved it, put up an obstacle to its solution.—To come to know
> means now to stumble over petrified words that are as hard as stone,
> and to break one's leg rather than a word.

Wittgenstein? No, Nietzsche.[39]

It is an ending a little like that of Goethe's *Tasso* where a man, a poet with all his certainties shattered, holds fast to his last possession: language. And it has remained an open question of literary interpretation whether that ending promises an ultimately happy consummation or a tragedy. Be this as it may, Wittgenstein was not a poet but a philosopher. And philosophy enters with Wittgenstein the stage which has been reached by many another creative activity of the human mind— by poetry, for instance, or by painting: the stage where every act of creation is inseparable from the critique of its medium, and every work, intensely reflecting upon itself, looks like the embodied doubt of its own possibility. It is a predicament which Nietzsche uncannily anticipated in a sketch entitled "A Fragment from the History of Posterity." Its subject is "The Last Philosopher." Having lost faith in a communicable world, he is imprisoned within his own self-consciousness. Nothing speaks to him any more—except his own speech; and, deprived of any authority from a divinely ordered universe, it is only about his speech that his speech can speak with a measure of philosophical assurance.[40]

In *Philosophical Investigations* Wittgenstein said: "What is your aim in philosophy?—To show the fly the way out of the fly-bottle."[41] But who asks? Who answers? And who is the fly? It is an unholy trinity; the three are one. This way lies no way out. This way lie only fly-bottles, and more and more fly-bottles.

# NIETZSCHE'S LAST WORDS

# ABOUT ART VERSUS TRUTH

"For a philosopher to say 'the good and the beautiful are one' is infamy; if he goes on to add, 'also the true', one ought to thrash him. Truth is ugly.

We possess *art* lest we *perish of the truth*."

This utterance, at once crystalline and tumultuous, brilliant and violent, was written by Nietzsche in 1888, the year preceding his mental collapse. It is contained in one of the posthumous notes that have been collected in *The Will to Power*\*[1] and has the resonance of last words, words spoken or cried out with that assured despair or hope that allows for no debate; and perhaps it was really meant as Nietzsche's last word concerning a problem of which—apropos his rereading, in the same year, of his youthful *Birth of Tragedy*—he said that it was the earliest which compellingly demanded his serious attention; and even today, he added, this dilemma filled him with "holy terror."[2]

The problem, so terrifying to Nietzsche from beginning to end, is the relationship between art and truth. Even in the context of *The Birth of Tragedy* it is exceedingly difficult to grasp. For whatever meaning is given to the word "truth," no common denominator can possibly be found among the endless varieties of "art": a sculpture of ancient Egypt, an archaic Apollo, *Antigone, King Lear,* Michelangelo, Bach, Mozart, Beethoven, Bizet or Offenbach, not to mention a short poem of Goethe's or Mallarmé's. Even if we equate art with ancient tragedy, as *The Birth of Tragedy* might suggest, just as it proclaims tragedy's rebirth in Wagner's music drama, the question is whether the dilemma, whatever its "true" nature, was resolved and the terror diminished by the terrifying "We possess *art* lest we *perish of the truth*." Has the ugliness of the ugly truth increased so drastically since Plato's time that now anyone associating truth with beauty commits a philosophical felony? Has truth become so militantly aggressive in its unpleasantness that art must serve as a fortification against its invading our lives?

---

\* W followed by the numeral indicating the numbered section refers to *The Will to Power*, translated by Walter Kaufmann and R. J. Hollingdale, New York 1967.

That we should not be able to live with the truth, the whole truth, has surely been said before, and by no one more memorably than by Plato in the cave parable; and it has been repeated again and again, by Lessing, for instance, who, had God given him the choice between the truth and the infinite search for it, would have asked him for the endless striving because the truth, he wrote, was only for God Himself; or by the story of the veiled image of Sais, the mysterious image of "the truth," whose unveiled sight would have been deadly. In all these instances, and many, many more, it is a matter of the whole truth being unattainable or not meant for the treasury of man. But that truth would kill us *because of its devastating ugliness* has never been said— surely not with Nietzsche's aphoristic vehemence. As the "truth" in Nietzsche's saying obviously means the true character of existence, and not merely this or that experience in our individual lives that may shock us to death, what, once more, can "art" mean as its radical contrast and "remedy"? There are many reasons for our hesitation in answering this question.

There is above everything else the indisputable fact that, since the generation of Rilke, George, Mann, the idea of art as the quasi-religious opposite of "life" has run its course. Who among the young can understand Stefan George's imperial pronouncement that *"kein Ding sei, wo das Wort gebricht"*—there ought to be no thing where language fails in naming it—which in the end meant the same as Karl Kraus's celebrated and notorious declaration that where the task was to find the right words for the rule of Hitler, language had to abdicate: *"Mir fällt zu Hitler nichts ein."* Certainly, there is no longer an artist who would look upon his art as an all but ecclesiastical, indeed monastic, devotion. "I have many brothers in cassocks," Rilke wrote, and the young Thomas Mann's Tonio Kröger even thought of having to sacrifice "life" in the service to his art: Not one leaf from the laurel tree of art, he said, may be plucked without the artist's paying for it with his life. Meanwhile, art has come to be as "ungodly" as life itself, and the evergreen laurel tree, for Tonio Kröger so dangerously in foliage, has been badly damaged by an autumn in which more has withered than the leaves of deciduous trees. "O trees of life, when will your winter come?" Rilke asked at the beginning of the darkest of the *Duino Elegies,* the fourth, written entirely in the deep shadow of the First World War. "Now," is the unison answer of modern literature. It is not for its practitioners to dedicate themselves to literature with that idolatrous religiosity that was Flaubert's, Thomas Mann's, Rilke's, and— amid the endless curses he uttered against the idol—Franz Kafka's.

Indeed, art is no longer as *"heiter,"* as serene, as Schiller believed it should be; yet it has ceased to be as serious as to demand the sacrifice of "life."

Then, there is the unsettling fact that during Nietzsche's lifetime, and even before, a species of literature emerged that hardly earned his praise but that, for the sake of his consistency and our intellectual comfort, he ought to have judged even more harshly. Sometimes he did, but only selectively (although when he did so, he discriminated with his unfailing artistic instinct). What I have in mind is realism and of course naturalism; and the naturalists pride themselves upon forcing "the truth of life," as they see it, not "art," as Nietzsche understands it, upon the attention of the public. Nietzsche would have approved of our using the word "forcing"; for he once, and more than once, characterized "modern art," above all naturalism, as "the art of tyrannizing." Those "artists," he wrote, were in the habit of employing an "overwhelming mass"—an ugly mass, it is to be presumed—"before which the senses become confused," and "brutality in color, material, desires" (W.827). One wonders, with regard to both the tyranny and the brutality, what his vocabulary would have been if he had lived to witness the productions of the cinema—a form of presentation that is, quite apart from any content, by its very nature incomparably more "tyrannical" than any art that preceded it: the very darkness in which it is being watched opens the spectators' eyes and minds to the vision of the film's maker with a hypnotic exclusiveness that is unique in the history of the arts—or what he would have said, with regard to "brutality," about Eugene O'Neill or Tennessee Williams or Thomas Bernhard.

Or did he anticipate all this when in 1888 he wrote: "The ugly, i.e. the contradiction to art, that which is outside the scope of art, its No; every time decline, impoverishment of life, impotence, disintegration, degeneration are suggested even faintly, the aesthetic man reacts with his No" (W.809). Or when he said in the same year of the increase in civilization "that it necessarily brings with it an increase in the morbid elements, in the neurotic-psychiatric and criminal" (W.864) all of which is as "depressing" as it is "the symptom of a depression," and "takes away strength, impoverishes, weighs down . . ." (W.809). It is exceedingly doubtful whether history is bent upon teaching lessons; but if it does, it proves right the grand gesture with which Nietzsche dismisses the revolutionary claim of "naturalism." Is it, he asks, a critique of social ills? By no means, it is a pathological fascination with them and a foreboding of ever more pathology: ". . . the artist, re-strained from crime by weakness of will and timidity, and not yet ripe for the *madhouse*" makes himself the bearer of the message "of the Revolution, the establishment of equal rights," and becomes the para-gon "of the instincts of decline (of *ressentiment,* discontent, the drive to destroy, anarchism and nihilism), including the slave instincts . . . that have long been kept down" (W.864). That much, then, about Nietz-sche and naturalism.

As examples of the tyrranical force employed by modern art, Nietzsche quotes the creations of Zola and Wagner. Zola and Wagner may seem a surprising pair of brothers in the art of hypnotic brutality, yet their features do display a family resemblance. (Thomas Mann, in his essay on Wagner* made a great deal of this and thus provoked some guardians of the "German genius," intellectual warriors that, under the rule of Hitler, happened to live in 1933 in the "Wagner City" Munich, to that notorious "Protest" that certainly helped to keep the author of *Buddenbrooks* residing outside the frontiers of Germany for the rest of his life).

In the order of aphorisms collected in *The Will to Power* the succinct proclamation of the function of art—to make the unbearable bear-able—is preceded by an observation that, of course, denies the possi-bility of pessimism in art: "There is no such thing as pessimistic art.—Art affirms. Job affirms" (W.821). This is an old Nietzschean theme; and what he says here is true on the level where even tragedy "cele-brates" the tragic human destiny, although one may not without some scruples accept the abrupt inclusion of the Book of Job in the category of Art. And there is no mistaking the religious resonance of the voice that pronounces: "What remains essential in art is its being bent upon perfecting existence, its creating perfection and plentitude. Art is es-sentially *affirmation, blessing, deification* of existence . . . Schopenhauer is *wrong* when he says that certain works of art (what is meant is once more Attic tragedy) serve pessimism." And in case Nietzsche's *Birth of Tragedy* was not yet understood—as late as 1888—he emphasizes again that tragedy does *not* teach resignation, as Schoenhauer believed. No, for an artist "to represent terrible and questionable things shows in itself his instinct for power and magnificence: he does not fear them" (W.821), but affirms even evil in its transfiguration through art. He affirms like Job.

*Thomas Mann, *Gesammelte Werke,* IX, Frankfurt 1960.

To descend from such heights into the lowlands of grammar looks like seeking shelter in banality. Yet it is really banal to enquire whether the verb "affirm," a transitive verb, does not stand in need of an object? My Latin teacher, a kindly Cistercian monk, rigorously insisted on his pupils' asking "whom or what?" to find out whether a verb was transitive. If it responded positively to the question, it was. "Affirm?" he would have said: "whom or what?" and might have failed Rilke on the famous opening line of the Orphic sonnet *"Rühmen, das ist's!"* "Praising, that's it!" "Whom or what?" he would have asked and waited for a considerably more particular answer than "life as such." "Life is not 'as such.'" The language of poets has become accustomed to the—as it were—intransitive use of such verbs as "affirm" or "praise." This is more than a matter of grammar: grammatical usage, as often it does, mirrors the grammar of consciousness itself. It is impossible to make articulate sense, and not merely an ecstatic-intoxicated dithyramb, of the praiseworthiness of praise; or simply of affirming affirmation. *"Ein Gott vermag's,"* "A God may do it," Rilke's third sonnet says; but, before Rilke took charge of him, Orpheus was no god. Rilke raised him to the status of a god by merging him with Nietzsche's Dionysus; and he, the god, surely succeeds where a mere human being is bound to fail: in the lavishing of unconditional yea-saying upon an existence in which the No of disaster, sickness, murder, cruelty and senseless death is as inescapable as the Yes of love and happiness. With Job the object is easily supplied—in as un-Nietzschean a manner as can be: Job affirms God. Even so, the story of Job is never easy to take, and had Job received and in the end believed Nietzsche's message of God's death, it would be a downright unbearable tale.

He who is not inclined to dwell on such questions, may meditate for a while the song of the Watchman on the Tower in the fifth act of *Faust II.* It is one of Goethe's most beautiful lyrical poems, a song of praise intoned by one who is at that moment in the state of pure, "will-less" contemplation, the ineluctable condition of what Schopenhauer calls aesthetic experience—the experience that is untouched by any self-interest. Lynceus sees, *sees,* and only the happiness of seeing does matter to him. *What* he sees, is almost irrelevant. It is beautiful, because he sees it with eyes that are undistracted by anything that is not pure seeing: nearby the wood and the deer, and high above it the moon and the stars; and beside himself with ecstatic yea-saying, he speaks the words that are always quoted as proof of Goethe's affirmation of life. Yet these words lose sight of any definable or even particular grammatical object:

> *Es sei, wie es wolle,*
> *Es war doch so schön.*

Be it as it may (in the sight of those blessed and blessing eyes—"*Ihr glücklichen Augen//was je ihr gesehn . . .* ") it has been beautiful.

In the whole range of literature there is no purer lyrical expression of the jubiliant yea-saying affirming the world as "aesthetic phenomenon," as young Nietzsche, in *The Birth of Tragedy,* renames what for Schopenhauer was the artist's intuition of the Platonic Idea beyond the mere appearance of a thing. But because Nietzsche, as early as the otherwise faithfully Schopenhauerian *Birth of Tragedy,* robs this vision of its transcendental object, the Platonic Idea, it is bereft of any object whatever. This is a surgical act of the greatest consequence. It is representative of the dominant poetic perception in nineteenth century literature: "absolute" or "pure" poetry.

The monologue of the Watchman on the Tower, celebrating the "*ewige Zier*" ("*kosmos*" in Greek), the "aesthetic phenomenon," is interrupted with catastrophic suddenness; and what breaks into it is hardly ever quoted in the anthologies. Indeed, it is no longer a song and differs from what precedes it by the changed rhythm: Goethe has separated it from the celebration by the stage instruction "pause." And what a pause is this!

For abruptly the Watchman's aesthetic contemplation ends when he is reminded of his task as an active human being, placed upon the tower not to praise life as an aesthetic phenomenon, but to guard Faust's estate against threatening dangers. And what he sees now is the smoke rising from the little house of the dear old couple Philemon and Baucis. And the fire is due to Faust's megalomaniac orders to remove the two ancient people from the smallholding on Faust's empire; and the fire may spread, destroy not only the two but cause more disasters. Thus the Watchman's glorious yea-saying ends. He now reminds himself of his duty as a Watchman: he was up on his tower not merely in order to delight in the view, "*Nicht allein mich zu ergetzen, bin ich hier so hochgestellt,*" and is now terrified by the horrible threat from out of the dark world:

> *Welch ein greuliches Entsetzen*
> *Droht mir aus der finstern Welt.*

The indiscriminate object of praise has been replaced by an occasion for terror. Only a few verse lines before, the Watchman's eyes were happy to see *whatever* it was; but now he deplores that his sight reaches even as far as the burning hut:

> *Sollt ihr Augen dies erkennen!*
> *Muss ich so weitsichtig sein!*

Transitive verbs cannot easily be cheated of their transitiveness.

Is this, then, the way in which art affirms even what is ugly in life, "art understood as the potent incentive to living, as the eternal urge to live, to live eternally," as Nietzsche wrote in preparing *Zarathustra?*[3] We have only just heard of an art that deifies life and blesses it as Lynceus does before he espies the flames, an art that refutes Schopenhauer's belief that tragedy teaches resignation; and immediately upon the yea-saying Job there follows, with a question mark, Zola, this time not in the company of Wagner but in that of the—for Nietzsche— equally questionable Goncourts. What is wrong with those Frenchmen? "The things they display are ugly: but *that* they display them comes from the pleasure they take in the ugly." One is tempted to interject: "from the pleasure taken in the truth?" And how does this "pleasure in the ugly" differ from the artist's fearlessness in "representing terrible and questionable things," a courage that shows "his instinct for power and magnificence," as Nietzsche had just said? No doubt, this instinct does not seek *that* pleasure. Yet Nietzsche now continues: "It's no good! If you think otherwise, you're deceiving yourselves.—How liberating is Dostoevsky!" (W.821)

This is a psychological coup and shows Nietzsche's superb literary instinct: praise for Dostoevsky and sometime before of Stendhal, despite their practising "realism" and even "naturalism" in literature. We do not know for certain how much of Dostoevsky Nietzsche had read, but it must have been more than *Notes from Underground* (a book that undoubtedly had prompted him to call himself in the preface to *Dawn*—1881, preface of 1886—an "underground man"); it is certain that he knew *Crime and Punishment,* too. When he chanced upon Dostoevsky late in his life, he said not only that finding him was one of the most welcome strokes of good luck (even more so than his "discovery of Stendhal") but also that the Russian was "the only psychologist from whom I had something to learn."[4] The question "What?" although it lures us into the unknowable, is irresistible. Dostoevsky is "liberating," and differs in that from the Goncourts and Zola, the "naturalists," who took pleasure in showing the ugly, non-artists who did not know that just because the truth of life was its spiritually killing ugliness, we need art, the beautiful illusion, the redeeming untruth, the bewitching lie. Indeed, Zarathustra calls himself a liar insofar as he is an artist.[5]

The beautiful illusion versus the ugly truth: surely, it cannot be in this aesthetic sense that Dostoevsky could possibly have proved "liberating." His world can be as ugly as any naturalist's, and is as inelegant as his style. Well then, how is the sentence "We possess *art* lest we *perish of truth*," a dictum that is the extreme formula of the mature Nietzsche's philosophy of art, to be reconciled to his praise of Dostoevsky? The answer is "It is impossible." What, then, is it that Nietzsche could have learned from Dostoevsky, the *psychologist,* that he might not have learned from, say, Shakespeare, or indeed—from himself, incomparable psychologist of crime and criminal that he was, and the tireless, even if sometimes tiresome, explorer of the *psychological* roots of religion, asceticism and saintliness; the Ivan Karamazov, as he inhabits Dostoevsky's book?

At this point we need only mention the names of Zossima or Alyosha—despite the improbability of Nietzsche's having read *The Brothers Karamazov*—not to feel too insolent in our venture. We venture then, hesitantly, timidly, the answer to our question: how the philosopher who called himself "the first psychologist of Europe" had profited from Dostoevsky's "psychological novels" and what might even have "liberated" him. Liberated from what? From the fetters of his own psychology? For reading again and again what Nietzsche—again and again, and in a voice that sounds shriller and shriller as the years go by—says about the origins of "ascetic ideals" and the Christian religion, we sense that this immensely intelligent man had sometimes to deafen the gentle voice which within himself kept insinuating that all was not well with the monotony of his psychologizing. True, there are moments when the drumming subsides and that voice makes itself heard, for instance in *The Genealogy of Morals* when the "torture" of the psychologist's compulsion to guess "the true nature"—and that is, of course, the ugly nature—"of great men"[6] suddenly relents and quite a different voice is heard, namely the psychologist's confession that a man who in his determination to disclose the ugliness beneath the masque of greatness, violates the rule of respect and discretion and, revealing the "truth" about others, only reveals his own character. For greatness and "finer humanity," he says, is also in a man's respect for the masque.[7] It is as if Nietzsche had just read another psychological observation about psychology, the German Romantic Novalis's saying that psychology, or what goes by that name, is one of "the ghosts . . . that have usurped the place in the temple where genuine images of the divine ought to be."*

What then could Nietzsche have learned from Dostoevsky? First, that psychology may indeed affect a man's pieties but most certainly cannot *establish* the worth or unworth, the beauty or ugliness, the truth or untruth of what has grown from roots sunk deeply into the psyche; as little as botany or soil analysis or meteorology or geology can prove or disprove the justification of the sense of autumnal glory one may have in the sight of a yellowing birch tree before one's window or of the play of sunlight on the rugged faces of the mountains that rise beyond it.

That a man may be too weak to endure the tribulations of his existence—its "truth"—without faith in God (would Job have endured them?); or that the strongest sensual impulses may have led to Dante's *divine* love of Beatrice; or that Nietzsche, the unsuspecting teacher of Freud, might be right in assuming that "without a certain overheating of the sexual system a Raphael is unthinkable"; or that "making music is another way of making children" (W.800)—all this may be the case and yet would not in the slightest touch upon the question of the validity or falseness of Job's faith; or upon the true nature of Dante's love or the beauty of the poetry celebrating that love; or on Raphael's artistic integrity in painting his chaste madonnas; or on the greatness of Bach's B minor Mass (was he really in need of making music in addition to making twenty children?). If a believer, in the agony of his dying, is comforted by the thought of a Beyond, or a pagan hero, deadly wounded, by the promise of national glory, both the believer and the hero may consolingly deceive themselves with illusions. Yet what is certainly *not* proved by the torments that bring forth such consolations, is the absence of a Beyond or the emptiness of posthumous glory.

And Nietzsche's work itself? Would we grasp *anything* of his intellectual passion or of the quality and style of his thought if we merely remembered that he was the son of a mentally endangered Protestant pastor and a mother as ordinary as anyone can be (child of the same parents that a little later produced the notorious, rather than famous, Elisabeth)? Deplorable that it is still necessary to insist upon the obvious: the utter inconclusiveness of all conclusions drawn from origins when the question is the moral or aesthetic worth of the resulting phe-

---

*Novalis, *Fragmente,* ed. Ernst Kamnitzer, Dresden 1929, p. 381.

nomenon. No, the value of a pearl cannot be assessed by referring to the grain of sand that had pathologically irritated the oyster's mucous membrane.

"It is exceptional states that condition the artist—all of them profoundly related to . . . morbid phenomena—so it seems impossible to be an artist and not to be sick," Nietzsche noted in 1888 (W.811), but at the same time he maintained that "artists if they are worth their salt . . . must be—also physically—of strong disposition, excelling in vigor, powerful animals . . ." (W.800) This is a blatant contradiction, one with which he began to live even two or three years earlier when he knew how to be at his most "healthily" Dionysian. He would at that time ask "in regard to all aesthetic values: 'Has hunger or superabundance become creative here'?" (W.846) The question was undoubtedly meant to establish a difference in artistic rank: Homer, Hafiz, Rubens, Goethe were given as examples of artists who, in the fullness of their creative powers, "eternalize", "apotheosize" existence, while the others, the "hunger artists", were Nietzsche's unloved Romantics. Profoundly conscious as he was of the uncertainty that prevails in the relationship between origins and outcomes—first naming unavoidable morbidity and sickness as the source of art, then naming inexhaustible riches of health and strength as its wellspring—Nietzsche should not have been in need of Dostoevsky's instructions.

It may have been Dostoevsky, the liberating teacher, whom Nietzsche had in mind when, in the later part of the above note in *The Will to Power* (he used it almost verbatim in the *Joyous Wisdom,* section 370) he acknowledges, as if to make ambiguity still more ambiguous, an art whose abundant sources of energy spring, as it were, from hunger, expressing themselves in "the tyrannic will of one who suffers deeply, who struggles and is tormented."[8] The reading of Dostoevsky might indeed have taught him this. But after all is said and done, the bewilderment induced by the psychologist's scrutiny of the inner states that bring forth art could not be worse. There are, in the first place, such plentiful resources of vitality that cannot be contained in the ordinary pursuits of life. Whereupon the psychologist, anticipating the approval of Freud, equates that overflow of energy with the strength and urgency of sexual desires that, given the unavoidable limitations socially imposed upon them, have to be "sublimated" in music, painting, poetry. And it does apparently not matter whether the music is expressive of the subtlest designs of Eros as it is in Mozart's operas, or the contemplation of the divine as in Bach's oratoria, or in wild sensual intoxications as in Stravinsky's "Rite of Spring"; or whether the painter's subject is a madonna or a reclining nude; or whether the poetry is by Dante or Rimbaud. But this is not the end of the psychologist's explorations. For, we learn, there is also the kind of art that, like will-o'-the-wisps from swamps, rises from the morbidities and perversities of the mind or, like the fantasizing of the starving, from the mind in the enfeebled body. Finally, the psychologist will even discover that *real* healthy strength may grow from sickness. And the more the psychologist becomes entangled in the meshwork of the roots of art, the less likely it is that he will emerge from the murky depth better equipped to judge whether the work above ground is good or mediocre or worthless. Yet our initial aphorism can only mean: "We have *good* art lest we perish of the *ugly* truth."

Thus to discriminate is not, as Nietzsche was determined to say if not to believe, simply a "bad" habit, instilled in us by an injurious religious tradition, by upbringing, or even by language itself. No, we simply cannot overcome the "habit" of discriminating. For this "habit," like breathing, is a necessity. Indeed, language itself refutes the very title that Nietzsche gave to one of his late works: *Beyond Good and Evil*. There is no such Beyond. For if we miraculously ever reached that terminus, he who deems it desirable that we should, would exclaim: "How *good* it is to have attained the state beyond good and evil!" *And what applies to good and evil, does in equal measure apply to the distinction between good and bad, or true and false.* The Twilight of the Idols (1888), one of the last of the books Nietzsche wrote shortly before his mental breakdown, contains an astonishing and astonishingly condensed "narration," entitled "How the 'true world' (once again we have returned to 'truth') finally became a fable." It claims to trace "the history of an error" and ends thus: "We have abolished the true world"—and when he speaks here of the "true world," he means the "world of ideas" or of the Beyond, the only really real worlds that have dominated many of our philosophies and religions ever since Plato, the "true world" as distinct from the world of our ordinary experience. This true world, then, "we have abolished: which world is left? Perhaps the apparent one? Certainly not! *Together with the true world we have also abolished the apparent one!*."[9] Are we to respond by saying: "How true! The distinction between a true world and an apparent world, and thereby between true and false, is false!"?

Once more, Nietzsche appears to disavow himself and to embrace the very nihilism which he desired to conquer. For if one has even the slightest feeling for the communications inherent in language that, to spite the credulous semioticist, is capable of "meaning" incomparably more than it actually says, then one cannot but doubt that Nietzsche, in his "fable," announced only what is logically self-evident; for the logically self-evident does not need the rhetorical support of the accents of prophecy. As soon as we deny the reality of that ideal world— and Nietzsche is by no means the first to do so—we are clearly left with nothing but the world of our immediate experience, the world that for Plato was merely the world of shadow appearances. If that dualism collapses, there exists only *one* world. Who would doubt that? Every high school boy who has ever heard of the doctrine of positivism is able to comprehend it. Whereupon one ought to listen a second time to the conclusion of Nietzsche's "fable": "We have abolished the true world: which world is left? Perhaps the apparent one? Certainly not! Together with the *true world we have also abolished the apparent one!*" What is the appropriate response to these hammer blows of language? Should we say, "This is clear enough! What is the agitation about?" No, but rather to share the deep spiritual apprehension which is conveyed by the voice that says what the opinion it utters does not say: namely not merely that from now onwards we shall have to make ourselves at home in *one* world, but much more: that now we must be prepared to exist in *not even one,* at least in no world which would allow us truly to exist. Two or three years before this, Nietzsche drew up a sketch of a preface—it was replaced by that of 1886—for the new edition of *The Birth of Tragedy.* It says: ". . . there is only one world, and this is false, cruel, contradictory, seductive, without meaning.— A world thus constituted, is the real world" (W.835). And, therefore, one is led to ask: a world—false, he calls it—that Nietzsche's *Übermensch* would experience as being beyond good and evil? Not likely, unless he succeeded in what not even he could succeed in, namely in ecstatically "transvaluing" that world which, in Nietzsche's description, teaches us that *horror vacui,* the horror of nothingness, of nihilism, that determines the *style* of the "fable." And how could he succeed as long as he *knows* that it is a false, cruel, meaningless world?

Can anyone accept such a world which is, decidedly, not a human world? Even if we achieved the impossible and found the appropriate language for it, a language that would be able to renounce what Nietzsche's langauge cannot do without: namely such words as "true" or "false," "good" or "evil"? Would then our inner nature be so radically changed as to enable us to discard those distinctions? Perhaps we might; but only if they no longer corresponded to anything deeply within ourselves—and so we never shall, unless our nature ceases to be human nature.

Yet if this ever happened, we would no longer know what, for instance, could possibly be tragic in Sophocles' *Antigone*. It would seem absolutely senseless to us that a woman should risk her life by obeying the divinely ordained law which demands the burial of her slain brother; and is obeying it because she holds it sacred, its sanctity rendering invalid the contrary decree issued by the king. And the tragic metamorphosis that, according to Nietzsche, is the "true" and "good" effect of tragedy: the transformation of terror into bliss, the ecstatic yea-saying that triumphantly resists the most forceful temptation to negate, would inevitably be lost on us. Or we would, reading *King Lear,* no longer perceive any moral difference between Cordelia and her sisters, or between Gloucester's sons, and thus judge the whole course of action, the grand sublimity of the poetry and the ending a tiresome futility. Or we would be unable to grasp the brilliance of Nietzsche's paradox: "Truth is the kind of error without which a certain species of life cannot live" (W.493). Or indeed of "We possess *art* lest we *perish of the truth.*"

With this we are back at our beginning and forced to ask whether Nietzsche himself, at that time of his life, allows us to make sense of this sentence. Of course, to ask thus goes against the grain. The sentence instantly *shocks* us into understanding it. But do we really? It may appear to us that we know "what he means" and may even marvel at the marvelous power with which "truth" is her endowed: it kills through the force of its ugliness; and by thus cutting short our lives, brings Nietzsche's philosophy of art to its climax. For until Nietzsche arrived on the philosophical scene, it had always been regarded as a blessing to live "in the truth." Plato may have looked upon it as a dangerous, even a blinding blessing, but a blessing nonetheless. Has it now transpired that we have to make a living of absurdity? For we appear to be so absurdly constituted that one of our deepest and most honorable desires, the desire for truth, would lead to our perdition *if there was no art.* But this is an echo from that "once upon a time" which we remembered before. Once upon a time—or once in the past—it may have seemed that art could save us from the fatal attacks of truth. In the meantime, it is often joining the commissioners of the ugly, thus becoming the kind of art which could never have inspired him to say what the young author of *The Birth of Tragedy* might have confessed (as he later did): that he was "passionately in love with art" and finally "saw art in everything that is." [10]

Long before Nietzsche wrote that philosophically breathtaking reflection on "How the true world became a fable," this consummation was well-prepared by the very logic of the aesthetics at work in *The Birth of Tragedy.* This is the book that could not have been written without Schopenhauer, whether it is obedient to him or whether it flagrantly violates his teachings by undermining the foundation on which it rests, namely the thesis that the work of art is a *revelation of the truth,* truth in the metaphysical sense of Plato's ideas. Without as yet declaring war on Schopenhauer, *The Birth of Tragedy* quietly topples the "aesthetic phenomenon," the work of art, from its Platonic base, from "truth." Instead, "truth" is replaced by "illusion" and its "redeeming power."

The German word is *Schein.* It is an uneasy compromise with philosophical respectability: Appearance (*Erscheinung*) would be the word that traditionally goes, as its contrast, with the Platonic Reality, the ultimate reality of the Ideas—or, as Christianity would have it, of that God whose reality is not the reality of "this world." To show the way that leads from Appearance to appearance, *Schein,* illusion and finally to the "fable" that"the true world," that ruinous invention of Plato and the Christian religion, was to become, we could quote endlessly from Nietzsche's later writing. We won't. A few passages will have to suffice to make the dramatic point: "Assuming the true world, it could still be a world less valuable for us; precisely the quantum of illusion might be of a higher rank on account of its value for our preservation." And then Nietzsche adds in brackets: "Unless appearance (*Schein*) were ground for condemnation?" (W.583 b). But who would be able to believe in the higher rank of the illusion once he *knows* that it *is* an illusion?

No, this reversal of Platonism will not work. "Assuming," on the contrary, that the empirical world is only apparent, an assemblage of shadows cast by the ideal Truth, who will hinder those who are hungry for initiation into the ultimate knowledge to set out on the Platonic quest? They will be unlikely to heed Nietzsche's instructions that the "true" opposition is "the apparent world and the world invented by a lie," even if "hitherto" this mendacious invention has been called the "real world," "truth," "God," all those notions "we have to abolish" (W.461). Would this not be also the abolition of art? And once we have succeeded in abolishing that world? Then we would have reduced the juxtaposition of true world and apparent world to its "true" meaning, namely "the antithesis 'world' and 'nothing'" (W.567). This is Nietzsche's most succinct equation between the "true world" of Platonism (or Christianity) and Nihilism. It is an equation as forceful as that between the *one* world, that "false, cruel, contradictory world," with which we are left after the toppling of Plato's "true world," and the Nihilism of this one world's meaninglessness. Either way leads, it appears, to spiritual Nothingness, at least according to that unpublished preface to the second edition of *The Birth of Tragedy*. Even more than the published one, it would have insisted on the "gloom" and "unpleasantness" of the book's basic conception: the disappearance of the Platonic distinction between a true and an apparent world; and because the *one* "real world" is false, cruel, contradictory, meaningless, "*we have need of lies,*" in order to "live." "The terrifying and questionable character of existence" is borne out by this abysmal necessity. But there is worse to come. Remembering that art is an illusion, a lie, and the artist an illusionist, a liar, we shall be struck by the enormity of the sentence: "The will to appearance, to illusion, to deception . . . counts as more profound, primeval, 'metaphysical' than the will to truth, to reality . . . ," because "art is worth more than truth" (W.853).

Where the truth is as intolerably ugly as this, a ceaseless offense to the spirit, and the lie as beautiful as the beauty of art (surprising how consistently Nietzsche clings to beauty as the foremost criterion of art); where the "real" is man's worst enemy, and illusion, therefore, becomes the redeeming deceiver, there the human world has been torn asunder. A vast gap has opened, attracting swarms of demons. Some of them—these need not be failed artists, bad painters—would noisily claim that it is their mission to fuse the severed worlds again by appropriating the real as if it were the raw material for the making of a work of art, a pseudo-aesthetic phenomenon, a totally controlled body politic, a "perfect" society. This is the connection, if any, between the philosopher of art and the devastating usurpers of the human estate. But it is of course only one of modernity's many elements that disastrously connect.

# NIETZSCHE'S TERRORS: TIME
# AND THE INARTICULATE

There are many records of Nietzsche's early life that may cautiously be interpreted as signs of a pathological condition existing long before any symptoms of the presumed syphilitic insanity could possibly have shown. This is certainly so in the case of the report from Schulpforta, the distinguished boarding school to which the exceptionally gifted and penurious scholarship student was admitted in 1855. Describing the eighteen-year-old youth as exceedingly myopic, this report speaks of frequent strong headaches and advises careful observation because Nietzsche's father had died young from an inadequately diagnosed brain disease with which he was afflicted even when the child was conceived. But the most ominous of these documents is an autobiographical note of 1868–69. It was the time during which the student of classical philology met Wagner. He was twenty-five then and studied in Leipzig. The note is about a hallucination and reads: "What I am afraid of is not the terrifying figure behind the chair, but its voice. No, not the words, but the horrifyingly inarticulate sound of that creature. If only it spoke in the manner of human beings!"[1]

There is, of course, always the danger that an interpreter may make too much of such casual if uncanny autobiographical offerings. Yet here the temptation is reinforced by this reader's wonder, mixed of disquiet and intellectual delight, at Nietzsche's impassioned flow of articulation—which one might call loquacity were it not for the brilliance of its style. Sustained by an apparently inexhaustible energy which it may be too innocent to call inspiration, much of his writing is characterized by a kind of ecstatic meditativeness. One imagines this lonely wanderer, notebook in hand, walking along the sea between Santa Margherita and Portofino, where, as he said, "the Bay of Genova sings the last notes of its melody" drowned out these days by incessantly passing cars, the bay having long since ceased to be "the little forgotten world of bliss" that Nietzsche remembers in *Ecce Homo*. According to that unique autobiography, it was there that Zarathustra ambushed and overpowered him. Or one thinks of this almost perpetually sick man who only rarely felt well during the years of his maturity—at best one day in ten, he once said—imperturbably writing, writing, writing, on mountainous pathways, in unheated and poorly furnished rooms, in the wintry solitude of a Genova attic, writing as no philosopher before or after him ever wrote, in a language that rushes on in glittering cataracts, giving the impression that it never was in need of a pausing or correcting hand. Is it too extravagant to suspect that the driving force behind this orgy of wordmaking is the terror of the inarticulate, not unrelated to the hallucinated figure behind the chair, "the horrifyingly inarticulate and inhuman sound" uttered by that ghost? It is as if Nietzsche were constantly in flight from it, or else engaged in a war against it, raiding the inarticulate or trying to defeat its inhuman voice with the *vox humana*.

It is this that almost defines the total war that Nietzsche wages against the inarticulate, a war without end, for no articulation is capable of decisively winning it, and no language can forever prevail over the howls of the primeval jungle. Even the harmony of the spheres is always in danger of being upset by the cries of the chaos, and only for happy intervals can Apollo live in friendship with the unruly Dionysus.

The precariousness of all articulation is obvious enough. Articulation, whether it is linguistic or musical, consists in a complex system of dams, dykes, and canals warding off the threatening ocean of the inarticulate. It is fenland, fertile but exposed, elaborately drained as it is and fortified against the high tides of the turbulent elements. Widening the influx of the surrounding waters may indeed be enriching if they are controlled and tamed. Yet this may also prove as destructive, to an extent ever more clearly discernible, as the greedy and self-conscious reception of "the primitive" by a late and tired tradition. Judgment, aesthetic or ethical, is, in such situations, a delicate exercise of tact and intellectual instinct, and the indiscriminately positive use of the ungainly adjective "innovative" betrays vulgarity. Although Nietzsche cannot possibly be held to be the most exemplary thinker in the history of thought, he *is* exemplary in his scrupulous weighing of the formidable risks a society runs by welcoming the spectacularly different, very old or very new, only because it denies the validity of the traditional. It may sound odd to say this of a man who so ferociously fought what had been handed down by the past, diluted as it was by routine and the enfeebled spirit. Yet often he showed himself to be faithfully wedded to inherited possessions, and did so with surprising discrimination. Surprising because it was hardly to be expected that one born into the country vicarage of a village in Saxony and raised in the stuffy mediocrity of a provincial town (later he would sarcastically speak of the *"Naumburger Tugenden,"* the Naumburg virtues) would be almost infallible in his aesthetic discernment.

Indeed, his thought was a form of dynamite, or he used it, he asserted, as a hammer, particularly with regard to Christianity. But surely, no explosives or other means of destruction were at work when this tormented mind remembered the *Rosengeruch des Unwiederbringlichen,* the aroma of roses and loves, withered now and irretrievable. Or when he allowed Claude Lorrain to sing for him, with paint, the melody of the Mediterranean. Or when he sought and found comfort in the repose of Goethe's prose. Or when his recollections of human encounters suggested to him that it was only among Christians that he ever met with truly noble minds. Or when this "Anti-Christ" ridiculed the superstition of scientific gentlemen, priding themselves upon having overcome religion. Not so, Nietzsche countered. "Christ on the Cross is the most sublime symbol—even today."[2]

Contradiction? It is regrettable that there is no other word for it because it is, in Nietzsche's case, a misleading term. For what we have no choice but to call contradiction is both too easily shown by pointing to the self-evident, and unreachable by such demonstrations. It is, for instance, close to obtuseness to accuse him, as is sometimes done, of illogicality on account of his all-too-famous pronouncement that God, who by definition is immortal, "is dead"; close to blindness not to see that this is meant as a shocking paradox. His contradictions belong to the pattern of a most complex mind. They are woven into it just as colors and figures are woven into tapestries. It is inconceivable that anything less than a kind of *coincidentia oppositorum,* rooted in the very ground of Nietzsche's thought, could move him to prepare, on the one hand, the most venomous diatribe against Wagner, accusing him of corrupting the musical taste of the nation, of having indulged a *ne plus ultra* of histrionic mendacity, of Christian mimicry, with *Parsifal* (from its first performance in 1882 he pointedly stayed away in nearby Tautenburg); and, on the other hand, to write to Peter Gast (January 21, 1887) that the *Parsifal* music contained the best that Wagner had ever composed, namely the musical expression of a "sublime and extraordinary emotion and experience of the soul" and of "compassion felt with everything." "Things of this kind," Nietzsche continued, "may be found in Dante and nowhere else." Is there an artist, he asked, who has ever painted so melancholy an aspect of love as is heard in the last notes of the prelude to *Parsifal?* Yet scarcely two years earlier, Nietzsche had said of such music (to Malwida von Meysenbug, March 13, 1885) that it was the work of a decadent composer, a "badly turned-out musician and man who yet is a great actor." And one year after he had praised the *Parsifal* music in that letter to Gast, he gave free rein to his rejection of the "great actor" in *The Wagner Case* and *Nietzsche contra Wagner.*

As early as 1871, at the time of *The Birth of Tragedy,* Nietzsche was convinced that contradiction is the essence of what truly is, and tragedy its art;[3] twelve years afterward, in "The Afterworldly" portion of *Zarathustra I,* we read that the world itself is the projected image of an eternal contradiction.[4] The very name of Zarathustra, another name of the ancient Persian prophet Zoroaster whose religion was founded upon the primeval antagonism between Good and Evil, is in extreme contradiction to Zoroaster's unrelentingly moralist religion. For Nietzsche's prophet Zarathustra points the way toward a world "beyond Good and Evil."

Existential contradictoriness: this would be the category under which Nietzsche must be subsumed. His contradictions are far too obvious to be looked upon as mistakes or oversights. They are the outcome of his fear of curtailing articulation; and such curtailment is, lamentably and unavoidably, the result of logical consistency, as it is of any imposition of a philosophical system upon the totality of things. Indeed, this is true of language itself; for linguistic order is attainable only by abstraction and exclusion. One must turn to the Eskimos to learn what a betrayal of subtle differences our one word "snow" is. And the *casus belli* of Nietzsche's war against Socrates is the Athenian's insistence upon the virtuous pursuit of logic. Socrates enjoyed nothing more, Nietzsche wrote, than to prove his partners in dialogue wrong by the "vulgar" method *("pöbelhaft"* is the word Nietzsche uses) of entrapping them in logical contradictions. But, Nietzsche said, this plebeian zeal for logic is the worst offense against the fullness of life; for it is its plenitude of contradictions that nurture the sense of tragedy. Socrates, therefore, has poisoned the wellspring of ancient Greek art; and art is the embodied acknowledgment of life's resistance to a purely rational order.[5] Once again we hear the terrifying inarticulate voice from behind the chair that appears to prompt Nietzsche's hostility toward Socratic dialectics, toward the impoverishment of the articulation of life. And art, for him, is the only articulation in which the fundamental contradictoriness of life is kept intact. In this respect, at least, music is superior to language. *The Birth of Tragedy from the Spirit of Music* is, after all, the full title of his first book, a work unthinkable without Schopenhauer. And in Schopenhauer's philosophy of art it is music that is capable of sounding the note of existence itself; even in his acts of philosophical desertion Nietzsche remained faithful to Schopenhauer with regard to music. Clearly, Nietzsche aims at Socrates when he says in a letter to Peter Gast (December 12, 1887) that he himself distrusts logic "and even reasons. What a man *dares* to accept as true is the real measure of his strength. . . . I myself have only rarely the courage of my knowledge." (How much, at times, he needed such courage is shown by that moving letter to Franz Overbeck, July 2, 1885), in which he said: "My life is now comprised in the wish that the truth about all things be different from my way of seeing it. If only someone could convince me of the improbability of my truths!" Has any philosopher ever said anything like this?)

The Inarticulate comes to rule supreme in oblivion, either in the individual's forgetfulness or in those long stretches of the collective past that have never been and never will be raised into the—necessarily incomplete—articulations of History, the record of human existence that is profusely interspersed with dark passages. This accounts for the continuous questing of archeology, paleontology, anthropology, geology; and accounts, too, for Nietzsche's warnings against the "insomnia" of historicism. With regard to the individual, the same drive is behind the modern fascination with the unconscious and, thus, with dreams; and it was Nietzsche who, before Freud, spoke of forgetting as an *activity* of the mind. At the beginning of the Second Essay of his *Genealogy of Morals* he claims, in defiance of all psychological "shallowness," that the lacunae of memory are not merely "passive" but the outcome of an active and positive "screening," preventing us from remembering what would upset our equilibrium.[6] Nietzsche is the first discoverer of successful "repression," the burying of potential experience in the inarticulate that is, at the same time, enemy territory for him.

It is a chronological mishap that Nietzsche could not know Proust. He who excitedly discovered for himself Stendhal and Dostoevsky would have deeply and critically appreciated Proust's enchanted and all but monstrous attempt to recall the wholeness of a life's experience: *A la recherche du temps perdu.* For it would have been impossible for Nietzsche not to be struck by the poetic selectivity that continually frustrates the most pedantic literary ambition ever entertained: to achieve perfect recollection; impossible not to be impressed by Proust's forgetfulness, the subterfuges of the creatively active and busy memory, the writer's transformations, his elusive hints and pseudonymous hiding places—all that would prove the truth of one of Nietzsche's aphorisms: "'This I did,' my memory says. 'This I cannot possibly have done,' says my pride and remains inexorable. In the end my memory does give in."[7] A large part of psychoanalytic theory is anticipated as well as outshone by the brilliance of this observation, which acknowledges pride, not to say the sense of human dignity, as the principal ally of his fiend oblivion, the totally inarticulate.

The refusal of a person's memory, a refusal as obstinate as it is wholesome, to retain all his failures, humiliations, pains, moods, betrayals, and inconsistencies, proves the futility of the attempt to recollect the entirety of experience—even that of one single day. Although Nietzsche may be wrong in morosely believing that we "remember only what does not cease to *hurt*,"[8] the memory is always in some ways the loser in its bargains with time; and the most profitable compromise with its rapacious flights into forgetfulness may well be those in which the material to be stored up has been gradually changed into *forms* that are, as articulations, more durable: anecdotes, stories, myths, poems. The original "experience" is, then, the mere occasion of such metamorphoses. The original experience? Can it ever be reconstructed? Hardly, for to remember is to distort, whether the distortions tend to turn into articulate nightmares or sweet dreams.

In many passages Nietzsche comes close to seeing nothing but the deceitful maneuvers of Time in what we do or do not remember. And when he said of memory that it tends to pour recollection into hardened molds, that is, clichés, he was obviously unmindful of the artist's imagination which, re-*creating* the "deceit," transforms it into something livelier, purer, more abundant. Clichés: their solemn name is ritual. And what clichés, rituals, conventions, even melodies, epics in hexameters, and sonnets have in common with the rules of any game is the disciplining of spontaneity, the bridling of sheer "authenticity," the limiting of potential expression, much of which is left to the inarticulate—for the benefit of articulation. Indeed, the game of life, like any other game, can be played only on the strength of rules to which the players submit. Therefore, it seems devoid of any sanction, "authenticity," "true" or "real" meaning outside the fixed designs, the man-made orders, or the pleasure it may give to players or spectators. If anything were permissible, if there were no drastic curtailments of the players' freedom, no authoritative sanctions, no forceful lawgiving, there could be no game whatever.

Nietzsche did indeed experiment with the possibility that "everything is permitted"[9]—the belief, by the way, of Dostoevsky's "refuted" a-moralists such as Raskolnikoff or Ivan Karamasoff. It is a devastating experiment, for although it has been undertaken for the sake of the uninhibited fullness of life, it is terrifyingly self-defeating. Certainly, every moral taboo grievously diminishes the richness of life's possibilities, the range of its infinite contradictions and contradictory articulations. But at the same time, that moral nihilism would, like a game without rules, issue in chaos and thus frustrate the intention to articulate *anything*. After the demise of God, the supreme lord of the game's rules, the chaotic movements on the field will count for nothing. *Es ist nichts damit.* Nothing, *nichts, nihil;* and as this *nihil* has no speech, all it can utter are the inarticulate and inhuman sounds of that ghost that, it seemed, could be exorcised only through the total victory of articulation. Yet, if "everything" were "permitted," the outcome would be the totally inarticulate.

Nietzsche, from early on in his life, inclined towards the belief that true philosophy can be found only among the pre-Socratic minds of Greece, and the focus of his philosophical affection had always been Heraclitus of Ephesus, the philosopher of a world of perpetual change, endlessly moving toward no goal. Nietzsche made Heraclitus after his own image, and saw the world as he presumed Heraclitus saw it: as a place without "meaning," aim, or divinely ordained end; for if there is an end and purpose, Nietzsche rather questionably questioned, has there not been enough endlessness of time behind us to fulfill it? Often Nietzsche falls back upon the Heraclitean image of a god who, like a child, plays a game with the world, a solitary game without rules, just as an infant plays on the sandy beach, building castles to destroy them again as his fancy wills it, resuming the senseless play in the senselessly shifting sands that shift for ever and ever.[10] Despite appearances and language, there is nothing in the world of which it could truthfully be said that it *is*. Even the rugged chain of Alps that greets its 'invader' summer after summer only pretends that it remains identical. Imperceptibly, it changes all the time.

Nothing *is*, *everything* is changing—becoming something different: *everything* at least after the disappearance of the One of whom it was held that He possessed perfect and, therefore, constant Being: God. But this is no concern of Heraclitus', perhaps not even of Goethe's when, in his poem "*Selige Sehnsucht*," he commanded "*Stirb und werde,*" die and become! But while Goethe's vision comprehended the essential identity of every individual's entelechy, the innermost being that is indestructable in death, Heraclitus knew only eternal change as the model of existence, implicitly dismissing, according to Nietzsche's perspective, the hypothesis of *Sein,* of Being. Yet one may well ask whether it is not necessary for change to have roots in Being? For change is unthinkable without anything that *is,* anything that makes change perceptible. It was Heraclitus' contemporary, Parmenides, who was the composer, as Nietzsche puts it, "of the prelude to the theme of ontology," of the philosophy of Being,[11] a theme which, to the Heraclitean Nietzsche, is the most effective trap that language, with its unyielding and seductive "Is," has laid out to catch our thought. This doubt, attacking the justification of something seemingly so innocuous as an auxiliary verb, leads straight into the most revolutionary of all philosophical-literary revolutions after Goethe: the subversion of the authority of traditional language. The ultimate outcome of this subversion would be the enthroning of the speechless ghost. Did Nietzsche, the lover of the paradox, know and not mind this ultimate stage of nihilism? He did mind and boasted, hardly more than a year before his collapse, that he had lived through all the radical consequences of nihilism, "leaving it behind, outside himself," after having been "the first perfect nihilist of Europe."[12] Both these superlative claims are somewhat tinged by the lurking megalomania.

God is dead. The terror with which this event—and he did call it an *event*—filled Nietzsche is hardly understood any more. Yet to that latecomer in a long line of theologians and believers it meant the disapperance of meaning from the sentiment of life. This, as Nietzsche feared, pointed the way to nihilism. "A nihilist," he wrote, "is a person who says of the world as it is, that it better were not, and, with regard to the world as it should be, that it does not and cannot exist."[13] And it does not exist because God is no more. Therefore, there cannot be any belief in a Beyond, an ineffable life beyond the grave, not even in the possibility of that "godless" peace of Buddha and Schopenhauer that is indistinguishable from the peace of God and attainable only through the overcoming of all worldly desires and aspirations.

Nihilism, Nietzsche believes, is the fate of all religious traditions if along the road their fundamental assumptions are lost. This, according to him, is so with Judaism because of its all-pervasive "Thou shalt not" that, in the long run, can be accepted and obeyed only within a rigorously disciplined community of the faithful; and it is so with Christianity, not only because it was, to a large extent, heir to the Jewish moralism but, at the same time, tended to judge the whole domain of the natural to be a conspiracy against the divine spirit. For the Christian, the Here and Now with its deceptive promises of happiness—all of which promise, when it comes to it, an inevitable loss, and with its illusions of achievement, all of which conceal for a while the imminence of failure—is nothing but the testing ground for the soul to prove that it deserves the bliss of the Beyond. Nietzsche, like many before him, is philosophically outraged by this doctrine that conceives of Eternity as, at some point, taking over from Time, projecting it into endlessness, and of Time as being an outsider to the Eternal and, after the death of God, forever an exile from it. Everything, therefore, exists only for a while in its individual articulation and then never more. From this void, the black hole, there arises Nietzsche's Eternal Recurrence. It is to cure time of its mortal disease: its terminal destructiveness.

Nietzsche, believing that the traditional religious beliefs had become untenable, set out to seek "a new center." Yet, as he confessed in a note of the 1880s, he soon recognized the hopelessness of this quest. Therefore, he said, he "advanced further down the road of disintegration," finding there "new sources of strength for some individuals." "Against the paralyzing sense of universal dissolution, I held the *Eternal Recurrence*." [14] This is an important fragment from Nietzsche's intellectual autobiography and may serve as a footnote to the first and most "lyrical" invocation of what he later repeatedly called the most powerful thought of his prophet Zarathustra.

The first hesitant enunciation of the Eternal Recurrence is contained in the penultimate section of *The Joyous Science**; that is, at the end of the *whole* work as it existed before its fifth book was added in 1886 upon the completion of *Zarathustra*. I have quoted and discussed *Das grösste Schwergewicht,* as that section is untranslatably subtitled (it means approximaely "the greatest weight") in the essay "Zarathustra's Three Metamorphoses," included in the present volume. In 1883, then, the "weightiest thought" made its first appearance, but not without having been amply rehearsed in unpublished notes Nietzsche jotted down in preparing *The Joyous Science.* In the book itself it is cast in the form of interrogations and conjunctives, just as if it were not quite sure of itself. Indeed, it is not, certainly not as a doctrine. For the passage hinges on the extraordinary question raised by an extraordinary intruder: a ghost.

What, the ghost asks, would be his victim's response if the uncanny

---

* Walter Kaufmann published his excellent translation of the work under the title *The Gay Science* in obedience to Nietzsche's own subtitle *La gaya scienza,* the Mediterranean, "non-German," Provençal appellation given to the poetic spirit by the troubadours. Kaufmann used "gay" in learned and intelligently reasoned defiance of what is now the deplorably common usage of the word. Still, there comes a point where one cannot but yield to the tyranny of vulgarization. Yet even before sexual meaning had been imposed upon the defenseless adjective, I would have preferred "joyous" or "cheerful." Emerson, loved by Nietzsche, once called himself "Professor of the Joyous Science" as Kaufmann mentions in the Introduction to *Gay Science,* New York 1974, p. 8f.

visitor assured him that he must live his life once more and an infinite number of times, repeating every detail? Would the prospect of such an unending sequence of imperfect lives utterly dismay him? Would he curse the messenger, as Nietzsche himself might have done even at the very time his Zarathustra preached the Eternal Recurrence? For Zarathustra's author wrote in his notebook, "I do not wish to live again,"[15] confessing that only his imaginative power to create the *Übermensch* made life bearable for him. And in *The Joyous Science,* the ghostly question of that ghostly questioner is followed by the grand alternative to despair. It is an "Or" that reaches to the very center of Nietzsche's spiritual existence, to the very heart of his anxiety, the "existential *angst*" that, he feared, was bound to set up its rule over man after any expectation of transcendence was felt to be in vain. It is this that gives the "Or" with which the ghost's question continues, its weight: *Or* have you ever experienced a moment so tremendous that, if only to recapture this one timeless moment, you would bless the ghost and his "divine" news?

Here, at its first published emergence, the ancient and "impossible" idea of the Eternal Recurrence ("impossible" Nietzsche called it early on, in 1874, when he wrote the second of his *Untimely Meditations*)[16] is revealed as the imagined counterweight to the rapacity of time that takes with it into oblivion even those moments that insistently demand, as it were, life everlasting. Although Nietzsche thought of the Eternal Recurrence as intolerable if it meant the endless repetition of all the fragments, frustrations, losses, and imperfections that all but make up the lives of men ("I don't want to live again"), there is also the promise offered by the "tremendous moment." This belongs to a mode of experience that, in utopian perpetuity, would be distinctive of the life of the *Übermensch* and defeat Time, the all-poweful eraser, through the lasting form and lucid articulation that hitherto had been provided only by poetry and art. Nietzsche, as early as *The Birth of Tragedy,* allowed *only* "the aesthetic phenomenon"—that is, the world perceived in the perspective of art—to "justify world and existence into all eternity."[17] When he repeated this three times in the course of the treatise, the young writer unknowingly prepared himself and his readers for the later translation, half poetic and half pseudoanthropological, of this "phenomenon" into the prophecy of reality (or the reality of prophecy). And only the *Übermensch* would survive the lethal gloom of the Eternal Recurrence. Indeed, he would be *created* by this devastating message: The *Übermensch* would not only be able to live with the Eternal Recurrence but would demand it; for only the Eternal

Recurrence could accommodate the abundance of his "tremendous moments."*

This is the prevalent meaning that the Eternal Recurrence has in Nietzsche's thought and imagination. It is the school that teaches eternity, and only those who graduate from it, here and now, joyfully receive this conqueror of time. The rest, the "herd," are destroyed by it. True, Nietzsche repeatedly made the attempt to base the Eternal Recurrence upon the doctrines of nineteenth-century physics: the constancy of energy and time's infiniteness, arguing that *therefore* the given amount of energy had no choice but at some point to produce the *same* configurations in limitless time: "The law of the conservation of energy demands *eternal recurrence*" is one of the notes assembled in *The Will to Power*.[18] He ignored, absurdly, that "the same" would also mean the sameness of states of consciousness, which in turn was bound to preclude the "tremendous" effect Zarathustra's message might have on the mind: Live your life in such a way that you should desire nothing more than to live it again and again. But *without* the memory of having lived this same life before, this would not make any difference, and *with* that memory it would not be the same. Nonetheless, it is the hoped-for prophetic effect of the Eternal Recurrence and certainly not its "scientific" validity that caused Nietzsche to love this "impossible" idea so much.

On the verge of his collapse into insanity, at the onset of clinical megalomania, Nietzsche, concluding *The Twilight of the Idols* in the late summer of 1888, called himself: ". . . I, the last disciple of the philosopher Dionysus.—I, the teacher of the Eternal Recurrence."[19] Here, obviously, he is not the *author* of *Zarathustra*, but Zarathustra himself. If the prophet succeeded in "transvaluing" all traditional values, as was his madly grand intention, if it did come to pass that the "philosopher Dionysus," with the hammer of the Dionysian philosophy or the explosive thought of the Eternal Recurrence, changed the character and the consciousness of human beings, this would surely be *unique,* a change that could not have taken place before. Never before had mankind received *and* accepted the message of the Eternal Recurrence. If it had, it would not be in need of the lesson now, for the *Übermensch* would long ago have come into being, gloriously overthrowing the regime of the mediocre "herd." To be sure, Nietzsche believed that with the doctrine of the Eternal Recurrence of All Things

---

* To lend the weight of eternity to what, without it, would be "the unbearable lightness of being." Milan Kundera owes the title of his novel to Nietzsche's, "Eternal Recurrence" and acknowledges it.

he had produced what he called "the hardest possible thought."[20] Sometimes he must have assumed that this thought would not only prove lethal to the mediocre but would change man as such, man as hitherto he has been. Therefore, he added in the notes from the time of *Zarathustra*: "Now *let us create the creature* who will accept it light-heartedly and blissfully."[21] Of course, the creature to be created was the *Übermensch*. Nietzsche's jottings from that time show that he had planned the prophet's death for the moment when his followers answered the question, "Do you desire to live the whole of your life once again?" in the enthusiastic affirmative. At that moment Zarathustra would die "of happiness."[22]

After this formidable revolution of consciousness, history would change magnificently. A new epoch would begin, the epoch of the *Übermensch*, the golden age that could never have come before: "Only now, with the *death of all gods*, we *will* the *Übermensch* into life." This is Zarathustra's Last Will. It will be the "Great Midday" of Man when he celebrates his going-down as his highest hope, "for it is the way towards a new morning."[23] And a few pages into the second part of *Zarathustra*, the prophet indeed does say, "Never yet has there been an *Übermensch*."[24] Which means that the visions of *Übermensch* and Eternal Recurrence are the paradigm of logical incompatibility, and are, momentously proclaimed as they are by the same prophet, the most dramatic articulation of Nietzsche's contradictoriness.

It is amazing that Nietzsche, the master psychologist—"There was no psychology before me,"[25] he wrote in *Ecce Homo*, once more in obvious defiance of the Eternal Recurrence—did not see or pretended not to see that the change of consciousness, a change so profound that it was to bring about a new and unique kind of human being, could not have a place in the chain of the Eternal Recurrence. Yet this crass contradiction is revealing. It shows the overpowering strength of Nietzsche's desire to escape from transience, oblivion, the inarticulate—from the voice behind the chair. If the world is in the condition of permanent, inescapable flux, it is in its *totality* as elusive as every moment in it. And it is inaccessible to clear articulation through a language whose dominant mode is the indicative of being: I *am*, it *is*. The eternal Recurrence, so it appeared to the Heraclitean Nietzsche, is the world's only chance to become wholly articulate. For articulation presupposes a measure of duration for what is to be articulated, and the Eternal Recurrence, Nietzsche wrote, is the closest approximation to Being of a world that otherwise knows only what is transitory. One of the jottings collected in *The Will to Power* reads: "To impose upon

becoming the character of being—that is the supreme will to power." [26]
It is certainly the supreme will of the Eternal Recurrence.

Many pages of aesthetic speculation have been devoted to defining
the "significant moment" in sculpture and paintings that, in their static
medium, depict bodies and things in motion. In the Eternal Recurrence the problem disappears; every moment is significant by virtue of
its eternal return. The Eternal Recurrence is the extreme *epic* philosophy—epic to the point of grandiose absurdity, a cosmic therapy
against the terror of the passing of every moment, a vanishing into
nothingness, into absolute oblivion. A mathematical magic is at work
in this philosophy. The endless repetition of a senseless life is assumed
to yield an immensity of spiritual significance, as if one could arrive at
an overwhelmingly positive sum by fanatically multiplying zero. It is
the "tremendous moment" that is assumed to work the miracle.

Will it? The answer is probably that the words "*Incipit tragoedia*"
that introduce *Thus Spoke Zarathustra* at the end of *The Joyous Science*
must be taken seriously. The tragedy begins when the prophet descends from his solitary mountain to teach the people down in the
valley what he himself has gradually learned: about the death of God
and gods and the fearful consequences that are bound to ensue unless
the *Übermensch* comes into being and breaks man's intolerable bondage
to Time. This is a bondage not unlike Macbeth's enslavement by the
"tomorrow and tomorrow and tomorrow" that, to the last syllable of
time's record, will take its foolish victims "the way to dusty death."
Only the *Übermensch* would be able to transform the "tale told by an
idiot" into a divine story. This, and only this, would be the transfiguring articulation that Nietzsche hopelessly hoped for. While he
waited, he sometimes—impatiently, recklessly, unforgivably—uttered words that appeared to advocate the most brutal, impious gov-
ernance of human affairs; and yet he does speak truthfully of himself
when, in the "Retired" section of *Zarathustra*,[27] he makes the Pope,
desolate in his unemployment, call Zarathustra, that ill-starred lover
of eternity, "the most pious of those who do not believe in God."

# NOTES

Works frequently cited have been identified by the following abbreviations:

J.A.   Johann Wolfgang von Goethe, *Jubilaums-Ausgabe,* 40 vols., Stuttgart and Berlin, 1902–1912

M.A.   Friedrich Nietzsche, *Gesammelte Werke,* Musarion-Ausgabe, 23 vols., Munich, 1922–1929

## Chapter 1. THE IMPORTANCE OF NIETZSCHE

1. M.A., VI, 133ff.; *Untimely Meditations,* I; "David Strauss," no. 1.
2. Letter to Paneth, May 1884.
3. Letter to his sister, mid-June 1884.
4. M.A., XIV, 81; Notes from the time of *Thus Spoke Zarathustra,* Single Notes.
5. M.A., III, 260ff.; Notes for planning "Empedocles" (autumn 1870).
6. M.A., XII, 156f.; *Joyous Science,* III, no. 125.
7. M.A., XIV, 193; Notes from the time of *Zarathustra,* Plans and Fragments.
8. M.A., XVIII, 3, 52; *Will to Power,* nos. 2, 57.
9. M.A., XXI, 277; *Ecce Homo,* "Why I am a Destiny," no. 2.
10. M.A., XIV, 121; Notes from the time of *Zarathustra,* Plans and Fragments.
11. M.A., XVIII, 8; *Will to Power,* no. 1.
12. M.A., XIX, 96ff.; *Will to Power,* no. 618.
13. M.A., XVIII, 8; *Will to Power,* Plans, no. 5.
14. M.A., XXI, 282; *Ecce Homo,* "Why I am a Destiny," no. 6.
15. M.A., XV, 243f.; *Beyond Good and Evil,* no. 269f.
16. M.A., XV, 246, *Beyond Good and Evil,* no. 270.
17. M.A., XV, 248; *Beyond Good and Evil,* no. 275.
18. Karl Kraus, *Beim Wort genommen,* Munich, 1955, 351.
19. M.A., XVII, 29, 286, 351, 367; Cf. *The Wagner Case,* no. 9, *Nietzsche Contra Wagner;* XIX, 384; *Will to Power,* Plans for *Will to Power.*
20. M.A., XV, 437; *Genealogy of Morals,* III, no. 24.
21. Cf. M.A., VI, 8, 50, 51; Plans of 1872 (autumn and winter); X, 238; *The Dawn,* no. 304; XI, 120; Notes from the time of *The Dawn;* XVI, 50; Notes from the time of Transvaluation; XVII, 101; *Twilight of the Idols,* "What Germans Lack," no. 3; XIX, 80, 85, 225, 230, 263; *Will to Power,* nos. 585, 588, 815, 824, 864.
22. M.A., VI, 50; Plans of 1872 (autumn and winter).
23. M.A., XVIII, 20; *Will to Power,* no. 19.
24. M.A., XVIII, 24; *Will to Power,* no. 27.

25. M.A., XI, 309; Notes from the time of *The Dawn*.
26. M.A., XVI, 80; Notes from the time of Transvaluation.
27. M.A., XVI, 44; Notes from the time of Transvaluation.
28. M.A., XIX, 329; *Will to Power*, no. 983.
29. Cf. M.A., XV, 293f.; *Genealogy of Morals*, I, no. 8f.; XVI, 226ff., 326; Notes from the time of Transvaluation; XVII, 47f.; *The Wagner Case*, Epilogue, XVII, 153f.; *Twilight of the Idols*, "My Debt to the Ancients"; XVII, 199f.; *The Antichrist*, no. 26; XVII, 351; "Art and Artists."
30. M.A., XIII, 118; *Zarathustra*, "Zarathustra's Speeches."
31. M.A., XIV, 173f.; Notes from the time of *Zarathustra*, Plans and Fragments.
32. M.A., XIV, 179; Notes from the time of *Zarathustra*, Plans and Fragments.
33. M.A., XIV, 187; Notes from the time of *Zarathustra*, Plans and Fragments.
34. M.A., XVIII, 45; *Will to Power*, no. 55; XIV, 187; Notes from the time of *Zarathustra*, Plans and Fragments.
35. M.A., XIX, 229; *Will to Power*, no. 822.
36. M.A., XIII, 166f.; *Zarathustra*, "Zarathustra's Speeches."
37. M.A., XIV, 121; Notes from the time of *Zarathustra*, Plans and Fragments.
38. M.A., X, 247f.; *The Dawn*, no. 327.
39. Letter to Franz Overbeck, July 2, 1885.
40. M.A., IX, 7; *Human, All Too Human*, II, 2, Preface of 1886.
41. M.A., XIV, 176; Notes from the time of *Zarathustra*, Plans and Fragments.
42. M.A., XIV, 62; Notes from the time of *Zarathustra*, Single Notes.
43. M.A., XVII, 51; *The Wagner Case*, Epilogue.
44. M.A., XXI, 276; *Ecce Homo*, "Why I am a Destiny," no. 1.
45. M.A., XIV, 131; Notes from the time of *Zarathustra*, Plans and Fragments.
46. M.A., X, 22f.; *The Dawn*, no. 14.

Chapter 2. NIETZSCHE AND GOETHE

1. J.A., XXXVII, 102–5.
2. M.A., VII, 204; Plan for "A Future Philology."
3. M.A., XVII, 364; from "Art and Artists."
4. *Wilhelm Meisters Wanderjahre*, Book I, chap. 6, J.A., XIX, 72.
5. Ibid., chap. 10, J.A., XIX, 132.
6. Ibid., 146.
7. *Faust II*, verses 11127–42.
8. Letter to Wilhelm von Humboldt, March 17, 1832.
9. J.A., XXXVII, 104.
10. J.A., V, 247, 248.
11. M.A., XIX, 85; *Will to Power*, no. 588.

12. *Wilhelm Meisters Wanderjahre*, Book I, chap. 10, J.A., XIX, 138, 139.
13. M.A., XVI, 235; Posthumous Notes 1882–1888.
14. M.A., XVII, 149, 150; *Twilight of the Idols*, "Skirmishes of an Untimely Man," no. 49.
15. J.A., XXXVIII, 266.
16. Ibid.
17. J.A., IV, 219.
18. *Wilhelm Meisters Wanderjahre*, Book III, chap. 13, J.A., XX, 187.
19. M.A., XVII, 48; *The Wagner Case*, Epilogue.
20. M.A., VII, 207; Plan for "A Future Philology."
21. M.A., VII, 349; "Thoughts about Wagner."
22. J.A., XXVII, 175.
23. Goethe, from the cycle *West-Östlicher Divan.*
24. Ibid.
25. M.A., III, 365; Plan for a treatise "Music and Tragedy."
26. M.A., XVI, 8; Posthumous Notes 1882–1888.
27. M.A., XVII, 150; *Twilight of the Idols*, "Skirmishes of an Untimely Man," no. 49.
28. *Faust II*, verses 11600–603.
29. Ibid., verses 7438–39.
30. Ibid., verses 11404–7.
31. Goethe, from the cycle *West-Östlicher Divan.*
32. M.A., XVII, 344; from "Art and Artists."
33. M.A., IX, 174, 175; *Human, All Too Human*, II, 1, no. 408.
34. M.A., XIV, 109; Notes from the time of *Zarathustra*, Plans and Fragments.
35. M.A., XXI, 73; Posthumous notes about *Human, All Too Human.*
36. M.A., IX, 55, 56; *Human, All Too Human*, II, 1, no. 99.
37. M.A., IX, 245; *Human, All to Human*, II, 2, no. 109.
38. M.A., III, 247; Notes from the time of *Birth of Tragedy*, "Socrates and Tragedy," no. 88.
39. M.A., IX, 448; Notes from the time of *Human, All Too Human.*
40. M.A., XVIII, 65; *Will to Power*, no. 83.
41. M.A., XIV, 11; Notes from the time of *Zarathustra*, Main Ideas.
42. *Faust II*, verses 6222–27, 6246–48.
43. M.A., XVII, 346; from "Art and Artists."
44. M.A., XIX, 352; *Will to Power*, no. 1031.

## Chapter 3. BURCKHARDT AND NIETZSCHE

1. Jakob Burckhardt, *Gesamtausgabe*, Stuttgart, Berlin, and Leipzig, 1930, V, 21, 22.
2. Burckhardt's letter to Hans Riggenbach, August 28, 1838.
3. Burckhardt, *Gesamtausgabe*, VIII, 3.
4. Ibid., V, 215.
5. Ibid., VII, 14.

6. Ibid., 15, 16.
7. Ibid., 15.
8. *Maximen und Reflexionen,* J.A., XXXVIII, 261.
9. Burckhardt's letter to Willibald Beyschlag, June 14, 1842.
10. Burckhardt, *Gesamtausgabe,* VIII, 5.
11. Ibid., VII, 52.
12. Ibid., 2.
13. Ibid., 1.
14. Ibid.
15. Ibid., 2.
16. Nietzsche's letter to Carl von Gersdorff, November 7, 1870.
17. Schopenhauer, *Sämmtliche Werke,* Grossherzog Wilhelm Ernst Ausgabe, Leipzig, II, 1217–19.
18. Burckhardt, *Gesamtausgabe,* VII, 3.
19. Ibid.
20. M.A., III, 138; *Birth of Tragedy,* no. 20.
21. Nietzsche's letter to Carl von Gersdorff, November 7, 1870.
22. Burckhardt's letter to Hermann Schauenburg, March 5, 1846.
23. Burckhardt, *Gesamtausgabe,* VII, 28.
24. M.A., VII, 369; from the preparatory notes for *Richard Wagner in Bayreuth.*
25. M.A., XV, 245, 246; *Beyond Good and Evil,* no. 270.
26. Nietzsche's letter to Burckhardt, January 6, 1889, first published in Edgar Salin, *Jakob Burckhardt und Nietzsche,* Basle, 1938, 227.
27. Ibid., 226.
28. Burckhardt, *Gesamtausgabe,* VII, 6, 7.
29. Ibid., 202.
30. Burckhardt's letter to Friedrich von Preen, June 16, 1888.
31. Burckhardt's letter to Max Alioth, November 19, 1881.
32. Burckhardt's letter to Hans Riggenbach, December 12, 1838.
33. Burckhardt's letter to Albert Brenner, March 16, 1856.
34. Burckhardt, *Gesamtausgabe,* VII, 126.
35. H. Gelzer, *Ausgewählte kleine Schriften,* Leipzig, 1907, 325.

Chapter 4. THE TEACHER OF "FREE SPIRITS"

1. See footnote at the beginning of this essay.
2. M.A., XIX, 373f.; *Will to Power,* no. 1067.
3. M.A., XV, 243f.
4. Ibid., 245.
5. Ibid., 248.
6. Ibid.
7. M.A., VIII, 410f.
8. Ibid.
9. M.A., XIX, 13.
10. M.A., XIX, 248; *Will to Power,* no. 851.

11. M.A., XI, 82; Notes from the time of *The Dawn.*
12. M.A., XIII, 166; *Thus Spoke Zarathustra*, II, "On Poets."
13. M.A., XIII, 237; *Thus Spoke Zarathustra*, III, "The Return Home."

Chapter 5. ZARATHUSTRA'S THREE METAMORPHOSES

1. M.A., XXI, 251f.; *Ecce Homo*, "Zarathustra."
2. M.A., XIII, 25; *Zarathustra*, "Zarathustra's Speeches."
3. M.A., XIII, 25, 26f.; *Zarathustra*, "Zarathustra's Speeches."
4. M.A., XV, 13; *Beyond Good and Evil*, no. 6.
5. M.A., IX, 7; *Human, All Too Human*, II, 1, Preface, no. 4.
6. M.A., XIII, 166; *Zarathustra*, II, "On Poets."
7. M.A., XVI, 36f.; Notes from the time of Transvaluation, "The Species of Philosophers."
8. M.A., III, 5; 1886 Preface to *Birth of Tragedy.*
9. M.A., XIII, 321; *Zarathustra*, IV, "The Magician."
10. M.A., X, 22; *The Dawn*, no. 14.
11. M.A., X, 247f.; *The Dawn*, no. 327.
12. M.A., XIX, 19; *Will to Power*, no. 493.
13. M.A., XV, 243f; *Beyond Good and Evil*, no. 269.
14. M.A., XV, 246; *Beyond Good and Evil*, no. 270.
15. M.A., XV, 248; *Beyond Good and Evil*, no. 275.
16. M.A., XII, 253f.; *Joyous Science*, IV, no. 341.
17. M.A., XI, 187; Notes from the time of *The Dawn.*
18. M.A., XIV, 121; Notes from the time of *Zarathustra*, Plans and Fragments.
19. M.A., XIV, 187.
20. M.A., XVIII, 45; *Will to Power*, No. 55.
21. M.A., XIII, 26; *Zarathustra*, "Zarathustra's Speeches."
22. M.A., XVIII, 3, 52; *Will to Power*, Preface, no. 57.
23. M.A., XIII, 27; *Zarathustra*, "Zarathustra's Speeches."
24. M.A., IV, 183, 310ff.; *Philosophy in the Tragic Age of Greece* and "The Pre-Platonic Philosophers"; lecture on Heraclitus.
25. M.A., III, 46; *Birth of Tragedy*, no. 5.
26. Friedrich Schiller in the essay on "Naive and Sentimental Poetry."
27. M.A., XVIII, 356; *Will to Power*, Plans of 1888 (spring and summer).
28. Cf. M.A., XVIII, 62f.; *Will to Power*, no. 78.
29. M.A., XIII, 166f.; *Zarathustra*, II, "On Poets."
30. M.A., XVIII, 57, 309; *Will to Power*, nos. 68, 434.
31. M.A., XVII, 249; *The Antichrist*, no. 57.

Chapter 6. RILKE AND NIETZSCHE WITH A DISCOURSE ON THOUGHT, BELIEF AND POETRY

1. T. S. Eliot, *Selected Essays* (1917–32), London, 1948, 141.
2. Ibid., 135.
3. Ibid., 13.

4. Ibid., 137.

5. Ibid., 138.

6. First published in a Berlin literary journal and reprinted in *Erzählungen und Skizzen aus der Frühzeit*, Leipzig, 1930, 347–56.

7. *Ewald Tragy*, Munich, 1929–30.

8. Unpublished, but partly quoted in Ruth Mövius, *Rainer Maria Rilkes Studenbuch, Entstehung und Gehalt*, Leipzig, 1937, and in M. Sievers, *Die Biblischen Motive in der Dichtung Rainer Maria Rilkes*, Berlin, 1938.

9. Lou Andreas-Salomé, *Friedrich Nietzsche in seinen Werken*, Wien, 1894.

10. *Das Florenzer Tagebuch*, published together with other diaries in *Tagebücher aus der Frühzeit*, Leipzig, 1942.

11. *Ausgewählte Werke*, Leipzig, 1938, I, 14.

12. Ibid., 17.

13. M.A., XX, 158; *Poems*, "From High Mountains."

14. Letter to Malwida von Meysenbug, January 14, 1880.

15. *Tagebücher aus der Frühzeit*, 92.

16. M.A., XXI, 248; *Ecce Homo*, "Zarathustra," no. 1.

17. M.A., XIX, 359–65; *Will to Power*, no. 1049ff.; Cf. also Nietzsche on the Dionysian Goethe, M.A., XVII, 149, 150; *Twilight of the Idols*, "Skirmishes of an Untimely Man," no. 49.

18. Letter to Ellen Key, quoted in Paul Zech, *Rainer Maria Rilke: Der Mensch und das Werk*, Dresden, 1930, 118, 119.

19. *Tagebücher aus der Frühzeit*, 38.

20. Cf. Rilke, *Sonnets to Orpheus*, 1, III, and Nietzsche, M.A., XII, 156, 157; *Joyous Science*, III, no. 125; XIX, 228; *Will to Power*, no. 820.

21. M.A., XIII, 237; *Zarathustra*, III, "Return Home."

22. *Tagebücher aus der Frühzeit*, 89.

23. M.A., XX, 248; *Dionysian Dithyrambs*, no. 120.

24. *Ausgewählte Werke*, I, 176.

25. M.A., XX, 152; *Poems 1882–1888*, "Venice."

26. *Ausgewählte Werke*, I, 143.

27. M.A., XXI, 251; *Ecce Homo*, "Zarathustra," no. 3.

28. *Briefe*, Wiesbaden, 1950, II, 308–11.

29. Ibid., 382, 407.

30. *Selected Essays*, 135.

31. Ibid., 134.

32. Ibid., 135 (my italics).

33. Hegel, *Werke*, Berlin, 1835, $X_3$, 243, and $X_1$, 16.

34. *Rainer Maria Rilke*, Cambridge, 1952.

35. *Briefe*, II, 395.

36. *Ausgewählte Werke*, II, 297.

37. M.A., XIV, 80; Notes from the time of *Zarathustra*, Single Notes.

38. M.A., XII, 157; *Joyous Science*, no. 125.

39. *Briefe*, II, 480.

40. M.A., XIV, 234; Notes from the time of Transvaluation.

41. *Briefe*, II, 405.
42. *Tagebücher aus der Frühzeit*, 71.
43. M.A., XIV, 121, 125; Notes from the time of *Zarathustra*, Plans and Fragments.
44. M.A., XIV, 187; Notes from the time of *Zarathustra*, Plans and Fragments.
45. M.A., XIV, 191, 180; Notes from the time of *Zarathustra*, Plans and Fragments.
46. Cf. J. F. Angelloz, *Rainer Maria Rilke*, Paris, 1936, 3.
47. M.A., XIII, 97, 101; *Zarathustra*, I, "On the Gift-Giving Virtue," and II, motto.
48. *Ausgewählte Werke*, I, 364, 365.
49. *Briefwechsel in Gedichten mit Erika Mitterer*, Wiesbaden, 1950, 56.
50. M.A., XIV, 119; Notes from the time of *Zarathustra*, Plans and Fragments.
51. *Briefe*, II, 481–83.
52. M.A., XIV, 121; Notes from the time of *Zarathustra*, Plans and Fragments.
53. M.A., XI, 79; Notes from the time of *The Dawn*.
54. *Ideen 13*, Athenaum III, Berlin, 1800.
55. *Werke*, ed. Kluckhohn, III, 357.
56. M.A., XIII, 166; *Zarathustra*, II, "On Poets."
57. M.A., XX, 190; *Dionysian Dithyrambs*, "Mere Fool."
58. M.A., XIV, 326, 327; Notes for Prefaces.
59. M.A., XIX, 228; *Will to Power*, no. 822.
60. M.A., III, 10; 1886 Preface to *Birth of Tragedy*.

Chapter 7. YEATS AND NIETZSCHE

1. M.A., XVIII, 3, 52; *Will to Power*, nos. 2, 57.
2. M.A., XIV, 121; Notes from the time of *Zarathustra*, Plans and Fragments.
3. M.A., XIX, 292; *Will to Power*, no. 916.

Chapter 8. WITTGENSTEIN AND NIETZSCHE

1. Norman Malcolm, *Ludwig Wittgenstein, A Memoir*, London and New York, 1958, 35f.
2. Ibid., 98.
3. Ludwig Wittgenstein, *Philosophical Investigations*, transl. G. E. M. Anscombe, Oxford, 1953, no. 255.
4. M.A., XXI, 81; Posthumous notes about *The Dawn*.
5. Malcolm, *Ludwig Wittgenstein*, 55.
6. M.A., IX, 183; *Human, All Too Human*, II, 2, no. 5.
7. Robert Musil, *Der Mann ohne Eigenschaften*, Hamburg, 1952, 114.
8. Malcolm, *Ludwig Wittgenstein*, 70.

9. Ludwig Wittgenstein, *Tractatus Logico-Philosophicus*, transl. D. F. Pears and B. F. McGuiness, London and New York, 1961, no. 6.421.
10. Bertrand Russell, *My Philosophical Development*, New York, 1959, 216ff.
11. Wittgenstein, *Tractatus Logico-Philosophicus*, no. 6.13.
12. Ibid., no. 6.54.
13. Wittgenstein, *Philosophical Investigations*, no. 108.
14. M.A., XIX, 27f.; *Will to Power*, no. 515.
15. Wittgenstein, *Philosophical Investigations*, no. 109.
16. Malcolm, *Ludwig Wittgenstein*, 2.
17. Wittgenstein, *Philosophical Investigations*, nos. 126, 129.
18. M.A., II, 29; "Homer and Classical Philology," plans for the Introduction, no. 20.
19. Wittgenstein, *Philosophical Investigations*, no. 129.
20. M.A., VI, 45; Plans of 1872 (autumn and winter).
21. Wittgenstein, *Philosophical Investigations*, no. 115.
22. Wittgenstein, *Tractatus Logico-Philosophicus*, no. 5.4711.
23. M.A., VI, 78; Notes from summer 1873.
24. M.A., XV, 304f.; *Genealogy of Morals*, I, no. 13.
25. Wittgenstein, *Philosophical Investigations*, no. 109.
26. Ibid., no. 119.
27. M.A., XIX, 34; *Will to Power*, no. 522.
28. Wittgenstein, *Tractatus Logico-Philosophicus*, no. 6.41.
29. Wittgenstein, *Philosophical Investigations*, no. 116.
30. Ibid.
31. Ibid., no. 120.
32. Ibid., no. 124.
33. Ibid., no. 109.
34. Ibid., no. 111.
35. Ibid., nos. 106, 107.
36. Ibid., no. 19.
37. Cf. M.A. XIX, 252; *Will to Power*, no. 853, III.
38. Wittgenstein, *Philosophical Investigations*, no. 118.
39. M.A., X, 49; *The Dawn*, no. 47.
40. M.A., VI, 36; Plans of 1872 (autumn and winter).
41. Wittgenstein, *Philosophical Investigations*, no. 309.

Chapter 9. NIETZSCHE'S LAST WORDS
ABOUT ART VERSUS TRUTH

1. M.A., XIX, 229; *Will to Power*, no. 822.
2. M.A., XIV, 326; Posthumous notes of 1888.
3. M.A., XIV, 328; Posthumous notes of 1888.
4. M.A., XVII, 145; *Twilight of the Idols*, "Skirmishes of an Untimely Man," no. 45.
5. M.A., XIII, 166; *Zarathustra*, II, "On Poets."
6. M.A., XV, 243; *Genealogy of Morals*, no. 269.

7. M.A., XV, 246; *Genealogy of Morals,* no. 270.
8. M.A., XII, 311; *Joyous Science,* no. 370.
9. M.A., XVII, 76; *Twilight of the Idols,* "How the 'True World' . . . ," no. 6.
10. M.A., XXI, 68; Posthumous notes about *Human, All Too Human.*
11. M.A., III, 40ff.; *Birth of Tragedy,* no. 5.

## Chapter 10. NIETZSCHE'S TERRORS

1. *Historisch-Kristische Gesamtausgabe,* V, 205. This edition, Munich, 1937, interrupted by war in 1939, has never been completed.
2. M.A., XVIII, 162; *The Will to Power,* no. 219.
3. M.A., III, 326; Notes from the time of *The Birth of Tragedy.*
4. M.A., XIII, 32.
5. Cf. M.A., III, 206, 212; Notes from the time of *The Birth of Tragedy,* 1870.
6. M.A., XV, 319; *The Genealogy of Morals,* II, no. 1.
7. M.A., XV, 90; *Beyond Good and Evil,* no. 68.
8. M.A., XV, 322; *The Genealogy of Morals,* II, no. 3.
9. M.A., XIX, 80; *The Will to Power,* no. 602.
10. M.A., IV, 183; *Philosophy in the Age of Greece,* no. 7.
11. M.A., IV, 199; *Philosophy in the Age of Greece,* no. 1.
12. M.A., XVIII, 4; *The Will to Power,* no. 4.
13. M.A., XIX, 79; *The Will to Power,* no. 585A.
14. M.A., XVIII, 291; *The Will to Power,* no. 417.
15. M.A., XIV, 121; Notes from the time of *Zarathustra.*
16. M.A., VI, 246f.; *Untimely Meditations,* II, "On the Use and Misuse of History," no. 2.
17. M.A., III, 46; *The Birth of Tragedy,* no. 5.
18. M.A., XIX, 370; *The Will to Power,* no. 1063.
19. M.A., XVII, 159; *The Twilight of the Idols,* "My Debt to the Ancients."
20. M.A., XIX, 368; *The Will to Power,* no. 105.
21. M.A., XIV, 179; Notes from the time of *Zarathustra.*
22. M.A., XIV, 173; Notes from the time of *Zarathustra.*
23. M.A., XIII, 99; Conclusion of part I of *Zarathustra.*
24. M.A., XIII, 118; *Zarathustra,* conclusion of the section "On Priests."
25. M.A., XXI, 282; *Ecce Homo,* "Why I am a Destiny," no. 6.
26. M.A., XIX, 330; *The Will to Power,* no. 617.
27. M.A., XIII, 327; *Zarathustra,* IV, "Retired."

# INDEX OF NAMES

Aeneas Silvius, 42
Andreas-Salomé, Lou, 74, 75, 89, 90, 94
Anzengruber, Ludwig, 145
Aquinas, St. Thomas, 2, 6, 72, 88, 108, 131, 142, 156
Aristotle, 6, 44, 72, 142
Augustine, St., 3, 46, 72, 142

Bach, Johann Sebastian, 16, 158, 166, 167
Baglione, Astorre, 39
Baglione, Atalanta, 39–40
Baglione, Grifone, 39–40
Baudelaire, Charles-Pierre, 10, 129, 135
Beethoven, Ludwig van, 158
Benn, Gottfried, 2, 14–15
Bernhard, Thomas, 160
Bizet, Georges, 59, 158
Blake, William, 132, 133
Bosanquet, Bernard, 141n
Bradley, F. H., 141n, 147
Büchner, Georg, 48
Buckle, Henry Thomas, 43
Buddha, 180
Burckhardt, Jacob, 39–54, 57, 60, 85
Bury, J. B., 43
Byron, Lord, 63

Camus, Albert, 1
Cardanus, Hieronymus, 114
Claude Lorrain, 16, 175
Claudius, Matthias, 109
Common, Thomas, 130, 132, 133, 139
Constant, Benjamin, 9
Copernicus, Nicolaus, 7

D'Annunzio, Gabriele, 134
Dante Alighieri, 2, 9, 88, 108, 112n, 123n, 131, 166–68, 175
Descartes, René, 59, 142, 148, 154
De Wette, Wilhelm Martin Leberecht, 40
Donne, John, 109, 154
Dostoevsky, Fyodor, 1, 3, 164–67, 177, 178

Eckermann, Johann Peter, 16, 87, 106, 108
Einstein, Albert, 1
Eliot, George, 55

Eliot, T. S., 87–89, 90, 105–9, 112n, 123n, 130, 140
Emerson, Ralph Waldo, 181n
Empedocles, 3–4
Epicurus, 33, 59

Flaubert, Gustave, 9, 10, 135, 159
Frederick the Great, 58
Freud, Sigmund, 1, 7, 58, 166, 167, 177

Gast, Peter, 125, 127, 175, 177
George, Stefan, 2, 68, 129, 134, 159
Goethe, Johann Wolfgang von, 15, 16, 18–38, 43–44, 49, 59, 67, 105–8, 156–58, 162–64, 167, 175, 179, 180
Gogol, Nikolai, 63
Goncourt, Edmond-Louis Antoine Huot de, 164–65
Goncourt, Jules-Alfred Huot de, 164–65
Gregory, Lady, 132, 138
Grillparzer, Franz, 47
Gryphius, Andreas, 109

Hafiz, 167
Hegel, Georg Wilhelm Friedrich, 44–46, 53–54, 65–66, 83, 85, 109, 138–40
Heidegger, Martin, 1, 2, 116–17, 151
Heine, Heinrich, 34, 59
Heraclitus of Ephesus, 33–34, 82, 179–80, 184
Herbert, George, 109
Hermann, Gottfried, 18, 22
Herodotus, 46
Hitler, Adolf, 14–15, 112n, 156, 159, 161
Hölderlin, Friedrich, 3, 109, 133
Holthusen, H. E., 110–11
Homer, 8–9, 167
Humboldt, Wilhelm von, 21, 26

Jaspers, Karl, 2, 117
Jesus Christ, 6, 12, 16, 47, 49, 64, 97, 175
John, St., of the Cross, 109
Joyce, James, 131, 154
Jünger, Ernst, 2

Kafka, Franz, 2, 146, 159
Kant, Immanuel, 72, 142, 144, 147, 154, 156

Kaufmann, Walter, 181n
Keats, John, 111, 156
Keller, Gottfried, 47, 154
Kepler, Johannes, 148
Kierkegaard, Søren, 1, 3, 72, 81, 117, 142, 145
Kleist, Heinrich von, 34, 35, 48, 63, 84–85, 138
Kraus, Karl, 8, 68, 146, 152n, 154, 159

Lawrence, D. H., 138
Leibnitz, Gottfried Wilhelm, 148
Leonardo da Vinci, 70
Leopardi, Giacomo, 63
Lessing, Gotthold Ephraim, 59, 159
Lichtenberg, Georg Christoph, 67, 145, 146, 154
Locke, John, 142
Loos, Adolf, 146

Machiavelli, Niccolò, 88–89
Malcolm, Norman, 141n
Mallarmé, Stéphane, 129, 135, 158
Mann, Thomas, 2, 57, 58, 75, 134–35, 159, 161
Marx, Karl, 1, 58, 83
Matarazzo, Francesco, 39–40, 42
Matthew, St., 82, 83
Michelangelo, 158
Milton, John, 109
Mitterer, Erika, 119
Montaigne, Michel de, 33, 59, 88–89
Moore, G. E., 141n
Moreau, Gustave, 135
Mörike, Eduard Friedrich, 47
Mozart, Wolfgang Amadeus, 130, 158, 167
Musil, Robert, 2, 145, 146
Musset, Alfred de, 63

Napoleon, 54
Nestroy, Johann Nepomuk Eduard Ambrosius, 145
Newton, Isaac, 20, 23, 26, 44
Novalis, 165–66

Oeri, Jacob, 44
Offenbach, Jacques, 59, 158
O'Neill, Eugene, 160
Overbeck, Franz, 177

Pascal, Blaise, 3, 12, 27, 33, 35, 59, 67, 72, 81, 110, 117, 142, 145
Paul, St., 3, 92

Plato, 33, 45, 59, 72, 82, 142, 154, 156, 158–59, 168–72
Poe, Edgar Allan, 63
Proust, Marcel, 155–56, 177
Puvis de Chavannes, Pierre-Cécile, 135

Ranke, Leopold von, 1, 40, 42
Raphael, 29, 39–42, 166
Rée, Paul, 60, 65
Rilke, Rainer Maria, 2, 84–85, 87–126, 129, 138, 143, 159, 162
Rimbaud, Arthur, 129, 168
Ritschl, Friedrich Wilhelm, 57
Rohde, Erwin, 60
Rousseau, Jean-Jacques, 33, 59, 83, 154, 155
Rubens, Peter Paul, 167
Russell, Bertrand, 141n, 146–49, 153

Salomé, Lou. *See* Andreas-Salomé, Lou
Sartre, Jean-Paul, 1
Schiller, Friedrich, 30, 83, 85, 106, 138, 160
Schlegel, Friedrich, 121
Schönberg, Arnold, 146
Schopenhauer, Arthur, 14, 33–34, 44–53, 56, 59, 61, 62, 67, 93, 127, 154, 161, 163, 171, 176–77, 180
Seneca, 88–89
Shakespeare, William, 9, 37, 59, 87–89, 106–8, 123n, 154, 165
Socrates, 78–79, 176–77
Sophocles, 170
Spengler, Oswald, 1, 18
Spinoza, Baruch, 24, 33–34, 59, 89, 156
Stendhal, 8–9, 164, 177
Stifter, Adalbert, 16, 47
Strauss, David, 55–56, 61
Stravinsky, Igor, 167

Tasso, Torquato, 87–89
Tawney, R. H., 131
Theocritus, 59
Thucydides, 43
Tolstoy, Leo, 155

Verlaine, Paul, 135
Villiers de l'Isle-Adam, Auguste de, 134
Voltaire, 58–60

Wagner, Cosima, 56, 58, 60, 74
Wagner, Richard, 14, 16, 28, 34, 56–62,

65, 69, 73–74, 96, 127, 158, 161, 164,
173, 175–76
Weber, Max, 1, 131
Weininger, Otto, 143, 146
Wilamowitz-Moellendorff, Ulrich von,
57
Williams, Tennessee, 160
Winckelmann, Johann Joachim, 35

Wittgenstein, Ludwig, 141–57
Wordsworth, William, 84
Wright, Henrik von, 141n, 150

Yeats, William Butler, 16, 127–40

Zola, Émile, 161, 164–65
Zoroaster, 176